Laurence M. [signature]

Through
HELL
to
FREEDOM

The astonishing life story of Julian Bester
Farmer, slave labourer, soldier and builder.

Julian Bester [signature]

As told to
Laurence Macpherson Jones

To my dear parents:

Anniela and Francisek Bester

British Library Cataloguing-in-Publication Data. A catalogue record for this book is available from the British Library.

ISBN 978-1-873257-82-1

CONTENTS

PART ONE

End of Part One

PART TWO

ACKNOWLEDGEMENTS

Firstly my deepest thanks to Anita, Linda, Rina and Julian. He is a truly remarkable man. In many hours of conversation with him, Anita and Rina, covering every facet of their lives, I so appreciated and admired their selfless co-operation, scrupulous attention to detail, crystal-clear memories and infectious enthusiasm. I hope that in some very small way I have done justice to them and the Polish people who died in the Second World War.

I thank Julian most sincerely, for allowing me to write his biography.

I also wish to especially thank Helen and Gary James for their support and wartime photographs. Gary has been of inestimable assistance with the final editing, liasoning with 'Tucann' and extensive publicity.

The Polish Embassy, London. Oxford University, Department of Russian. Library of the Imperial War Museum. R.A.F. Cranwell Officers College Library. The Bodleian Library, Oxford. The Welsh Books Council. Wayne John and staff, Neath Library. Claire Smith and Jeanette Jones of the Reference department, for their cheerful assistance and professional help with a myriad of enquiries. Gill Griffiths and staff of Skewen Library. Staff of Swansea Public Library. Rhin Jones and staff, Carmarthen Public Library. Peter O'Brien for his computer skills, advice and photography. Jim Caddick for his invaluable assistance and work on the early editing. Elizabeth Caddick-Lees for her dedicated proofreading of the book. My brother Adrian, for a range of line drawings throughout the book. My dear friend, former Petty Officer Jim Murphy, of the 'C' class destroyer 'Beagle' and cruiser 'Jamaica', for his first-hand experience of merchant

convoy operations during World War Two. Maggie and Barry Long, Joy King, Robert King, historian, Remo Moruzzi for kindly giving me information on the 'Arandora Star', Carla Underwood, Paul Underwood, Shirley and Dorino Moruzzi, for information, photographs and especially their kind permission to view and photograph family artefacts of the 'Arandora Star' tragedy. Lewis Stuart, Des Morris, Angela and Luigi Domeio, Anna and Angelo Sidoli, Angela Marzella, Nigel Pledger, historian, for maps of the Russian Front 1941-43. Nantlais Jones, Tony Cottle, chaitman of the Mumbles Railway Society, Christian Bradshaw. Robert Cole, for an interesting piece he sent to me outlining his long career in the building trade with Julian. My thanks to Macmillan publishers, for permission to re-print photographs from General Wladyslaw Anders 1946 memoirs, 'An army in exile'. Angela Pockley, for photographs of Monte Cassino Monastery and her enthusiasm and encouragement. Peter Jenkins of Cefngolau House, Llandeilo. Anne Williams of St.Teilo's church, Llandeilo. Ieuan G Jones.
Julie Griffiths, Head Teacher, Tregib Comprehensive School, Llandeilo. Dame Vera Lynn O.B.E. D.B.E. for a signed photograph and letter. Peter Evans and Tom Jones of the Vera Lynn Trust, Billingshurst, Sussex. Reverend Fathers Chris Fuse, Eugene Monaghan and Bill Curran of St. Joseph's Catholic Church, Neath. Sisters of the former Poor Clare Monastery at Hillside, Neath. My personal thanks to so many friends and family for their constant encouragement and interest, during my attempt to detail Julian's amazing life. Thanks to my publishers for their superb professionalism, advice, distribution and publicity.

Laurence Macpherson Jones. Neath, July 16th 2007.

FOREWORD

It has been 12 years since I first met Julian at his family home in Neath, South Wales. An incredibly amiable and extremely modest man, I had no inkling about the life he had led. For a few of his teenage years his life was as hard as any human could endure but he has come through it with an amazing humility and selflessness. It would be understandable for a man with his experiences to hide himself away but that is not in his nature. Julian is a pillar of the community in Neath and never hesitates to help his friends and neighbours even in his Golden years.

All of Julian's family knew very little of his experiences because, like most men of his generation, he decided not to speak of it, even to his nearest and dearest. Indeed when I first started to ask Julian about his life he would only manage a few sentences before becoming quite emotional. The reason for his reluctance was to save himself from facing his demons and to save his family from any upset. It is only really since I joined the Royal Air Force as a Navigator in 1996 and become a 'veteran' of Gulf War II and subsequent tours to Iraq and Afghanistan that our bond has grown stronger and Julian can finally open up and speak at length about his WWII life. Coincidentally we have been to similar places in our Service lives.

Over time it has become more and more evident what a fascinating life Julian has led so far. It has been an honour to hear his tale, especially as he had not told his children. I like to think that the whole process has been a cathartic experience for Julian as well as making an excellent read for others.

An extra factor in this book is the current debate about immigration into the United Kingdom. Due to media hype as much as ignorance many people see the influx of people from Eastern Europe and further afield as a threat to our society. Without wishing to make this book political, Julian is a shining example of how much of our society has been both complemented and improved by his decision to live in Great Britain. Admittedly not all new arrivals decide to intergrate as Julian has done but we should maybe be less quick to judge all by their standards.

I have the utmost respect for Julian and I have all the time in the world to listen to his stories. We have a lot in common including being Brothers in Arms despite the generation gap, both calling Neath our home town and, probably the strongest connection, we are family; I married his youngest daughter Helen!

Enjoy the book.

Flight Lieutenant Gary James BSc RAF

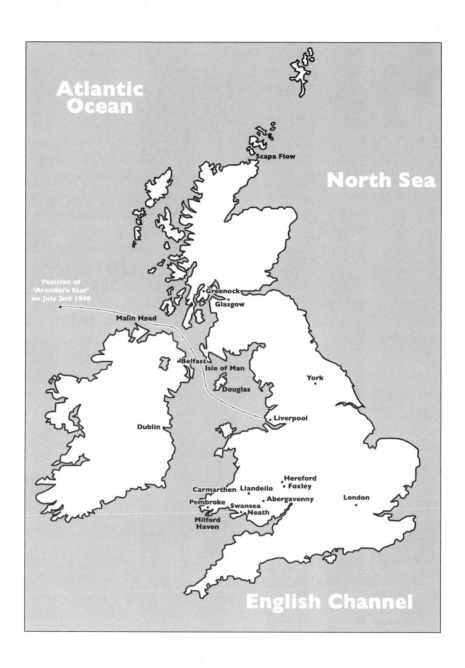

Atlantic
Ocean

North Sea

Scapa Flow

Position of
'Arandora Star'
on July 2nd 1940

Malin Head

Greenock
Glasgow

Belfast

Isle of Man

Douglas

York

Dublin

Liverpool

Hereford
Foxley

Carmarthen Llandeilo

Pembroke

Swansea Abergavenny

London

Neath

Milford
Haven

English Channel

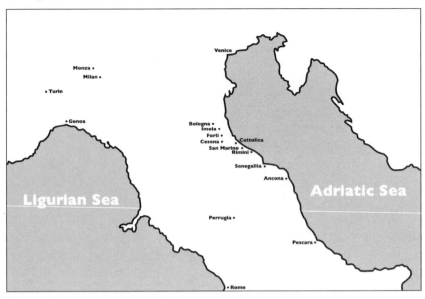

Northern Italy

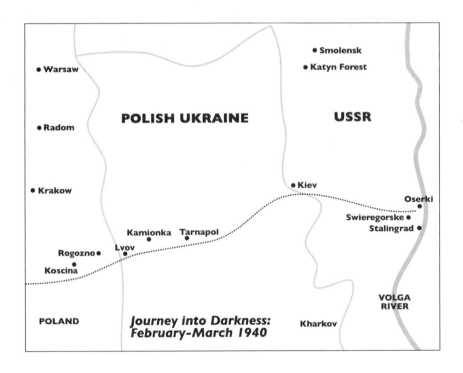

Southern Italy

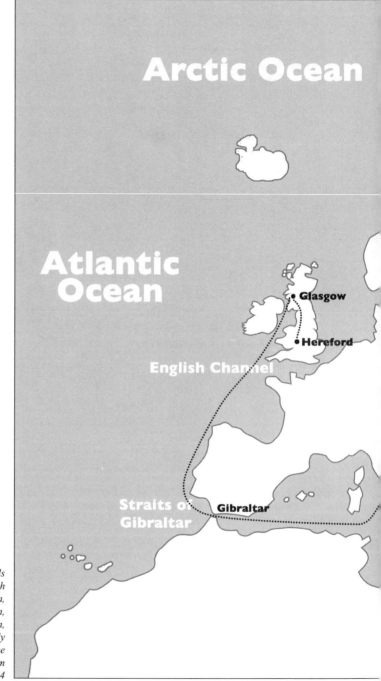

Julian Bester's travels across Poland, Polish Ukraine, Russia, Kazakstan, Uzbekistan, Iran, Iraq, Jordan, Palestine, Egypt, Italy and the United Kingdom from 1940 - 1954

Kara
Sea

Novaya Zemyla

Barents
Sea

Murmansk
Archangel

White Sea Canal

'The GULAG'

SIBERIA

Vorkuta

Moscow

Leningrad

Volga River

Swieregorske   Oserki

KAZAKHSTAN

Katyn
Forest

ltic Sea

Kiev

Stalingrad

Kamionka

gozno   Lvov

Kharkov

Tashkent

UBEKISTAN

Caspian
Sea

Black Sea

Krasnovodsk

Pahlevei

Kirkuk

Kinokin   Baghdad

IRAQ

diterranean Sea   Palestine

Tel-Aviv

Bergigi

Alexandria

Ismaillia

Cairo

EGYPT

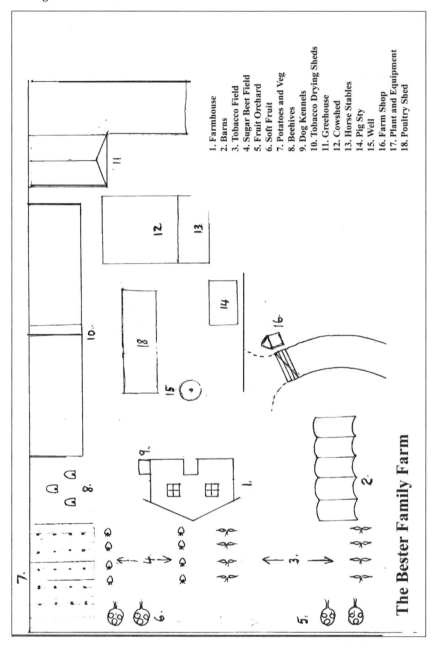

The Bester Family Farm

1. Farmhouse
2. Barns
3. Tobacco Field
4. Sugar Beet Field
5. Fruit Orchard
6. Soft Fruit
7. Potatoes and Veg
8. Beehives
9. Dog Kennels
10. Tobacco Drying Sheds
11. Greehouse
12. Cowshed
13. Horse Stables
14. Pig Sty
15. Well
16. Farm Shop
17. Plant and Equipment
18. Poultry Shed

CHAPTER 1
Village Life

I was born on the fifteenth of March 1925 in the village of Rogozno, a farming area in Poland surrounded by the villages of Pszework, Wacud and Szezunt. The nearest city was Lvov, fifteen kilometres to the east. My father, Franciszek Bester, had lived and farmed in Rogozno all his life. He met my mother, Anniela Kielb, in 1913 and they were married in 1914, just before the First World War. In 1919 he was called up to serve in the 1st Krakoviecki Lancers in the Russo-Polish War. During the Battle of Plock in 1920, he was wounded and repatriated. I was the youngest of three children, with an elder brother Joseph and sister Wlatka. I was told much later that my grandparents had died before I was born. We were a predominantly Catholic community in Rogozno, of around five hundred, and each Sunday we attended the family Mass at the newly renovated church of St. Joseph at Koscina, about one and a half kilometres away. There was just one priest for a fairly large area and two weeks after my birth I was baptised by him and afterwards, so I'm told, we had the customary family celebration.

My early childhood was very much the same as that of all the children in this very friendly community, where everything revolved around the farm and the seasons. Family friendships really came into their own at Christmas and everything was prepared and the farm decorated for weeks before December 25th. A sumptuous feast took place on Christmas Eve. It began at eight p.m. with all the family seated around the farmhouse table, which had been covered with straw representing Jesus' manger at

Bethlehem. First course was a thick vegetable or pea soup, followed by goose, chicken, beef or pork with a range of vegetables. The pork had been steamed in the kitchen pot and the calf roasted in our coal-fired oven. For dessert, we had Mum's cakes with custard.

At eleven p.m., we walked to St. Joseph's, as there was always an hour of carols, readings and rehearsing the music for the Midnight Mass. The Mass was in Latin and the congregation, who packed the church for the two-hour service, was always devout and enthusiastic. An earlier service was always held outside at Our Lady's grotto and many villagers attended that as well. In addition, as was the custom in Poland, the parish priest visited every family in the village over the Christmas period. Santa Claus came to the farm on Christmas morning and we had our presents and treats.

Over the New Year, we always visited close relatives for a meal and celebratory drink. One visit was always made to my cousins who lived nearby: Stefa, Salka, Joseph, Edek and Tadek. Although Tadek was much older than we were, we always got on well with him. Salka was always great fun to have around and Stefa, although young, was a very skilful seamstress, always busy designing and making clothes. Who knows, she might already have set her sights on working for a Paris haute couture fashion designer in the future! Helena, another cousin, came to Rogozno later than us and her family's farm was nearby. Edek's parents had died when he was very young so Dad was his official guardian and he helped on our farm. Another cousin named Joseph was a very successful tailor and a barber in the village.

We had been a farming family for generations and in 1930 we had twenty acres of potatoes plus the usual vegetables, hay, sugar beet and tobacco. The livestock consisted of two horses, ten Friesian cows, fifty pigs, fifty poultry and twenty beehives plus two cats and two collies, but no sheep. In 1937, when I was twelve, Dad decided that we should move away from Poland to a much larger farm at Kamionka in Tarnopol County, Polish Ukraine, eighty kilometres west of Rogozno. Land in the Ukraine was much cheaper than in Poland and its rich soil was ideal for all our crops, especially tobacco, the main source of our income. When the sale of the farm in Rogozno was completed, the family possessions, equipment, timber and dismantled sheds, were taken by horse-drawn carts to the small railway halt which we had always used for transporting our produce around the area. The timber, farming tools and household possessions were loaded aboard open freight wagons and the animals led onto two cattle trucks. The only family member left in Rogozno was cousin Joseph, our celebrated tailor and barber. His business was well established and it would have been a mistake for him to leave with us. More importantly he didn't fancy starting all over again and could well have struggled against existing competition in Kamionka.

Our new farm was situated on a hill overlooking Kamionka village and surrounded by four lakes. There were beautiful views in every direction and the fields were green and lush; evidence of the rich red soil in this peaceful part of Polish Ukraine. After Dad had met some villagers, we discovered to our great shock that during the past years, life in the Ukraine had been far from peaceful. Stalin, the Soviet dictator, had become jealous of the success of the peasant farmers, whom he derisively called 'kulaks'. He wanted them all to join his State-run collective farms or 'kolkhoz', and levied punitive taxes on their grain harvests. When the peasants defaulted on the payments, his gangs seized all their grain and deported the families to labour camps in Siberia. Thousands of tons were exported and the region which had always been known as the 'bread basket of Russia' was laid waste. This evil act resulted in mass starvation for the poor peasants: millions, yes, millions died and the country was devastated. The period was known as 'The Great Famine'. What a terrible man this Stalin must be.

We soon set up our new home in Kamionka, building a very large shed that would be used for drying the harvested tobacco leaves in the late summer. We also erected barns and various outbuildings to house the equipment and tools and a large stone compound in the yard for the pigs. The milk from our Friesians wasn't collected by a dairy, but made into butter and cheese and sold to shops in the village and we also helped Mum with her shop at the farm gate. Above all, the new farm ensured we could increase our acreage of sugar beet, with additional fields for the large tobacco crop. Following an inspection visit, the Kamionka authorities realised the potential of our farm for the local economy: they generously offered Dad an interest-free loan to maximise production of tobacco and sugar beet, which would be processed by the state factories in Tarnopol.

The cultivation procedure for the tobacco was especially prolonged and needed very careful attention. Tobacco grows best in a warm climate and in carefully drained and cultivated soil. After the seeds were planted in beds in late winter or early spring, they grew to fifteen centimetres tall in about twelve weeks and were then transplanted into the fields in rows, with a three feet gap in between each plant to allow for the wide leaves. The upper part of the plant was topped when it flowered, enabling the remaining leaves to become heavy. The plants were watered frequently until they were five feet high and turning yellow. During August and September, the crop was harvested and strung on lines in the drying shed until November, by which time they turned brown, again being frequently doused with water to prevent cracking. Finally the leaves were cut, boxed and taken to Kamionka station to be transported to the factory in Tarnopol. There was always great excitement when the large cheque arrived from the local government in December. (Our euphoria would indeed have been short-lived if we had known that the December 1939 remittance was to be the last we would receive, as in two months we would be taken away from our farm and livelihood forever).

Tobacco Plant

Twice a year, inspectors arrived to carry out checks on the management of the tobacco crop and to ensure that the government grant was being used correctly. For instance, on one visit, they suggested that another drying shed be built to further increase production the following year. We became friendly with the inspectors and they invariably stayed for several days, paying Mum for their food and lodging. During the long, hot summers it was quite usual for Dad to rise well before dawn, work until noon, and rest for two hours after lunch, then work until dusk at around eleven p.m. We hired contractors during the harvesting and they cut and bound the hay into stooks. These were turned over periodically to ensure the hay was dry and in late September it was stored into sheds for winter feed for the cattle. Each summer, on average, we produced about twenty tons of sugar beet for refining. The friendly manager always sent us a two-hundredweight sack from the first batch that was refined, so that was a nice addition to our winter store. 18

So much work had to be done in the summer that we couldn't manage without help from the villagers, as all the production, packing and distribution was a huge task on its own, without the on-going farm duties, like milking and feeding the animals.

In November, a large pit was dug in the yard to hold the twenty tons of potatoes that had been stored in a shed since the summer. The walls of the pit were lined with straw to prevent frost damage during the severe winters. The potatoes were boiled in a coal-fired oven for the winter feed for the pigs, which were regularly sent to the slaughterhouse in Tarnopol.

Along with five hundred other pupils, I attended the village school, situated one kilometre from the farm. It was staffed by a headmaster and five friendly teachers, with classes starting at 8.00 a.m. and ending at 3.00 p.m. When the afternoon bell sounded, I always rushed home to have tea, do my homework and help with the remaining farm chores before joining in games of basketball or volleyball with Wlatka, Stefa, Salka, Joseph and other village children.

As the farm was situated high above the village, it was an ideal winter sports playground for us. Dad encouraged our alpine skills by buying us brand new skis and skates in Tarnopol and making us toboggans. We imagined ourselves as the future Winter Olympic champions of Poland, yelling excitedly as we careered down the hill, skilfully negotiating our improvised slalom and downhill courses and always visualising the three of us securing Olympic podium places and medals! The four lakes on the valley floor were a skater's paradise as the very low winter temperatures ensured the ice was frozen solid until March and we took full advantage of the frequently extreme winter conditions. The lakes were teeming with trout, so from May onwards we again hired contractors to catch the fish with nets, after they first diverted the feeder streams and lowered the water level in the lakes. They put the trout into barrels and we took them to shops in Tarnopol. Again, this was a very profitable sideline.

Cranes were one of the species of bird-life in the area and these huge, magnificent birds would nest on rooftops, buildings or in high trees. Each September, as many as two hundred would gather and circle endlessly in the late Summer sky, waiting for stragglers from all over the Ukraine to join them in migration to the warm climes of Africa. When the leader decided it was time to depart, he soared like a rocket into the cloudless sky, followed by the rest of the flock. We watched their departure ritual with great excitement. When the leader reached a cruising altitude to take advantage of the wind, he levelled off, hovered until the others joined him and like a silvery ribbon, they vanished over the horizon.

For Catholics, May is traditionally the month of the Blessed Virgin Mary so we had a service every evening at a small shrine outside the church, dedicated to Our Lady of Czestochowa, Patroness of Poland. Hundreds of people would attend these services. On one occasion, I clearly remember a lady parishioner who, on glancing down into the small stream running alongside the shrine, noticed that the sun's rays striking a piece of wood in the water appeared to give a clear image of the Madonna! Naturally this strange occurrence was widely reported and in fact the local priest came to see this phenomenon for himself.

In July 1939 I joined the local boys cadet troop in Kamionka. Meetings were held in a hut near the Catholic Church, with two groups consisting of about thirty members. The oldest members were from sixteen to twenty four and the youngest (including me), from twelve to fifteen. It was a tradition in Poland that young men joined the cadets for military training and later progressed to the armed services. My brother Joseph was already in the barracks in Tarnopol, having been drafted into the Polish Army along with thousands of other new recruits. Although I was young, I listened to Mum, Dad and other adults talking about the great danger to Poland, which could come at any time, from the National Socialists in Germany, led by Adolf Hitler. They explained to us that Hitler was seeking to extend Germany's borders and that his policies could lead to armed conflict between our two countries, as Poland would never accede to any of his expansionist plans. In fact, Dad, along with many other farmers and villagers was convinced that he was simply looking for an excuse to invade Poland, sometime in the future.

Meanwhile, we learned a series of drills and marches, working hard to reach a high standard as we would be combining with the local army corps in a parade in Tarnopol in May 1940, celebrating Polish Independence Day.

The Nazis invaded Poland on September 1st with a terrifying new style of warfare called a 'Blitzkrieg' or 'Lightning War', using fast, overwhelming air and armoured assaults. These attacks resulted in many Polish cities and towns being destroyed and thousands of civilians killed. Although the Poles fought and defended bravely, they couldn't halt this well-planned onslaught. The Polish government left Warsaw on September 5th and to secure a quick, decisive victory, the Germans unleashed savage air and artillery attacks on the surrounded capital after two ultimatums to surrender were ignored. Eventually, the Warsaw garrison surrendered on September 25th to save needless bloodshed, in what would have been futile resistance against overwhelming odds.

On September 17th whilst Poland was fighting for its very existence, Soviet Russia's Josef Stalin set into operation his own pre-arranged plans to occupy Poland from the East, having signed a 'non-aggression' pact with Hitler on August 23rd 1939. After signing the 'pact', Soviet Foreign Minister Molotov was heard to sneer to his German counterpart Ribbentrop: 'Well that's the end of the Poles!' Soviet forces advanced one hundred kilometres into Poland encountering no opposition from a country that was now besieged on two fronts. Stalin's dreaded secret police, the Narodni Kommissariat Vnutrennikh Del or NKVD (Peoples' commissariat for internal affairs) quickly arrested tens of thousands of Polish soldiers trying to escape from the Germans. They, and in many cases their entire families, were deported to labour camps in the Arctic Circle where many of them perished.

CHAPTER 2
The Russians

Many of the villagers and their relatives had sons in the Polish Army and they hadn't heard from them since hostilities ended on September 25th 1939. We were in a similar position, as Joseph also hadn't been in touch and Mum and Dad were extremely concerned about his safety and whereabouts in the confusion following the Polish Army's surrender. Worst of all, there had been disquieting rumours that many had been killed or captured by the Russians when their units tried to escape through Hungary. Parents were frantic about the soldiers' fate and kept asking everybody for any news, hoping that they would return home safely, but as the days progressed, they began to fear the worst. In fact Joseph was alive and a prisoner of the Germans, not the Russians. Later that week, thousands of Polish prisoners including Joseph, passed through Rogozno on their way to prisoner-of-war camps in Germany. By a stroke of luck, Joseph had somehow managed to escape from the column of prisoners. A villager told us that he was hiding in a loft on a farm in Wacud, but we didn't know what had happened to his unit and were just thankful that he was safe for the present.

We woke up one day in late October to discover that several divisions of Russian soldiers had arrived on the outskirts of the village overnight. They had no tents or facilities and lived in their battered lorries and trucks in the meadows and lanes. After everyone in Kamionka had got over the shock of their unexpected arrival, we children used to go and see them out of curiosity, as everybody spoke of their wretched living conditions, ragged green uniforms and unkempt appearance. Dad reckoned they were peasant conscripts who were half-starved, as there were no field-kitchens, toilets or eating arrangements and they existed on what kind locals gave them or what they stole from farms at night. We gradually got to know them, as some villagers spoke Russian and we communicated with sign language. They were so grateful when Mum made a huge container of tasty goulash for them to share out and complained bitterly of their situation and hatred of Stalin for sending them far away from their families to claim new territory for him.

The conscripts had to very careful not to be seen to fraternise with us too much, as they were watched by NKVD Political Commissars, who monitored their actions and in some cases, a few were punished. Soon the NKVD were going around the village in jeeps, stopping at people's houses and farms, questioning the inhabitants. They were making lists of all the adults and Dad knew exactly what they were up to. He told us that things were definitely going to change in the area and that this was the beginning. He had heard of the reputation of the NKVD and their methods. We didn't understand what he meant, but it was plain that the adults were very concerned for our future, although we had no idea of the nature of their concerns. As things turned out, we had plenty to be worried about.

During November, all the adults were ordered to report to the village hall. They were issued with ballot papers written in Cyrillic script, which nobody could read and told to cast their votes in a small cubicle. There was just one candidate in this apology for an 'election': Josef Vissaroniovitch Stalin! Anyone over twenty one who defied the edict and refused to vote would be forced from their homes and taken at gunpoint to the hall. Dad ignored the order, but sure enough, they came to the farm, pushed and punched him a few times and took him off to vote. At the same time, they had a good look around the farm and it was obvious they liked what they saw, especially our food store. We felt very uneasy after this unexpected visit and all the family were sure they'd be back one day.

Their next target was small arms and rifles, which they knew all farmers had, and an opportunity was given to villagers to surrender their weapons, before the searches began. A veiled threat was also made that if any arms were discovered hidden in houses, there would be severe consequences for all the families. Dad owned a pistol, so he hid it in the farmhouse loft. About fifty rifles were held at our cadet hut, so our unit leader, along with other older members, coated the rifles in oil, wrapped them in sacking, then buried them at the back of the hut. Unfortunately for us, the existence of our arms cache was betrayed to the NKVD, probably by one of our disaffected members, who may have been rewarded by the Russians.

Twelve of us were rounded up and taken to the police station in Kamionka and questioned three at a time, in a small interview room. We were resolutely determined, after our betrayal, not to divulge the place where the rifles were hidden, even if they used force and torture to extract confessions. The NKVD officer said, 'We know you've hidden the arms, so tell us where they are before we punish you!' Nobody said a word, so he signalled to soldiers waiting outside; they crashed into the room and started viciously attacking us. We were hit with rifle butts, kicked and punched from one side of the room to the other, until we were all dazed and bleeding. During the prolonged assault, the officer screamed at us to confess, but nobody answered him. They realised we weren't going to talk, so they locked us in an adjoining room while they started on the next group of cadets. Hours later, having had no food or water, we were all taken outside and roughly pushed onto a filthy lorry. We greatly feared this was to be our last journey and would end in our execution, deep in the forest. Having had no contact with our families all day, it was even more distressing to realise that we might not see them again. To our great relief, the lorry pulled up into a farmyard, a few miles from the police station. The soldiers hit us as we climbed down, and pushed us into a dirty cowshed. Again no food was provided and the officer snarled, 'You'll stay here until you talk!' Then they roared off into the night.

It was damp and freezing in the cowshed, its thick stone walls were coated in ice and we huddled together through the night, shivering and unable to sleep. How long were we going to be kept here was the thought on everybody's mind and would we be left to starve? The farm appeared deserted and even as dawn approached, there were only occasional sounds of animals. An hour later the lorry returned, screeched to a halt and the cowshed door was unlocked. There were fewer soldiers this time and two were carrying buckets of water and what appeared to be pigswill, which they had demanded from the farmer. It was to be our only meal that day and the same monotonous, tasteless, diet continued during the remainder of our imprisonment. Despite the constant threats and starvation, none of the lads gave them the information they wanted and I think the NKVD realised that they'd never find the arms.

Our ordeal lasted for a month, and then one day, we were awakened to hear wonderful news: as it was December 13th and Stalin's birthday, an amnesty was declared for certain categories of prisoners and we would be freed immediately! Nobody could believe this totally unexpected development and we were all so excited to be returning to our homes and families, thankfully none the worse despite the interrogations and brutal assaults. The family was ecstatic at my safe return and no doubt fervent prayers had been offered up continuously for our safe release, which occurred in such an unexpected manner. Now we could all look forward to our happiest family Christmas ever!

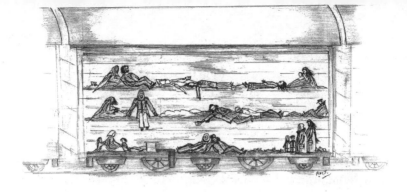

CHAPTER 3
Journey into Darkness

The weather deteriorated in January 1940, with constant sub-zero temperatures, bitter winds, and exceptionally heavy snowfalls. Farm life was restricted to essential daily work, with the animals being kept warm and well fed in their byres and sheds. Very deep snowdrifts surrounded the farm and access to the main road became so difficult that we had to dig tunnels through the snow. The school remained closed throughout the remainder of the month as the severe weather continued, so we had to study at home until conditions improved.

On February 10th at around 3.00 a.m., we were all woken by a frightening crash. I jumped out of bed and, looking out of the window, saw that a large army truck had smashed down the farm gate. The dogs were barking madly, when suddenly shots rang out and they were brutally killed by soldiers who were now surrounding the farm. The soldiers shone the lorry lights on the farmhouse and then started breaking down the farmhouse door with rifle butts. Dad rushed into my room shouting, 'Get dressed Julian, the Russians are here!' I scrambled into my clothes and ran downstairs. Four Russian soldiers were in the kitchen, motioning everyone to sit in lines on the floor. Mum and Wlatka were crying and we were all scared, wondering what was going to happen to us. They stood over us with rifles for an hour, determined that nobody would escape. In broken Polish, a Russian officer told Dad that we had to be ready to leave in an hour, taking no belongings, food or extra clothes. Dad had spoken to him on several occasions during their time in the village, so he asked him, 'What's going on Slava?' The officer quietly explained, 'Look Fran, I feel bad about this, but I have my orders and I can't tell you anything, otherwise the NKVD will arrest me too and I'll probably be shot!' 'But Slava', pleaded Dad, 'for God's sake, at least tell me, is it only the Poles that are being taken?' Slava hesitated, and then shamefacedly said, 'Yes Fran, only the Poles'. He then rushed out.

Soon the soldiers signalled for us to leave and we walked out of the farm into the deep snow towards the main road. It was moonlight and freezing cold, but thankfully not snowing. As we trudged along dispiritedly, families from neighbouring farms and the village joined us. I looked all around at our family and friends: Dad, Mum, Wlatka, Salka, Helena, Honorka, Stefa, Tadek, Martin, Mietek, Edek and Zybyshek. They had all been taken, so had anybody escaped? Cousin Joseph the tailor and barber in Rogozno was the luckiest, as he'd stayed in the village, not wishing to come to Kamionka. The soldiers' target was us supposedly 'rich' farming people, that's why the soldiers arrived in the middle of the night and they had obviously conducted similar operations many times.

Dad said that his worst fears of the soldiers' arrival in Kamionka had now been confirmed. He was convinced that evil Soviet officials had undoubtedly carried out many wholesale deportations during the 'Great Famine', seizing well-managed farms. Families had been banished to far-flung regions in Russia with no hope of returning to their villages and facing inevitable, slow deaths in terrible conditions in slave camps in the Siberian wastes. The Soviets knew that very few, if any, villagers would slip through their steel net. It seemed to me that the entire Polish population of Kamionka and district was disappearing from the face of the earth. Where were they taking us? God forbid it wouldn't be a mass execution. By now, Soviet troops with fixed bayonets were bringing up the rear of the long procession to prevent anyone slipping away into the black, freezing night. The guards walking alongside us ignored any questions we asked in Russian about our ultimate destination, and soon we arrived at the small country railway halt that we used to dispatch our goods and produce in summer. The station was in darkness, but in the moonlight I could see a line of cattle trucks, stretching for at least half a kilometre into the distance and faintly hear the steam hissing from the train's engine.

The double doors in the centre of each boxcar were already open and the soldiers signalled us to get on board and as the cars were only about a foot above the track, this was easy for everybody. We all helped the families with babies and young children during the loading and I certainly wasn't aware of any shouting or disturbances by villagers resisting the deportation. I'm pretty sure, anyway, that the soldiers had orders to shoot anyone who attempted to hide or flee from the station. Inside the car were two-storey wooden bunks and everyone tried to sort themselves out as best as they could, leaving the bunks for mothers and babies. The rest of us crouched on the floor, huddled together for warmth in the freezing conditions. There was no lighting or heating and the steel-bowled toilet had no privacy. The implications of this primitive system were apparent to everybody, especially if we faced a long journey to wherever the Russians were taking us and there were fifty six of us in the box-car. The soldiers were now rushing alongside the train, hurrying and shouting to complete the loading and ignoring any frantic pleas from mothers for food, milk and water for their babies. They slammed and bolted the doors and the train slowly pulled out of Kamionka station.

We all wondered if we would ever see our village and farms again. The mothers with babies were hysterical, crying and screaming uncontrollably. I listened to the men cursing Stalin for destroying a peaceful farming community. Dad told everybody to calm down, as he was sure that food and water would be provided at the next stop. He told us that regardless of events in the war now raging across Europe, our own battle would be one of survival during whatever lay ahead and we should be strong and look after one another. He finally led us in prayers, insisting that prayer would be our only hope in the days ahead, whatever Stalin and the NKVD had planned for us all.

The only light for the interior came from a one centimetre slit at the top of the wall of the car. If I stood on a bunk I could just see out onto the moonlit, snow-covered Ukraine countryside. I'd often seen cattle trucks at Kamionka station when we were taking produce there, and the upper sections had bar-covered windows to let fresh air in for the cattle, but this car had been designed for the transport of humans. There was no possibility of anybody escaping when the train slowed down and anyway, during the journey the train only stopped outside isolated stations, well away from the prying eyes of inquisitive locals. I did hear Edek, Martin, Zybyshek and Tadek talking about an escape attempt at the first opportunity, but nothing came of it and I think they decided to abandon

28

the idea. Even if they successfully got off the train without being shot by the guards, they would have to survive freezing conditions, without warm clothing and food. In this ill-prepared state they would be easily rounded up by local militias, who might be paid a bounty by the authorities for capturing the escapees.

After what seemed like days, the train ground to a halt. I think it was around midnight, but it was difficult to judge, because of the winter darkness and short daylight hours. We had no means of keeping track of time, as the soldiers had forbidden the adults to take their watches. No doubt these, along with all our possessions and animals had been looted by the Soviets the day after we left. The door was unlocked and two soldiers handed in a pile of enamel mugs, two buckets of soup and around twelve batch loaves of black bread. Dad, Mum and some mothers shouted at them, 'When are we going to get water, the children are very thirsty and they'll all die. We need water, please get us some!' They pleaded in vain, but the Russians ignored them and locked the doors. It took ages for the food to be distributed along the length of the train, but eventually they finished and our journey continued. The 'soup' was a concoction of rotten fish, vegetables and potatoes and already cold when we shared it out. As for the 'bread', it appeared to be a mixture of flour, sawdust and potatoes and had been only half-baked, with a type of clay outer covering. Having always been used to nourishing thick soups and Mum's tasty oven-baked bread, we were horrified. Everybody felt sick at the smell of the appalling soup and there was just enough bread for a small piece each. Dad, assessing the situation, warned everybody, 'Listen, if you don't at least eat some of it, you'll die. I don't know how long this journey's going to take; we could even be locked in here for weeks. Even they know that we must have water at the next stop, or we'll all die of thirst!'

The mothers desperately tried to coax the babies and children to eat a little of the soup, but the greatest need was for water. I tried to eat the soup, but after swallowing a few mouthfuls, I nearly vomited, such was the taste of the pieces of rotten fish floating in the liquid. What if this rubbish was all we were going to have from now on? I dreaded to think of our future health, and without water we wouldn't have a future anyway, wherever we were going in this dark, freezing, creaking truck of despair. Next I tried to eat a little of the bread. It was rock hard and tasteless, so I dipped pieces into the soup liquid, to at least have something in my stomach, which by now was pleading for food. I looked across at Wlatka, Salka, Helena, Stefa and Honorka and the other girls and women. Not surprisingly, they were also struggling to eat, but they gave up after a few mouthfuls, feeling nauseous and I later heard several vomiting into the toilet. We all had searing stomach pains later on and I think most people had already decided not to drink the soup and just eat the bread, assuming that the guards brought us some precious water to dip it in.

On and on went the train and once again, it was not until the middle of the next night that it stopped. The door opened and, thank God, the soldiers handed in buckets of water. Dad told the adults to issue it to the mothers, babies and children first and then we all had a mug full each. He warned everybody to drink slowly and make it last, as it could well be that we would only have water on alternate nights and so he was proved right, as at the next stop there was just bread and the hated soup. Heavy snow was now falling, with such deep drifts on the tracks that progress was very slow and it took another three days to reach Kiev, the Ukraine capital. Some of the adults standing on the bunks recognised the city outskirts, but as usual, we stopped outside the station.

The train was stationary for about an hour, then suddenly the doors opened and a guard pointed at Edek and me and motioned for us to come down onto the track. We walked in front of three soldiers who guarded us with fixed bayonets until we reached a small water tap which was enclosed in straw to prevent the water from freezing. They gave us each a bucket to fill from the slow trickle and as we waited, one of the soldiers, who spoke good Polish, apologised for our treatment. He admitted that he and all his colleagues were terrified of the NKVD and worried that there might well be an informer planted in their ranks. If this treacherous soldier betrayed them, they would be immediately arrested and deported to the Gulag. When the buckets were full, we staggered back to the train, nearly collapsing with hunger and weakness. Later, we all discussed what the soldier had told us. We felt sure that the 'Gulag' he mentioned must be a severe prison camp somewhere in Russia.

The Soviet Gulag Prison System

The Gulag (Glavnoe Upravlenie LAGerei: Main Camp Administration) was the name given to a vast network of labour camps in Siberia, where millions of prisoners were deported over the twenty year Stalinist era alone. The NKVD ruthlessly controlled these terrible places. The camps in Vorkuta, in the furthest extremity of the Ural mountains; Magadan on the coast of the Sea of Orkhotska; Chechotka and Kolyma inland; and the White Sea- Baltic Canal were notorious for the high death rate among prisoners working in slave conditions, in gold, lead and copper mines. In one camp, on the island of Novaya Zemyla, between the Kara and Barents sea, which was later used for Soviet underground Nuclear tests in the 1960s, it is widely believed that nobody survived incarceration. There were also reports of prison ships from other regions of the Soviet Union, bound for Siberia, sinking in bad weather. In one catastrophe, a ship was trapped in the Arctic pack ice. With no hope of rescue and all food supplies gone, the seamen and guards fled across the ice, leaving thousands of poor souls locked in the hold to freeze to death.

The conditions in the wagon were now appalling, especially the stench from the toilet, which sometimes overflowed and we had to use some of our precious water to wash it down periodically. We were now filthy and lice-ridden, and many were suffering from dysentery and continuous stomach pains and many children had hacking coughs. Some days, the train would pull up alongside mountains of coal at the side of the track. We could see the driver and fireman shovelling coal on board and filling the engine's boiler from water tanks. The soldiers commandeered locals to help, but they didn't use us, for fear that someone would escape in a blizzard 'white-out'. However, they always chose Edek and me to collect the water on alternate days.

As the days dragged on interminably, we were certain that we would starve or freeze to death and all the adults took turns to keep the children warm. Progress was slow because of the terrible weather. It seemed to become even colder and during early March, the train was diverted into a siding for a week to wait for the blizzards to die out. March 15th was my 15th birthday, but needless to say, there were no celebrations, just good wishes all round, everybody shouting the Polish birthday greeting: 'Sto lat!' (May you live for a thousand years!). Around this time, Dad proudly showed me his secret store of tobacco seeds! I was amazed that he had managed to fill a pocket with the seeds during our hurried evacuation from the farm. I thought he was very brave and extremely farsighted but as he said, they might well come in handy in the future, if he had a chance to grow a small plot of tobacco.

At last on April 9th, fifty-six days after leaving Kamionka, we arrived at a small run-down station. A rusty sign proclaimed: 'Swieregorske.' Nobody had the faintest idea where we were and there was still snow on the ground. The guards ordered everyone off the train, hurrying us towards a convoy of tractors, trailers and horse drawn carts. The drivers were wrapped in furs and sat resolutely in their seats, making no attempt to help anyone to climb aboard, even though they could see that everybody was weak and exhausted. Perhaps they'd done this trip many times before and we were just another army of cheap labour for Stalin, but I could now look around and see just how many villagers had been on the train. There must have been over a thousand queuing for their onward transport and thankfully, it appeared that all had survived the journey; at least I didn't see any bodies laid out on the side of the track. I had half expected many Kamionka people to have died from severe food poisoning after digesting the rotten soup. It later transpired that during the arduous journey many hadn't eaten the soup, just the bread and water. They saved up bread scraps to dunk in the water when it arrived on alternate days and their expediency probably saved their lives. As one told me later, 'Better to starve than die!'

There wasn't much room on the trailers and carts so we all crammed in; at least it was one way of keeping out of the bitter wind and sleet. Zybyshek, our Russian linguist, bravely attempted to engage the stony-faced driver in conversation, hoping to discover our destination. The man's response was a look of utter contempt and his reply a monosyllabic grunt followed by the goading of his horse into action. We travelled for an interminable distance that day, eventually arriving at a clearing in the forest, where there were about one hundred small huts. If this was a prison camp, it was very strange. It wasn't surrounded by a barbed wire fence and there were no watchtowers. Later, a local told me that there was no need for such security measures: any prisoner foolish enough to attempt to escape would be soon lost in the forest and die of starvation, or be attacked and killed by the packs of timber wolves that roamed the area.

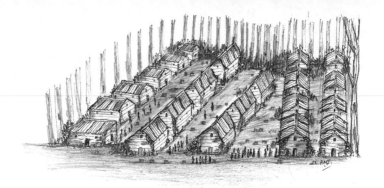

CHAPTER 4
Stalin's slave

A group of Russian soldiers were waiting for us to arrive and as soon as everybody had disembarked from the wagons, they told us to get organised in family groups of eight. I joined Mum, Dad, Wlatka, Salka, Edek, Martin and Honorka. Zybyshek later told us that he had asked one of the guards if we were in Siberia, but the fellow had laughed and shaken his head. He told Zybyshek that Siberia was at least another week's journey east, beyond the Ural Mountains. What a vast, inhospitable country Russia is! Our clothes were now stinking rags, but no replacements were offered and the soldiers left us to sort out our living arrangements. The huts had sloping; corrugated iron roofs and would be freezing at night, as there were just square holes instead of windows. Wooden boards covered the floor and at each end were benches to enable four prisoners to sleep head to head, with a wooden partition separating the men and women. There were no toilet or washing facilities, but fortunately the hut was heated with a central wood-burning stove and a flickering paraffin lamp cast shadows on the walls, lessening the gloom of the dreary place.

No food was provided that first evening, but we were so tired we all just lay on the hard benches and fell asleep. The next morning, we queued in long lines at the camp's food distribution hut for a miserable breakfast consisting of soup similar to that which we endured on the journey, accompanied by bread. Everyone groaned in disappointment at seeing that the hated soup had again appeared on the 'menu'. This time, it was liberally laced with salt and as there was no water, we had to eat snow to quench our thirst. I met Stefa during breakfast and she wasn't very happy, as her hut was very crowded and she was appalled at the non-existent washing and sanitary facilities. I told her that regrettably, the same ablution arrangements existed in all the huts and I didn't see how anything could be done about it. Quite a large village called Oserki lay near our camp, so later we decided to walk over to it. The inhabitants, who seemed very friendly, were amazed that we had been hardworking farmers like themselves. Apparently the NKVD had put a notice in the village news sheet, warning Oserkians of the imminent arrival of farmers and their families from Polish Ukraine. The notice branded the new arrivals as wicked capitalists, who starved their peasant workers and beat them savagely with whips. So this explains the attitude of the drivers at Swieregorske station!

There were a few small shops in Oserki, but the shelves were bare and the only items readily available were potatoes and bread. The latter was of only marginally better quality than that which we had been eating for weeks. We explained that we didn't have any money and they quite understood; in fact the shopkeepers seemed very nice people. Seeing our tired, emaciated condition, I'm quite sure they would have willingly have given us food, but I think they had barely enough to feed themselves and their families. We retraced our steps back to the camp for the evening meal and then, as we were all still exhausted after the terrible journey, decided to go straight to bed. Before we slept, Dad led us in prayers but afterwards reminded us not to forget that this was a labour camp and although the Russians had left us alone today, a prisoner had told him they would be setting up the work parties first thing in the morning.

Dad awoke us from our dead sleep at 6.00a.m. the next morning and we went to the food hut. Thankfully, this time we had water with the soup and bread. After breakfast, a soldier banged on the hut door and pointed to the area outside, where we all had to assemble. There were about a thousand prisoners milling about in the clearing; families and friends chatting to one another, all anxious about what was going to happen next. A party of Russian Political Commissars arrived and speaking through an interpreter, a brutal looking Commissar, who introduced himself as Comrade Sergei, addressed us. He said we had been brought to Russia to work for their great leader Stalin and after our lazy, capitalist lives in the Ukraine, things were now going to change. He berated us for our treatment of our workers and, his voice rising, repeatedly screamed one word, 'Rabotach! Rabotach! Work! Work!' So that was the thug's message and believe me, he meant every word. Thumping his greatcoat with a gloved hand, he emphasised that everybody had to work and inevitably some would die. Exceptions were to be made for young children and mothers with babies, who would be taken to a nursery in Oserki and luckily, Honorka was to work there. Other children were be looked after by Russian women in the camp, but disabled adults like Dad (who had suffered an injury in the First World War), would remain behind with Mum, who had to clean the huts every day. The soldiers later made him night watchman for the camp food store. We feared for his health as this job would involve long shifts, standing outside the hut in all weathers with totally inadequate warm or waterproof clothing.

When the soldiers had finished organising the working arrangements for the villagers who would live permanently in the transit huts, our large workforce was marched for an hour into the forest, eventually arriving at two enormous huts in a clearing. These had also been made from corrugated iron sheets, but the floors were earthen, and again had a central wood-burning stove and paraffin lamp. Wooden sleeping benches ran all around the walls and men and women slept head to toe with no privacy and no blankets were issued. As in the transit huts, there were no washing facilities and prisoners needing the toilet had to go outside in the trees. (These foul sanitary arrangements were to lead to rampant disease later on, as the summer temperatures soared).

Reveille next morning was at six and we were rudely awakened from our sleep by soldiers bashing the hut doors with rifle butts shouting, 'Rabotach! Rabotach!' There was a camp canteen nearby, and tired and shivering we stumbled out of the hut to join long lines of prisoners being served the usual poor food from a hatch by three cooks. They were very efficient and clearly were under orders to speed up the food distribution, so the working brigades could be fed quickly and lined up before leaving the camp. After breakfast, using sign language the guards told us to arrange ourselves into groups of three, so I asked Wlatka and Salka to join me, in case they needed help when the work started. The villagers in Oserki had already told us that we would be felling fir trees and it was very hard, dangerous work. There were about one hundred and seventy teams of three prisoners and we were taken to a large workshop where three Russian prisoners handed us a cross-saw, two axes and a pole with a spike on the end. They then gave us a brigade number and marked this on a tool rack for easy identification when we returned the equipment at the end of each day's work.

The worksite was about an hours march into the forest and all around were thousands of tree stumps from the labours of previous work parties. The Russians seemed to randomly select a starting point, then push into the forest for mile after mile. The trees seemed to go on in a never-ending silent green swathe and we could see small muddy tracks created by workers and guards tramping back and forth. No doubt tractors and carts would be used to take the trees away, but this was a long way off yet. The trees were about eighty metres tall and the problem of how we were going to manage to cut them down safely seemed insurmountable. We had no previous experience of tree felling and on the farm, there were only medium sized larch and birch trees, which were easy to handle. These gigantic firs were a completely different proposition and every time I looked up at them, the job seemed more daunting than ever. At school in Kamionka we had all seen pictures of lumberjacks working in the forests of Western Canada, but how we were going to manage to cut the trees down, I had no idea. To start with, our clothing was unsuitable for the work and weather conditions, as in this area, it seemed winter would never loosen its grip and bitter high winds blew incessantly all day. Surely the guards would ask some experienced Russian workers nearby to at least give us a quick demonstration of the safest method? Not a chance: the guards were already leaving and not in the least bit interested in how we would manage.

We watched the Russians working effortlessly, but to me it seemed a very dangerous procedure even in calm weather, let alone struggling in blustery conditions. I decided to go up to them and ask them to help us at least start correctly, to avoid an accident, as I was very worried as to how Wlatka and Salka would cope, especially if things went badly wrong. One called Ivan came back with me and he soon showed us the safest method. He said that he was glad that I had asked for advice, as there had been lots of accidents with previous inexperienced groups. Sadly, many had found to their cost that it was virtually impossible to control a tree weighing tons if it swung towards them in high winds when being lowered to the ground. He told us that the saw and axes were sharpened every night to a razor-like cutting edge and again, great care was needed using them, especially as we were not wearing gloves. Above all, he reminded us that there was no hospital in Oserki nor any medical supplies, doctors or nurses at the camp.

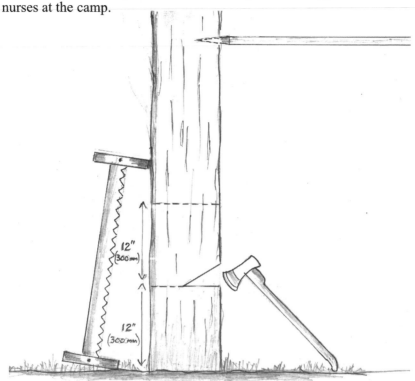

The procedure started by using the saw to make a nine-inch cut into the tree trunk, twelve inches from the base. This cut was then chopped carefully with an axe into a V shape and then another worker would stab the spike on the pole into the tree trunk. This was done about two metres above the V cut to secure the tree and stop it falling in the wrong direction in the high wind, or worse still, on top of us! The trunk was then sawed right through, twelve inches above the wedge-shaped cut and the tree slowly lowered to the ground. The branches were then lopped off and most importantly, any rough edges were smoothly shaped with the axes and finally the trunk sawed into four very precise measurements. Later, one of the Russians kindly warned us that it was imperative that the measurements were accurate, as a Soviet tree inspector would be periodically checking them and he would soon detect inaccuracies, which could lead to an accusation of 'sabotage' and a likelihood of severe punishment.

We then attempted this difficult operation ourselves and slowly got the hang of the complicated procedure, and anyway the guards weren't around, so we learned as we went along, gaining more confidence with each tree felled and cut up. Before they left, the guards had told us that there would no food until the evening and as it was late winter, there were no berries or fruits to pick. The only way to alleviate our thirst was by eating snow, which was still quite deep in the forest. Although the temperature hovered around freezing in the late afternoon, the work kept us warm and at five p.m. the guards returned to escort us back in the dark, so we collected up our tools.

Suddenly as we walked along, the chilling sound of howling wolves echoed through the forest and Salka and Wlatka were terrified, clinging on to me. The wolves boldly came closer and when I looked around I could sometimes see their yellow eyes glistening as they watched our party. The soldiers were used to wolves and a few of them moved to the back of the procession and then lit newspapers, to keep the animals at bay. It worked, as this was one thing that scared them off, and it certainly taught us a lesson. If we had to make this trip unaccompanied by the guards, we must bring newspapers and matches at all times, although this danger would recede when the days lengthened and the wolves retreated deeper into the forest. On arrival back at the huts, we first stopped at the tool workshop. Our saw and axes were carefully examined by the men there and hung up on the beam at our allotted place. One of these men, whom I met one day, told me that four men worked all night, sharpening and repairing the saws and axes for the next day's work. I will say that the tools were made from the finest quality steel and in pristine condition, so we had to be very careful handling them. Pity the prisoner who damaged, or lost one of them: I dread to think what punishment they would receive.

Our first working day ended with a wait of several hours for our food, as now the workers from all the brigades were back in the camp and there must have been a thousand people in the food queue. After the meal, I fell exhausted onto my sleeping bench, completely shattered, and this was just the first day! I looked around the hut and saw that many villagers were already fast asleep in their clothes. Luckily, one of the Russian women who cleaned the hut had kept the stove lit, so at least it would be warm for a few hours. As Dad was based in the transit huts there wasn't anybody to lead us in prayers, so I just whispered a heartfelt 'thank you' that I'd survived the first day, then fell into a deep sleep.

It was the usual noisy reveille the next morning at 6.00a.m. As the guards knew how tired we'd be, they shouted a threatening, 'Rabotach!' at the top of their voices and hammered the door and walls. I felt like death after yesterday and every bone in my body ached, as it was impossible to enjoy a comfortable night's sleep on those iron-hard benches. The day started with a visit for everybody to the 'toilets' in the nearby trees. I felt so sorry for the females, who were completely humiliated by this unpleasant ordeal. But there was nowhere else to go and in the days ahead we all got used to it. On the train, everybody was helpful and sympathetic, aware of each other's considerable embarrassment, but here, with hundreds of prisoners all around, it was very difficult and nobody cared. It would have taken a very brave person to have asked for toilets to be provided and a beating would have very likely have been the outcome.

After the usual scramble for breakfast, we collected our tools for the second day and marched out to the forest, but this time the Commissar Sergei accompanied the guards. Assuming that after just one day we were thoroughly competent, he gave a lecture on the importance of achieving our daily quota, or 'norm'. Each team was expected to cut down, trim and saw to the exact measurements, five trees a day. This figure was to be the standard 'norm' for all workers, without exception. Failure to achieve this, for whatever reason, would be punishable by deprivation of the evening meal! We were aghast at this ruthless warning as everybody realised that to even attempt to work hard, without regular food every day, would be impossible. What about the women, already too weak to manage the work on the meagre rations? Any poor team that repeatedly failed to reach the norm would eventually be too exhausted to even march to work and would die in their huts from starvation. A horrible, ghastly, thought and a sober one too, as anybody could be too ill to get up some days and if that was the case, they'd have nothing at all to eat, as the guards would punish them repeatedly. Thank God that Mum and Dad didn't have to work in the forest, as they'd die very quickly. I knew for a fact that Dad was finding his watchman's job very hard going, but neither would survive a week with us.

That evening we had a surprise visitor –my brother Joseph! He had been in the camp since November 1939, after being captured by the Russians. He looked very well, but had been shocked to learn on the camp grapevine that we had all been deported from the farm at Kamionka. He spent some time telling us about the camp regime, promising to later show us the ropes; for instance which guards to avoid, how to gain a little extra food and tellingly, which Russians would turn a blind eye to any rule-breaking for a small bribe. He warned us that the NKVD always had several paid informants among the prisoners in every labour camp and emphasised strongly that we must be very careful in casual conversations with strangers who were too friendly and ingratiating. Their usual ploy was to gain a prisoner's confidence, asking loaded questions in an attempt to procure useful information, which was passed on to their superiors. Joseph was delighted and roared with laughter when I told him about Dad's secret hoard of tobacco, saying that it would prove to be invaluable in the future for bribing and bartering both with the guards and villagers. Just before he left he said he would arrange for Edek, Tadek and Martin to stay in his hut, as three poor unfortunate prisoners had recently died, so there was room for three more.

Thankfully there was no work on Sundays, so we just rested, trying to recover from the previous weeks labour. Accidents were frequent, as my Russian friend predicted, because without sturdy gloves there was no protection from the axes bouncing off the smooth tree trunks. I sliced my index finger one day using the cross–saw, but there were no bandages, ointment or medical treatment of any kind. Wlazda treated the wound as best she could, using cloths to bind my finger and keep it clean, thus avoiding gangrene, a veritable death sentence in that hostile environment (I still have the deep scars today, sixty years later!).

A few weeks into the work, the starvation diet started to take its toll. People started to die in the night and in the morning the guards ordered us to carry the bodies outside, to be buried in long pits that other prisoners had dug near the huts. The soldiers sprinkled quicklime on the corpses and then told the prisoners to cover them with frozen earth. Some days, we found prisoners who were too weak to get up and they were left in the hut. Invariably they were dead when we arrived back after work. Even with the fire, the large hut was always freezing at nights and sometimes I awoke to find that my hair was frozen to the bench! I estimated that fifty prisoners had died in one terrible week, but later the toll was to rise inexorably. Everybody developed frostbite on their fingers and especially their toes, as our boots had holes in them and were always wet.

One bitterly cold day, we were all alarmed on finding that due to our lack of facemasks, the vicious wind chill had turned our noses white. I rushed over to the Russians to ask their advice, as we thought that soon our noses would drop off our faces! They laughed and soon sorted out our frightening predicament, by getting us to press a handful of snow against our noses for a few minutes: thankfully this strange remedy worked!

As a result of the rampaging lice in the huts, which were driving everybody insane, especially at night, the guards told us to light log fires in what appeared to be a delousing shed, twenty metres from the huts. Once the wood had been lit and was later smouldering, we poured water on the fire to create clouds of steam and acrid smoke. Finally our lice-ridden rags were hung on a rail above the fire, while we sweated in the heat, trying to remove the dirt and sticky tree sap from our bodies.

CHAPTER 5
The Death of Anniela

In early May, a Commissar named Dimitri told me that Mum was very ill in her hut outside Oserki that she shared with Dad and Honorka. He gave me permission to go to visit her immediately and later, once a month as her health improved. I would have obviously preferred to see her every week, but I was grateful for him telling me, so didn't argue and went to see her. Mum lay on her bench, looking very frail and listless but her face lit up when she saw me. The dreadful food and conditions had severely weakened her, but if it hadn't been for Dad and Honorka, she wouldn't have survived this long. As we talked quietly, she suddenly started sobbing uncontrollably, lamenting the family's situation and bewailing the loss of her lovely farm and home. She wondered wistfully who was living in the farmhouse now and what had become of the family possessions and heirlooms that she treasured so dearly. Over a year later, I learned from a Ukrainian who had also lived in Kamionka and whom I met in Uzbekistan, that a Soviet Commissar was cosily ensconced in our home with his family. The outbuildings were in a ramshackle state and there was no sign of the livestock. They had probably been slaughtered and eaten soon after the Russian seized possession. Doubtless all the fields had been left to grow wild, or had become another addition to Stalin's kolkhoz, or collective farms that now covered the entire Ukraine. However, any self-satisfaction that this thief may have had with his fortuitous acquisition would certainly have evaporated overnight, when Hitler suddenly attacked Russia, on June 22nd 1941.

It was imperative that I get some fresh milk for Mum, but none was available in the co-operative village shop. Luckily, a local told me that a family living in an adjacent hamlet had a cow and might be persuaded to let me have a few litres. There were only a few houses in this very poor village, which was half a kilometre from Oserki. I had no idea of its existence, as we were forbidden to go outside our work areas and anyway, I only had permission to visit Mum. I found the house, which was at the end of the village, and after listening to my urgent request in my best Russian and my admission that I had no money but would give her a small bag of tobacco seeds, the mother graciously let me have two precious litres. I thanked her profusely for her great kindness and started off back to Mum's hut. Suddenly two Soviet soldiers appeared on horseback, shouting, 'Prekrati ili eto sdelaiuia!' ('Stop, or we shoot!'). I ignored their commands and ran for my life as fast as I could into the safety of the forest. They immediately started firing with their rifles, the bullets hitting or ricocheting off the tree trunks and whistling past my head. Luckily, as the forest was very dense they couldn't follow me, so I ran in zigzags through the trees and shook them off. It was now getting dark, so I waited in the forest for about half an hour, listening intently for any sound of my pursuers, before carefully venturing onto the road. Satisfied that was no sign of the Russians, I safely returned to Mum's hut with the precious milk. I fondly kissed her goodbye, promising that I would come again as soon as I could arrange it with Dimitri.

I next decided that I would get some potatoes for Mum: perhaps Honorka or Dad could bake them on the hut stove and she would be able to eat a few. I remembered seeing a small field of potatoes on my near-fatal mission for the milk, but this could well be even more dangerous than the last attempt, as the soldiers would definitely be looking for me. On a Sunday night a week later, I returned to Oserki to try my luck. There was no moon, so I could easily get to the field without anyone seeing me in the village (I was a bit concerned that a villager would denounce me to the NKVD and claim a bounty of some kind if I was caught). I stealthily crept into the field, lay down alongside a patch of plants and very carefully and quietly, eased up a clutch of potatoes from the soil and put them into my sack. I repeated the process until the sack was half full but as I started to retrace my steps, a voice shouted, 'Rukiv verka!' ('Hands up!')

My blood froze in shock, as I couldn't see where the soldier was in the darkness. I instantly dived down among the potato plants and hid in the small ditch, praying that he couldn't see me. My heart was hammering so loudly in my chest I felt sure he'd hear it and finish me off there and then. He fired several times in my direction but missed, but at least from the gun muzzle flames, I knew where he was. I desperately tried to scramble away in panic, along the rows of potatoes and out of the field. Then I ran as fast as I've ever done down the road, tightly gripping the sack and thankfully it was so dark he had no idea in which direction I'd gone. I soon reached Mum's hut and literally collapsed in relief beside her, but I didn't breathe a word about my lucky escape and just showed her the potatoes!

After I had recovered from my second brush with death, I walked back to the camp and told everybody about my experience. They were all very relieved, but Wlatka and Salka told me very firmly never to take any more risks again, Wlatka saying, 'They'll get you next time Julian, you know that. For Heavens sake, Mum wouldn't want you to risk your life for her!' I reluctantly agreed and said that would be my last attempt to get food to vary Mum's meals.

In the morning, two days later, an urgent message came from Dimitri to go immediately to Mum. I rushed up to Oserki to be with Dad and the others. Mum was definitely not going to live very much longer: she was sleeping peacefully as we waited for the inevitable end, and sadly she died in the afternoon. Dad was inconsolable. He would dearly have wished that a priest had been present to administer the last rites during her final hours on this earth. I told Dad and Edek I was determined that Mum wasn't going to be buried in one of the bleak communal graves near the forest, so I chose a site on the grass verge adjoining the peaceful main road. Although it was now May the ground was still frozen to a depth of three feet, so I had to light fires for two days to thaw the soil. I cried continuously as I struggled to break up that hateful, flint-hard ground, using an iron rod and a small shovel and then asked Edek to help me with the burial in the morning. In the meantime, I had to somehow make a coffin and, scavenging around the huts, found a few pieces of wooden packing cases, so I nailed them together.

The following day, Dad, Joseph, Wlatka, Salka, Honorka, Stefa, Tadek and Edek joined me as we gently laid Mum to rest, said a few simple prayers of farewell and filled in the grave. The girls placed a posy of early spring flowers at the foot of the mound and finally, I planted a cross at the head of the grave, inscribed with her name and dates and we all sadly departed.

On reflection, it was thanks to Dimitri, the sympathetic, kind Commissar, who enabled me to make my visits to Mum and be in attendance with the family at her death and finally give her a decent Christian burial in that God-forsaken place.

CHAPTER 6
New Clothes

The next day it was back to work. I couldn't concentrate at all and after a few days, became very depressed at Mum's death. Finally I told the girls I'd had enough and all our anguish would end if we pulled a tree down on top of us. They were aghast at my suggestion, as they certainly didn't want to die! They told me very forcibly that it was a stupid idea, as we all might be badly injured and would endure lingering deaths. They asked me incredulously if I had forgotten that there weren't any medical facilities in the camp. Of course, Wlatka and Salka were right; it would have been a terrible act on my part. In my misery I just hadn't thought of the long-term consequences for us. I apologised to them and they encouraged me to put all such thoughts out of my mind for ever!

The mortality rate among the prisoners was now steadily increasing. The cumulative effects of starvation, exposure and the relentless, backbreaking work started to make a huge impact. Every day more and more bodies were being carried out to the burial pits. By now, the temperature was rising and the stench of the bodies, plus the human waste lying everywhere, was sickening. Surely, these conditions would eventually lead to a devastating epidemic such as typhus, which would wipe us all out. Those who collapsed and died during work didn't have graves, as the guards callously refused to allow us to dig any, even though this would have meant a superhuman effort in our weakened state. We all felt it was the very least we could do for dear friends and fellow villagers for them to have a decent burial. There was no compromise from the soldiers. Sergei, the heartless Commissar, repeatedly made it clear that as the dead workers were of no use any longer to Comrade Stalin and the

State, their bodies were to be dumped in the undergrowth and left for the wolves, foxes and other forest carrion to devour.

By now my boots were useless, with leaking, cracking uppers and large holes in the soles. I had to tie them with string to prevent them falling off my feet. Once again, the Russian workers came to my aid: seeing the state of my boots, they showed me how to cut the bark off a tree to use as a sole, which was then wrapped around with rags to make a decent foot covering. To supplement our food rations we were always setting traps for rabbits, which we'd take back and cook in the hut. We found out that if we dried the fur it made a very good foot covering, as it was softer and more comfortable then the tree bark. Ivan and his group were impressed with our ingenuity and some also used rabbit fur themselves and so we all adapted to these primitive methods of foot covering. Our clothes, which we had been wearing since our deportation, were now completely disintegrating and a substitute had to be found from somewhere before they completely fell off our backs.

This time the assistance of the Oserkians was invaluable. They were too poor to buy even second-hand clothes and instead, cut up food sacking to make into vests. We soon improvised in this way and found the vests very cool and hardwearing. None of the conscript soldiers that I came across in Russia were wearing decent uniforms and always gave the appearance of a down trodden, ragbag army. The NKVD bosses ignored the state of the men's clothing and never gave them replacements, so they too were reduced to wearing sacking vests and foot rags. The Commissars themselves wore very smart uniforms and some prisoners who had been to the NKVD barracks at Oserki were staggered at the luxuries they had seen there, including the finest food, cigarettes and copious supplies of the best vodka. Talking of tobacco, Dad had successfully planted the seeds that he had managed to bring from the farm. Later the tobacco grown would be very useful as a bribe to obtain extra food from the kitchen staff and we knew the poverty-stricken soldiers could be 'bought'. Maybe the tobacco would persuade them to make Dad's watchman's job easier and reduce the hours of his shifts. He needed all the support we could give him, as he was still heartbroken and bewildered following the grievous loss of Mum. As for the prisoners, they made their own tobacco from dried larch leaves, which were then wrapped in newspaper. Anyway, they didn't have any money to buy tobacco from the village shop, even if it was available.

One evening after work, I was having a chat with Ivan, our friendly Russian who had helped us so much at the start of our work in the forest. He had told us previously that he and his workmates had been at the logging camp since 1937, but never gave a reason for them being sent here. They had been suspicious that any one of us could be a stool-pigeon, cunningly inserted in our ranks by the NKVD and reporting back to them any grumbles or derogatory remarks about Stalin. He said the NKVD prison system was riddled with informers, who were well looked after by their bosses. Ivan and his pals had tested us out on several occasions since our arrival, but were happy enough that we were genuine; no doubt if one of us had been a plant, a very nasty 'accident' would have been arranged! He then told me his disturbing story: he was from Kharkov and like so many millions of innocent Russians, had been denounced to the NKVD by someone as an 'enemy of the people' during a frightening period in the 1930s called 'The Great Terror'. Like all dictators, Stalin was paranoid about assassination and conspiracy and especially afraid of the military, who he was convinced would mount a lightning coup d'etat at any time. He plotted with the Minister of the Interior, a monster called Lavrenti Beria, to pre-empt any move by these imaginary enemies, who were arrested and tortured into admitting their complicity in a plot against him or the State. In Ivan's case, although he was completely innocent, he was lucky just to be charged with 'sabotage' against the State and sentenced to ten years in a labour camp, in contrast to so many who were shot, or deported to the Gulag.

Ivan also told me that deadly purges were carried out against the military in the late 1930s. Massive show trials took place, these being elaborately contrived to give the outside world the pretence of Soviet 'justice'. (Stalin's obsession with perceived enemies would rebound on him years later. He foolishly had hundreds of his top officers shot during the 'Great Terror' purges and bitterly regretted this when in June 1941, Hitler suddenly invaded Russia and the Red Army was virtually leaderless, with only inexperienced commanders and officers to try to stem the Nazi invasion. Even his most senior general, Georgy Zhukov, was on Beria's original death lists and only escaped because of an administrative error).

After hearing Ivan's story, I was greatly relieved that we had lived well away from the big cities. Any jealous person wanting to settle an old score could easily have fabricated a story, telling the NKVD that Dad was a wicked capitalist plotter, wrecker, subversive, enemy of the state and so on. If that had been the case the entire family would have perished. At least we knew where we were here and, remembering my luck during the imprisonment in the cowshed, it was conceivable that if there were a change at the top in Moscow, we would be released!

CHAPTER 7
The Volga

The mighty Volga River flowed quite near our worksite, but it couldn't be seen because of the forest surrounding its steep banks. The Russians told us that the logs we had cut would be rafted downstream to the sawmills as soon as the ice 'break-up' had started, and this was usually in early May. However, since the ice had been around seven feet thick all winter, they said it would take a while for this operation to start, as blocks of ice the size of cars floated past for days after the 'break-up'. This seemed to me an enormous undertaking and I wondered how on earth it could be done. By now there were thousands of logs littering the forest. I calculated that our brigade of 170 teams cut up 680 logs a day. In a six-day week 4,080 were cut and a monthly total of around 16,320 logs could be achieved. That's without the extra logs cut by faster, experienced workers, who regularly exceeded the 'norms' and got extra rations. So the figures for a ten week stint in the forest were around 40,800 logs! Add on the output of the other brigades throughout the vast forests and Comrade Stalin was doing very nicely from his unpaid, slave army.

The May 'break–up' was under way when I was unexpectedly summoned to the NKVD barracks in Oserki. I hadn't been to the Commissars' H.Q. before and soon realised that their living conditions were somewhat different from ours. The large wooden building adjoining the barracks was comfortably furnished and well heated. Several prisoners had done odd jobs there and were very envious of the officers' superb accommodation. Some days they had worked near the officers' mess room and looked on hungrily at the steaming dishes served by women from the village. I did wonder what the conditions were like in the rough looking barracks where the conscripts stayed and wouldn't have been surprised if they lodged in cold, bleak dormitories. One thing's for sure; they most definitely would have been partaking of a distinctly different menu from their superiors! Why I wondered, had I been summoned to this meeting? Perhaps there was a perfectly straightforward reason? No such luck in Stalin's kingdom! The meeting had been arranged between selected prisoners and the Commissars to discuss new working practices. I had been asked to attend because they were pleased with my work. Sergei, the odious Commissar, offered me the position of foreman in charge of a brigade of thirty workers to supervise the movement of the logs down to the Volga. However, one important condition of my promotion would be that I speeded up the process, using any methods I felt necessary, even by physically punishing the workers or by denouncing perceived 'saboteurs' to the NKVD. I was also assured that if the output by my brigade increased, I would be rewarded with extra rations, new clothes and other privileges. I was appalled by this evil proposition and, slowly looking at the expectant faces of the assembled officers, immediately declined, as I could never ill treat my fellow workers, no matter what incentives were offered. Sergei looked hard at me, his face slowly changing into a vicious mask of hate and he became insanely angry. His cobra-like eyes bored into my soul, 'Julian you're a fool, we'd have looked after you, now you'll die with the others, we'll work you to death! Now you ungrateful Polish louse you can get out of here. Get out! Get back to your stinking hole before I put a bullet in you!'

I trudged sadly back to my hut, wondering what Sergei would do. He'd definitely punish me somehow, as his evil plans were now in tatters. He might even force me to do a job that nobody wanted, like dig more burial pits or latrines, working a twelve-hour shift including Sunday. How would the girls manage without me? He probably wouldn't give them a replacement and punish them when they failed to reach the daily 'norm'. But my mind was made up: whatever the outcome, I resolved never to even consider the despicable offer he had made, with it's attendant risk of blackmail and I would accept whatever lay ahead for us all in that hellish country. From now on, I would have to keep a sharp eye out for Sergei. He and Oleg were always hanging around, leering at the girls when we left the huts each morning, so I decided to march in the middle of the group and hope they didn't spot me and haul me out.

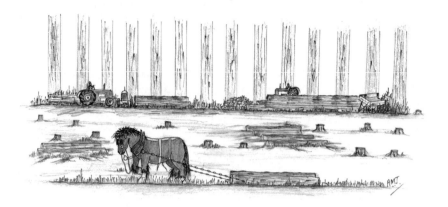

It was plain that the Russians had very few refusals from prisoners they were setting up as overseers and collaborators and were mystified and very angry with me. I think that many workers must have found the offer very enticing and soon overcame any initial disquiet when the extra food materialised. Yes, an extra calorie intake might have made all the difference between survival and death, but could they have lived with their consciences? I knew that some workers who had been transferred here from other slave labour camps were already brutalised by the hardship and degradation and would have done anything to live a few years longer. At least one admitted to me that he had assisted the NKVD in a massacre at a camp in the Ural Mountains for extra food. (I later repeatedly heard in 1943, dark, terrible rumours of cannibalism and of people reduced to eating family pets and even mice and rats during the long siege of Leningrad. Such was the desperation of the trapped, starving citizens, when supplies failed to arrive across Lake Lagoda because of atrocious weather and the German encirclement). Never mind, at least my fellow prisoners were proud of my bold stand and their future welfare and fair treatment was my only concern.

The next day it was decided to start moving the logs immediately, as the big ice-floes had diminished, with just occasional small lumps floating past. About fifty strong shire horses and their handlers had arrived, as they did this time every year, the animals being kept, fed and watered in sheds near the river. The handlers attached chains to the harnesses and the horses could pull two logs at a time to the river, a kilometre away. To facilitate this operation and make the muddy ground less slippery for the horses' hooves, a decking of small branches had been laid in a path, so when the first batch of logs was ready, we followed the horses down to the river.

The Volga River was enormous, but flowed very slowly, being far wider than I imagined and I couldn't see the mist-shrouded far bank. The chains were unclipped from the horses' harnesses near the riverbank and then the logs were rolled by six of us on to a steel slide, from which they tumbled down into the water. About ten men were waiting up to their waists in the freezing river and as each log came down they tied them in rows of ten. They then placed another two layers on top, making a raft of thirty logs, which was lashed together with heavy ropes. Finally, the huge raft was pushed out into the river and it started its slow journey downstream to the sawmills. Men and women were stationed with long poles on the bends to push away rafts that had become entangled in tree roots and other debris. Some of us walked along to find a low bank leading down to the water, to have a wash. We found that slapping the black mud on our faces and upper bodies and washing it off was both cleansing and invigorating and sheer heaven after months without washing. When their shift ended, the team who had been in the water all day without a break emerged, blue with cold and shivering uncontrollably. I was sure they would all eventually die of hyperthermia, as there wasn't even a fire for them to dry out. Although the sun shone all day, a piercing easterly wind ensured that the air was always freezing.

Summer came suddenly to the Volga in 1940 but as the temperature rose, the previously frozen ground became a quagmire. We slipped and fell continuously as we tried to push or roll the logs. It seemed to me that because of the conditions, the work was much harder and more frustrating than in winter. Some days there were violent thunder and lightening storms, with torrential rain and we were soaked through, but the biggest problem, (one that no one had foreseen) was the endless attacks on us by hordes of horseflies and mosquitoes. The guards gave us net hoods that resembled beekeepers' protective headgear. These had to be worn all throughout the long, sweltering summer, as these voracious insects thrived in the swamp-like conditions. Whilst they protected us from bites and potential malaria, the sweat poured out of us, so we had to repeatedly wash ourselves down. The insect attacks never abated as they came at us in never-ending clouds and it was impossible to avoid being

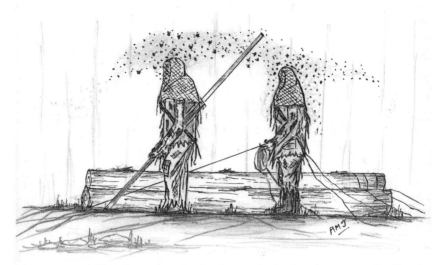

bitten, especially when we were having a dip in the river to cool off. The work would have been impossible in temperatures of thirty-five degrees centigrade and in constant humidity, without water. Thankfully, the thunder storms left pools in the holes in the boggy ground and although some days the water tasted brackish and smelled, it was always welcome after a sudden downpour to slake our constant thirst.

In the midst of this gruelling hard work, a funny episode occurred one day. The Commissar in charge, Oleg, who we hated because he was always trying to make us work faster, yelling 'Rabotach!' came to grief as he was helping to push a log on to the slide. Suddenly his feet went from under him and he rolled down into the river! Hearing our laughter, he scrambled out of the water, dripping wet and, beside himself with rage, started fumbling for his revolver, screaming, 'You Polish scum did that deliberately, somebody pushed me!' We denied this and said he slipped into the river accidentally. Things were very tense for a few moments, but he eventually calmed down, realising that it was his own fault. We kept well clear of Comrade Oleg after that, as he would definitely shoot without hesitation the next time he thought a prisoner was making fun of him.

Strange as it may seem, although I frequently returned from work soaked through and slept in my wet clothes, I never once caught a cold in

Russia, which was fortunate, as any chest infection could have resulted in tuberculosis and death. One condition that affected everybody was a form of blindness, accompanied by agonising pain in the eyes that persisted as the hot summer wore on: not having sunglasses to counteract the blinding glare of the sun on the water may have been a contributory factor. Everybody was worried and I began to think that we would all become blind. The guards said the condition was called 'chicken blindness' and was a result of vitamin deficiency. They eventually realised that medication had to be provided, otherwise they would have huts full of blind prisoners on their hands and the work would stop. Supplies of cod liver oil were urgently brought from a town on the river and a thousand prisoners treated. This basic medicine worked and we wondered why, as they obviously encountered this problem every year, there weren't supplies at the barracks. Quite obviously, it was yet another cynical NKVD ploy to save money at all costs. They would only get the supplies when the health of the workforce was threatened and the sawmills complained of the slow arrival of the logs.

Although we had now been working on the river for the summer, we still didn't know the location of the sawmills; they may have been many kilometres from where we were working. Nor did we know what the logs would be used for and the guards had orders not to tell us anything. There was such a continual emphasis by the inspectors on the precise measurements and smoothness needed before they stamped each log; perhaps the wood was to be exported, after being processed by the sawmills? Alternatively, the wood may have been made into expensive furniture for Party officials. If the latter were the case, they definitely wouldn't tell us that now would they?

CHAPTER 8
Strike!

For some time now, we had we had been discussing a plan to take positive action about our food and general conditions. It had above all, to be something that would not put our lives at risk, as we had no idea what the reaction of Sergei and his cronies would be if they were challenged by us. If they were as utterly ruthless as some suggested, any hint of an attempted go-slow or refusal to leave the huts for work would be construed as an uprising. Many felt that this action would be met with unparalleled ferocity from the Russians, who were heavily armed, and no doubt their NKVD bosses had arrangements in hand to suppress any revolt by the workers in labour camps. I personally was certain that they wouldn't negotiate with us prisoners and would immediately open fire if we refused to go to work.

Some of our colleagues decided not to wait for any discussions with the Commissars. They had already made up their minds to break into the food store, regardless of any reprisals. One night they broke down the storeroom door and carried off armfuls of food, which they victoriously brought back to our hut. The Russians didn't know about the thefts and as usual woke us up the next morning. To their utter disbelief, we told them that we weren't going to leave the huts and nobody was going to work that day: we were on strike! The soldiers quickly left to report to their officers; the alarm was raised and soon the hut was surrounded by fifty guards, all armed with tommy-guns. Trucks of reinforcements arrived from the barracks but no attempt was made to storm the hut. Clearly they had orders not to negotiate with us, so for the moment it was a stalemate and I think they wanted to see what we would do. They probably thought that we'd soon give up without food or water, but they hadn't reckoned on our stock of looted food, which would stop us from starving. The standoff continued for two days, during which time soldiers continuously surrounded the hut.

Eventually on the third day, Sergei shouted from outside that they wished to speak to us. We suspected a trap, and insisted that we would only let him in if four other officers accompanied him. Sergei and Oleg entered with three other Russians and said they were prepared to discuss any grievances we had, so that this unfortunate strike could end. Several people shouted that the soup was always bad, there was never enough of it, we all had dysentery and many had died, as they well knew. I was determined to let them know about our daily treatment and their continued injustices. I exploded in pent-up rage at Sergei, 'We've had enough! We're people, not pigs! In fact, we don't care if you shoot us now!' Sergei, taken aback and very uneasy, answered that they just wanted the strike to end peacefully. He realised that things had gone too far and that we were deadly serious about risking a massacre by his troops. He promised an immediate improvement in the food and conditions, but said we must return to work the next morning. They then immediately left to let us discuss his offer. The soldiers guarding the hut soon dispersed and I watched the trucks leave in a cloud of dust and diesel fumes. After a lengthy debate, we decided to return to work and see if things changed for the better. A few were disgruntled and said that Sergei had only agreed to our demands due to his panic, as the inevitable bloodbath would have made him accountable to his district superiors.

Our challenge to the NKVD did pay off, as the quantity and quality of the food at last improved, to everybody's delight. We'd taken a huge gamble and on this occasion, had been very, very lucky to have successfully called their bluff. Later that evening, I talked to Ivan about our confrontation, which he'd certainly heard about! He gave me many instances of NKVD massacres in labour camps for much lesser offences, as this organisation's penchant for killing was very well founded. Lastly, he advised me not to try anything like that again. Next time, the reaction of the Commissars would be violent and the consequences would almost certainly be execution of the entire brigade, as a salutary warning to the other prisoners.

CHAPTER 9
The Winter of 1940-41

At the end of September we finished the dragging of the logs to the Volga. The armada of slow-moving rafts had not decreased at all during the summer, resulting in hundreds of thousands of logs being despatched to the sawmills. Despite the dangerous job of the raft builders, there were very few accidents and no drowning that I heard of. All that was left to do now was clear up the banks and burn the tons of branches and off-cuts. Alas, the poor horses did not get off so lightly. Sometimes the logs weren't secure in the chains and they would fall on the horses' flanks and legs, badly gashing them or in some cases, breaking them. In wet weather the animals would slip and fall and the heavy logs would smash into them, breaking their necks. The badly injured horses had to be shot and so it was decided by the guards to switch to tractors and winches for the transportation instead of using the strong working animals. The herd was released to roam around the forest and riverbanks until the handlers took them away in the autumn.

'At the first opportunity we cut chunks of flesh off the animals that had been shot and hid the pieces in the bushes and trees during the day. After work, everyone contrived to hide the meat from the soldiers on the long trek back to the huts. Starvation does very strange things to even civilised people, which we certainly regarded ourselves as. I personally hadn't the slightest qualm or queasiness about eating horse flesh and the aroma from the juicy meat, cooking and spitting on its smoky wood fire wafted over the camp, making many prisoners crazy with hunger. When the grossly inadequate evening meals were dished up at the cookhouse, we added our roasted horse meat and devoured the lot in no time but still felt famished.

If prisoners died because they couldn't stomach eating horse flesh, which tasted like sweet meat to me, they were so wrong. However, I did draw the line at eating domestic animals. I regularly witnessed Poles and Russians skinning and cooking dogs and cats which they had somehow caught in Oserki. Other delicacies on their 'alternative' menus were rats, mice, voles, birds, wild mushroom and an array of forest roots and leaves which were roasted and eaten with relish by desperate people, anxious to somehow procure and other week's existence in Stalin's Slave Camps.

In late September it was back to the drudgery of tree cutting. The Commissars didn't even give us a break for a few days after all our Herculean efforts in the baking heat and being constantly tormented by the insects. One advantage of summer work was the abundance of fruits and berries all around us in the forest: at least we were able to assuage the gnawing pangs of hunger that made the work so much harder in winter. We greedily ate all we could and took pocketfuls back to the hut to eat after the evening meal.

There was no new cutting area designated by the guards, so we just carried on where we left off in May. Now that the horses had gone, the question was what mode of transport would now be used for the log transportation? That pair of rogues, Sergei and Oleg soon circumvent the problem. Awaiting our arrival the next day was a line of rusting tractors that looked as if they'd been manufactured around the time of the 1917 Revolution! Typical Stalin! So long as a piece of machinery or in the case of these ancient crocks of tractors, was still standing and somehow a terrified engineer had coaxed another day of life into them, on pain of a Gulag train ticket, they were to be used forthwith! I suddenly realised that this was my chance to have an unexpected sedentary job! I confidently swaggered over to Oleg and told him that I was an experienced tractor driver on our farm in Kamionka. He was pleased to hear this. Anything and anyone who could push on the transportation of the logs to the river was a bonus to his evil mind. If a volunteer unfortunately chose a vehicle that was dangerously defective and it toppled over and crushed the poor devil, it was simply regarded as a bad deal of the cards. Oleg knew full well that plenty more prisoners would risk anything to have eight hours 'rest' sitting on a tractor! My lucky start was shining and I experienced no real problems apart from the mud which I knew would soon freeze hard and prevent an accident leading to possible serious injury or death.

We had advanced three kilometres into the forest by the winter of 1940; such was the speed demanded, as they were always trying to increase the daily norms. We were always aware of attempts by the guards to increase output but we worked carefully and methodically. The soldiers, therefore, couldn't detect any sign of an organised go-slow, nor could there be accusations of sabotage, as the norms were being constantly met.

A sudden drop in temperature in early October appeared to be the harbinger of another dreaded Russian winter. Even the soldiers realised that we must be provided with warm clothing to withstand the snow and sub-zero temperatures. In Russia, winter came very suddenly and I just hoped we wouldn't be caught out by their slow response to our need, as happened with the chicken blindness debacle. At last, the next week we were each given two pairs of gloves and a padded jacket! What an improvement on the rags we froze in last winter, which cost so many unnecessary lives, and crippled hundreds with frostbite. Wlatka for instance, had suffered badly with frostbite on her legs and feet. For me, it was my feet, especially the toes and heels: eventually I lost the tips of two toes on each foot. Even today, my feet react adversely each winter and always became inflamed and very painful in cold weather. Strangely, there is a similar painful reaction during a thunderstorm and my doctor told me that the arteries shrink in limbs after frostbite, thus causing such intense pain.

The only advantage of working in the forests during the winter was that we were shielded from the incessant winds by the surrounding thick tree growth and the forest canopy. Still, I often wondered how many of us would be alive after another winter of slavery and starvation, without forest fruits, small birds, rodents and rabbits to keep our ravenous hunger at bay. We always chatted incessantly at night, lying on the benches and, being unable to sleep, we would think of the lovely food Mum used to cook for us. In my dreams I used to endure fantasies of her wonderful cooking, tantalisingly almost being able to smell the aroma of her famous goulash, tasty soups and bread, inevitably reflecting that she was much better off now.

We didn't need to visualise hell: it was visited upon us daily in this nightmarish place, the hopeless despair of their predicament plain to see on my fellow slaves' pale faces. Just who would be next to die was the unspoken question, as each of us battled through another day for survival. I felt so sorry looking at the girls, shivering and huddled together for warmth on those iron hard benches. How on earth would they survive another freezing winter? They looked so gaunt, tired and desperate in the flickering light of the solitary oil lamp. Several had red blotches and deep scratches on their skin and were raddled with rasping bronchial-like coughs that racked and shook their frail bodies. We knew that even the strongest prisoner would eventually succumb to the conditions; it was simply a stark question of when, not if, it would be my turn to die. I mused on the sad reality that none of the girls' lives would be fulfilled. They wouldn't marry and have families now, as it was painfully clear that they would all die in Stalin's hell on this earth. Perhaps they once had childhood dreams of falling in love with a local lad and even owning their own farm in Polish Ukraine. Still thinking about our situation I fell asleep and it only seemed minutes before the thud of rifle butts on the door and the shouts of 'Rabotach!' from our jailers.

A few weeks after we finished on the river, word started to filter through to us that the authorities in charge at the sawmills had complained that many logs sent to them had been incorrectly measured before cutting. We still had no idea what the logs were used for; certainly the fuss made by our inspector wouldn't have been necessary for telegraph poles, or fences. Anyway, another far more serious problem had come to light: the authority that periodically calculated the output for the area announced that there was a shortfall of several thousand logs, and this just had to be sabotage! They hauled all the inspectors before them to account for this deficiency and the outcome was that we never saw our irritating, fussy inspector again. He and his fellow supervisors had paid the price of failure, and no doubt the insatiable maw of the Gulag had swallowed more hapless victims and their families. After this disquieting incident, I asked Ivan what he thought had become of them. He replied that he had heard of terrible camps in the Arctic Circle, where no prisoners lived long. The winter temperatures often sank to a steel shattering minus fifty degrees, when all work had to stop. Slave conditions, starvation and uncontrolled savagery from convict trustee prisoners were all de rigueur for the NKVD and their criminal accomplices. The largest camps were in regions called Vorkuta and Kolyma. The latter was known as 'the land of gold and death.' He was pretty certain that if our inspector had been deported there for his 'crime', it was extremely unlikely he would ever return.

The winter of 1940-41 was, in comparison to the previous one, bearable for us as we now had good clothing and the improvement in food rations helped. We had also learned from our naivety in the past and knew how to recognise the signs of frostbite and the remedies. It was now a question of survival during the harsh days and a countdown to the arrival of spring. Our first Christmas in captivity was a very subdued affair when we realised that Christmas Eve and Christmas Day were definitely not on Stalin's calendar! There was no extra food or treats and the poor villagers in Oserki had nothing they could spare us. We tried to ignore these shortcomings and to maintain our family Christmas traditions, thinking all the time that this would be the first Christmas in our lives without Mum's cooking and careful attention to the festivities. We all met in the huts at Oserki: Dad, Joseph, Honorka, Stefa, Wlatka, Helena, Martin, Edek, Tadek, Zybyshek, Mietek and me. It was a real family gathering in such difficult circumstances. We all tried to cheer Dad up, but the memories of so many past happy Christmas and New Year family festivities must have been unbearable for him. One thing was certain, we were going to stick together and get through this, no matter what the future held and whatever difficulties we encountered.

The New Year 1941, as usual, started with heavy snow, so whether the Russians liked it or not, we couldn't go out to cut the trees and we enjoyed a few days in the huts.

CHAPTER 10
The German invasion

A fter our unexpected brief lay-off because of the blizzard it was back to work. We were by now very experienced at the cutting and it was so much easier than our first, very hesitant attempts. Also, the NKVD authorities had drafted in a new inspector: naturally, he was very keen to ensure that everything was in order and had no intention of suffering the same fate as his predecessor! It was very quiet in the forest now, after the heavy snowstorm; there was no wind for a change and few forest animals in sight. Flocks of crows wheeled above the firs, scanning the land for easy pickings and we often saw shy deer scratching at the snow-covered ground for lichen and moss. Packs of wolves scampered around, chasing each other, throwing up clouds of powder snow; in fact the skiing conditions were ideal! We wondered if Sergei, Oleg and Co. would have been impressed if we knocked some skis together and did a few circuits of the work site. Probably not!

That night we were awoken by the noise of wolves barking and howling. The disturbance eventually died down and I went back to sleep. The next morning we were only a few metres into the forest when Helena pointed to what looked like a pile of old clothes. The guards went across to examine the rags and we joined them. The clothes were in shreds and all around, the snow was speckled and crimson with what appeared to be human blood, but there was no sign of the body of the poor wretch. Oleg told us that occasionally villagers got very drunk and in this case the wolves' victim had become lost. Once the wolves picked up his scent, he was torn to pieces in minutes and every scrap of his corpse had vanished. Oleg warned us that the same fate would befall any prisoner who lagged behind the main body of workers returning in the evening, especially in foggy conditions. The wolves hid in the forests and were always watching for prisoners who ambled along. The pack would strike in seconds and drag their victim deep into the forest and only a fool would attempt to follow their tracks in the snow.

Although the depressing number of deaths continued as prisoners simply gave up the hopeless struggle for daily survival, there appeared to be a never-ending stream of labour, of all ages and from many regions of the Soviet Union. The army of forced labour that the NKVD had at its disposal (with emphasis on 'disposal'), must have been counted in millions. I just couldn't see how any of the Russian workers, who had been so helpful to us, would survive, as some of them had already been in the logging camp for six years. Indeed, I met some very old men who were well into their eighties and had been incarcerated in camps as prisoners of the Cheka secret police since Czarist times. They had virtually given up hope of ever seeing their families and homes again; that is, accepting that the families were still alive. Stalin, Beria, Kaganovitch (the murderous architect of the 'Great Famine') and their evil Kremlin henchmen, would have doubtless enjoyed their prisoners' misfortune.

The 'break-up' started earlier in 1941, as the ice wasn't as thick as in the previous years. The horses and their handlers arrived again to see if the animals could manage this spring and the removal of the logs started once more. From time to time, we had been receiving bits of news about the progress of the war, from some of the soldiers and especially the locals. The German armies had been sweeping all before them, in a seemingly unstoppable wave of military successes: France, the Low Countries and some parts of Scandinavia had all fallen to Hitler. However, the defiance of Great Britain, led by a man called Churchill, was paramount in preventing an invasion of that small island. Hitler was so enraged at their brave resistance that he launched continuous bombing raids to attempt to terrorise and eventually subjugate the population. Stalin must have privately been very uneasy at Germany's swift successes. Regardless of the pre-war 'non- aggression treaty' that their respective Foreign Ministers, Ribbentrop and Molotov had signed, he suspected that Adolf Hitler might well have his eyes on Russia in the future. Hitler regarded the Bolsheviks as 'Untermensch', or sub-human beings: a barbaric, inferior race, in contrast to his Nordic, racially pure concept, and second only to the hated Jews.

His persecution of the Jews had begun in earnest and we heard that ghettos had been established in several cities and towns like Warsaw, Krakow, Lodz, Chelmno, Lublin and even Lvov, near Rogozno. The poor people had been herded into overcrowded hellish enclaves where conditions were appalling. A thousand Jews were dying of starvation every month in the Warsaw and Lublin ghettos alone. A year later, the inmates were told they were to going to be 're-settled', but instead they were deported to death camps in Eastern Poland. Terrible places, with names that I hadn't heard of, such as Belzec, Sorbibor, Maidanek and Treblinka. The ghetto clearances, carried out by Nazi S.S. (SchutzStaffel - Protection Squads) and local militias, can only be described as a nightmare of blood and terror.

The key planners and organisers of the Eastern Poland transportations were two shadowy SS-Obergruppenfuhrer, Odilo Globocnik and Dieter Wisliceny, whose names, in contrast to Reinhard Heydrich and Adolf Eichman, (the architects of the 'Final Solution' of the Jewish 'problem'), are virtually unknown, even today.

On June 22nd 1941, we were awoken to incredible news sweeping the huts: Hitler had attacked Russia! The guards were devastated at this cataclysmic event and there were no shouts of 'Rabotach!' They left us in the huts and a few later returned to discuss the news that had changed everything overnight. The soldiers tried to gauge what Stalin's reaction would be to this totally unexpected turn of events. I also think they had decided that now we were their comrades in the fight against the Nazis! All sorts of wild rumours were now circulating in the camp and village, most without any foundation. The soldiers told us the Russian radio was broadcasting regular bulletins from the Front, interspersed with martial, patriotic music. Soviet commanders had also given confident interviews, assuring people that Hitler's aggression would be met with a devastating response. We laughed to ourselves at this Soviet propaganda, as our guards had admitted Stalin was totally unprepared for the sudden German invasion. I gleefully imagined Stalin's haunted face as he skulked in the Kremlin, frozen into indecision, awaiting the next batch of reports from the front announcing further catastrophic Soviet losses.

In the days following Hitler's lightning attack we didn't work: the NKVD authorities were in a complete tailspin, totally disorientated and unable to make decisions. The invasion had thrown all their plans out of the window and the very last thing on their minds was rafts, trees, 'norms' or us! A week later, a senior NKVD officer arrived and announced that the work would continue but comrades, (that's us!) were invited to work without pay on Sundays for the war effort. We would also be very welcome if we wanted to join the Red Army! What?! Me join the Red Army? There was more chance of Stalin joining the Corps-de-ballet of the Bolshoi! We could see that there was no enthusiasm from the officer about anything to do with the work: he was trying to boost his fellow comrades' morale with this pathetic, whining, speech and no doubt, at the back of his mind was the prospect of his inevitable call-up! What he was well aware of, but choose to ignore, was an atrocity carried out by the NKVD in Lvov, a week after Hitler invaded. Thousands of Polish political prisoners in three jails were murdered by the guards before they fled from the city.

The horrors perpetrated by both the NKVD and the Nazi SS Einsatzgruppen death squads seemed to almost rival each other in their barbarity. Jerzy, a newcomer from Kamionka, later told me of the execution of five hundred Jews outside the town. Sadly, Alter Kazyne a well-known Jewish writer and a broadcaster on Radio Lvov, was gunned down by two assailants as he cycled from Tarnopol to the radio station. Kazyne's murderers were never caught. Weeks later we heard of a terrible massacre carried out in September by an SS Einsatzkommando outside Kiev: nearly forty thousand Jewish men, women and children were shot in just two days and their bodies thrown into a gorge, at a place called Babi-Yar. More Jews had been murdered in the first eight weeks following Hitler's invasion than in the previous three years. Hadn't the poor people of the Ukraine suffered enough in the 'Great Famine' under Stalin?

Once more the dreary work on the river continued, but with only desultory interest from everybody, especially the soldiers, who were more friendly and open to us than they had previously been. The summer faded into autumn and our second full winter steadily approached. The winter of 1941-42 was not going to be taken for granted by us one little bit, but realistically, would anybody still be alive come the spring? In fact, it was the coldest winter for many years. The soldiers were now giving us daily reports of the fighting on the Eastern Front and they were very worried indeed that Hitler's armies were literally at the gates of Moscow, having made unbelievable territorial gains. But as the temperature dropped lower and lower, so the problems multiplied for the Germans.

The Red Army fight-back started, skilfully planned by Generals Zhukov and Konstantin Rokossovsky, using crack Siberian reserve troops who were able to fight in unimaginably severe weather, unlike their opponents. Partisans constantly harried the German supply lines and many soldiers began to seriously think that this time Hitler had made a colossal mistake in hoping to vanquish the Red Army in a few short years. After his initial catastrophic disregard of undoubtedly alarming Soviet intelligence reports of an impending German attack on Russia, Stalin had come to life. For months prior to the German attack (code-named 'Operation Barbarossa',after the nickname of Emperor Charlemagne: 'Redbeard'), Zhukov and General Semyen Timoshenko, who were receiving daily irrefutable intelligence reports of Hitler's intent to invade, pleaded with their leader to launch a pre-emptive strike at the massing German forces. Stalin always refused and in fact had decided to invade Germany in 1943, when the Red Army, which he had himself emasculated in the purges of the late 1930s, would be superior to Hitler's forces. He appointed himself Commander-in-chief of Soviet forces and set up a 'Stavka', or War Cabinet. From 1941 to 1945, he planned every move of the war, ruthlessly terrorising senior commanders and insisting troops fight to a standstill. Any commander who retreated, or worst of all surrendered a key city to the Germans, was shot.

(A vindictive bloodlust had always been part of the murderer's character and he always stealthily pursued his 'enemies' and had them eliminated. His first wife Ketevan Svanidze, whom he married in 1906, died of tuberculosis and he married Nadya Alliluva in 1917. In 1932, following several abortions, she was suffering from depression and hated life in the Kremlin, having had to endure a string of Stalin's very public affairs. After yet another evening of taunting and humiliation by Stalin during one of his drinking sessions with his cronies, Nadya went to her room, took out a gun she had hidden in a drawer and shot herself in the heart. Stalin later described her despairing action as 'treachery' and didn't go to her funeral or ever visit her grave).

One bitterly cold day in early December, I met a Russian guard called

Anatoly who had been particularly decent and I think he wanted to help us. He had heard on the army grapevine that a new Polish Army was being raised from prisoners at present in Russian hands, under the leadership of a General Anders: a brilliant General whom everybody revered after his bravery against the Germans in the desperate battles of 1939. I thanked Anatoly profusely and rushed off to tell the others. They were all amazed at the news and most of the lads were very keen on joining up, anything to get away from this Red hell. I would be sixteen in March and would certainly try to sign up, but Dad exercised caution, saying we should wait and see what the Soviets, (meaning Stalin), had decided for us, as he didn't trust them.

We had become very confident now in our dealings with the Russians, so it was decided that this Christmas Day there would be no work! Nothing was said to any of the guards as the 25th approached, so they would have a nice, unexpected present! Christmas Day dawned clear and frosty as we collected the tools and marched confidently out. When we reached the worksite, a huge bonfire was lit and we threw our axes, saws and poles on the ground in a gesture of defiance. The guards were astonished that we made no attempt to pick up the tools and start working. The Commissar angrily asked what was going on. We calmly retorted that as it was Christmas Day, we wouldn't be working. The look on his hard face was a picture, perhaps he'd never heard of Christmas? He exploded in a rage and immediately sent for reinforcements from the barracks. Nobody was afraid of them any longer, so I thought; here we go again comrades! We replenished our fire and waited for the inevitable show of force. An hour later, we were surrounded by a hundred soldiers, with their guns pointed threateningly at us.

The impasse continued and the usual threats were made; that we wouldn't be fed until we returned to work. This had no effect so, as in the previous strike, we faced up to their bullying and threats, regardless of the consequences. We were not going to work on Christmas Day and that was final! Once again, being unable to break our defiance, the soldiers buckled under the pressure of failure and sloped off back to Oserki. The real possibility of being them all being sent to the front lines if we had all been killed had swayed it in our favour and the whole incident was forgotten. This was a huge triumph, despite our aching, empty stomachs on Christmas Day 1941. We had once again beaten these godless, craven, cowards. Ivan, who hadn't been out that day, was mortified that we had again challenged the guards. Knowing their reputation, he couldn't believe that we hadn't all been killed. He rushed away, muttering to himself about 'These crazy Poles!'

New Year's Day, 1942. It was work as usual and the guards made no reference to the Christmas Day strike. There was only one thing on their minds, the containment of the German advances on the Eastern Front and the consequences for the country's future if the Red Army failed to win more battles. In early January, there was fevered speculation about the new Polish Army, but nothing had officially been confirmed. At long last, would we finally escape Stalin's clutches? Plans were excitedly made in an atmosphere of disbelief, hope and sheer exhilaration and there was much discussion about our next step, so we made enquiries at the barracks. Our tip-off was confirmed by the officers, who said that the army was being recruited in Tashkent, capital of Uzbekistan, in Soviet Central Asia. They estimated that tens of thousands of Poles, who had been prisoners of the Russians in Siberia since 1939, would be released and allowed to go to enlist in Tashkent. Travel arrangements would also be made for anybody wishing to leave Russia altogether. How things had changed! A few days later we were informed that those of us wishing to go to Tashkent (including women and children) would be transported there in mid-February, by train. I decided to go to talk to Joseph, to see what he had planned. He was adamant that he wanted to leave immediately for Tashkent and would make his own way there. He persuaded Martin, Tadek and Edek to join him and they left the next day.

Several times before our scheduled departure, I was asked by soldiers to remain in Oserki and they promised I'd be well looked after. I turned them down on the spot, as I couldn't get away from the wretched place quickly enough! Some prisoners did stay, including Honorka; she was quite happy working in the nursery and had made many friends in the village community but, with the war situation balanced on a knife edge for the Red Army, I was not alone in questioning the wisdom of her decision. The establishment of Hitler's armies on the West Bank of the Volga during the present siege of Stalingrad would certainly have made her and any other ex-prisoner's decision to stay distinctly problematical. If the Germans overcame the desperate defenders, I didn't think they would take kindly to Poles who had made their homes in Russia. (Little did we know that exactly the opposite was taking place: the long, bitter struggle at Stalingrad was leading to annihilation for the Germans. Hitler's Russian adventure, like Napoleon's one hundred and thirty years earlier in 1812, was turning into a nightmare and would become a pivotal episode in the outcome of the war).

I said goodbye to Ivan and gave him some tobacco, thanking him for his considerable help in our early days in Russia. He said he was going to make his way back to Kharkov and avoid the inevitable NKVD round-ups for the Eastern Front. It was in mid-February 1942 that we were to leave. I genuinely had a great fondness for the Russian peasants, who had often welcomed us into their poor hovels and shared their food. I was especially grateful to the people who, at great personal risk to themselves, had told me where I could get milk for Mum in those bleak, desperate days which now seemed so long ago. Indeed, many of the Oserkians were sad and in tears at the prospect of our imminent departure.

We had one final act to carry out before leaving: Dad, Wlatka, Salka, Stefa, Helena and I said 'goodbye' to Mum. All of us were heartbroken and made our last prayerful farewells to her, having miraculously survived nearly two years of captivity. We then departed to make our final preparations, before leaving Oserki forever.

CHAPTER 11
Through Hell to Freedom

Despite previous promises to help us leave Oserki, the Russians had cunningly made no arrangements for our travel to Swieregorske station. Joseph had been absolutely right to start off immediately with the other lads when he knew they were free to go. He said it was around two hundred kilometres to the station and was confident they would get there quickly and safely. I wasn't so sure, as being mid-February the weather was very bad and my main concern was Dad and the girls: Wlatka, Salka, Stefa and Helena.

I went to talk to a few villagers, who were somewhat alarmed when said that we intended to walk to the station. They told me that as well as the severe weather, in February the wolves were always bolder and would attack on sight. The farmers and woodsmen never went out into the forest at this time of year without their hunting rifles. They warned me never to veer from the small track and most importantly, to mark notches on the tree trunks every fifty metres, in case we had to retreat back to the village. With this advice in mind, I bribed one of the machine-room men with tobacco in exchange for an axe, which I buried in the snow outside the hut.

The villagers also said that the farmers or foresters would never turn away anyone caught out in the forest in severe weather, so that was a small comfort. Finally I asked the locals whether they knew how frequently trains went across the border to Uzbekistan, but they couldn't help. Although they had of course made regular trips to the station in their carts and wagons bringing new prisoners, not one had even been on a train! All they could expect under Stalin was a life of grinding poverty, from which in many cases, death would be a happy release. Now with the Soviet Union locked in a war with Germany, the few men remaining in Oserki could be rounded up and sent to the front any day. The wives accepted this with resignation, knowing that they would never see them again if they were conscripted.

Later that day Sergei came to the hut and asked me to come outside for a chat. 'Julian', he began, 'I hear you are going to walk to Swieregorske then?' I replied, 'Well, since you've reneged on your promise to get us to the station safely, we've got no choice have we? Why can't you ask the villagers to take us in their carts, the same way we arrived here? 'Sergei laughed at this, 'Why should we help you now? You lot aren't any use to Comrade Stalin any longer. It's over two hundred kilometres to the station and in this weather you'll never make it! Even if you reach the station, you won't have enough money to buy tickets and the inspector will throw you all off the train in the middle of the steppes even if there's a howling blizzard!' With that final rejoinder he walked off, still laughing. In my fury I could have hit him, but I restrained myself. He would have enjoyed shooting me, as he always regarded me as a troublemaker and would never forget my point blank refusal to co-operate with his insidious plans in 1940.

I decided to leave the next day as it was crucial for us to get going, in case the weather deteriorated. The only food we managed to scrounge from the cooks was scraps of stale bread, but if we boiled water we could make bread soup. As I bade farewell to the villagers, I could see from their expressions that they thought we were mad and would perish on the journey. Some were in tears, as they had become very good friends and just couldn't bear us leaving, but leave we must, if we were to get across the border. After breakfast I helped Dad to get ready and we met up with Wlatka, Salka, Helena and Stefa and left the village. It was snowing lightly and at the outset I decided to take control of our little group, during what could prove to be a very hazardous undertaking. Apart from Dad, the others were fairly fit and I was confident we'd make the station without any mishaps. I just hoped we'd find shelter at night as one of the villagers estimated that it may take two weeks to reach the station in this weather, allowing for frequent delays sheltering from blizzards.

The snow became very deep, as the wind had been blowing it along the forest track and it was banked against the trees, causing some of us to slide from the icy paths into the drifts. As I expected, Dad was really struggling and breathing heavily, trying to keep his balance on snow-covered icy patches. Suddenly the dreaded sound of howling wolves was born on the wind towards us. Wlatka and Stefa screamed in terror and I searched feverishly for some sheets of newspaper and matches: if I could light the newspaper in this strong wind, it might keep the animals at a distance from us. Luckily I succeeded, but now the wolves seemed to have gone off in another direction, so we hurried on, anxiously looking for a hut or farmhouse in which to spend the night. As there was no sign of a refuge and darkness was rapidly closing in, I decided to stop at a spot in the trees where I could build a small shelter and cut branches with the axe. Dad sat down in the snow looking exhausted while the girls helped me to finish our den.

I lit a fire and boiled water in our small pan, adding scraps of the dried bread to make soup. Dad had the first mugful and did appear to look a little better as the hot, thin gruel warmed his frail body. It was now dark, so after finishing the meal we huddled around the fire, which I kept replenished with branches. I warned everybody not to fall asleep as it could well be fatal in these temperatures, so we talked for an hour or so, and then dozed. The vicious cold slowly seeped into our bones and I kept banking up our fire, keeping an eye on the others. In the early hours, snow spindrift kept pouring down on us from the trees; it found its icy way inside my collar and trickled slowly down my back, until my clothes were wet and started freezing hard.

Time and again during that terrible night, I shook Dad awake and kept telling the girls to massage their feet and limbs. They were huddled up together and murmuring to each other trying to stay awake. Once, I heard a scream and it must have been one of them having a nightmare of an impending wolf attack. The icy fingers of the remorseless cold gradually penetrated our tired limbs. I rubbed my frostbitten, damaged toes for hours, telling Wlatka to do the same. She moaned in despair, expecting this time to lose all her toes and perhaps her fingers. I just kept on telling her to persevere, anything to keep the blood flowing to her extremities. It was so tempting to slide into a surreal and pleasurable, but fatal sleep. I tried with all my might to keep awake, to save us from a frozen death in the forest, on this hellish journey to freedom. Once or twice I dreamt I saw Sergei's evil face, grinning in expectation of our impending fate.

In the pre-dawn blackness I gazed at the starry mantle above our pitiful refuge. Dad had often pointed out the Pole star when we were working together in Rogozno. It was so bright and he assured me that the Three Wise Men had followed its lambent beauty to Bethlehem. I remember replying that it must be a lucky star, as it was named after us Poles! Dad laughed at my wit, but had no idea why it was named the Pole star. On the other hand, Venus was equally bright and perhaps she guided the Magi on their journey. I dwelt on our desperate plight as I watched the starry mantle. Surely we wouldn't die after all we'd been through, like the millions of tortured souls of the Gulag?

Dawn arrived eventually, after an eternity of paralysing cold. Everyone slowly stirred into life: covered in frozen snow, aching and cramped, having spent hours huddled up in a crouched position to preserve and maximise body heat. Dad whispered a heartfelt thanksgiving to God that we had all survived that terrible night. I quickly stoked up the fire and soon it was blazing furiously, fanned into life by a strong easterly breeze. One thing was certain; we had to find proper shelter the next night or it would be all over for us. Then that evil thug Sergei and his malevolent master Stalin would have triumphed.

We quickly devoured our breakfast of the soup and a mugful of hot water; everyone anxious to be on the move again before more snow arrived. A weak, watery sun struggled to dispel the mist but it was so cold that I doubted if Dad would survive another day and night in this frozen waste. We stopped for a short break and drinks mid-morning. Dad dissolved into tears of despair; he sobbed and moaned that he couldn't go on, remonstrating and pleading with us to leave him and save ourselves. He kept saying, 'Anniela, Anniela, please help me. I'm finished; I can't go on. I'm coming to join you in Heaven today!' The loss of his beloved wife weighed heavily on him now and it had torn his heart out. The poor man had given up the will to live and all he now wanted was to be re-united with Mum. I certainly hadn't given up hope of survival. I gave Dad another drink and told him I'd get him to the station, if I had to carry him every centimetre of the way on my back!

In late afternoon, I was frantic to find any kind of refuge knowing that failure to do so would condemn us all to certain death. Any thought of going back to Oserki was also ruled out, as we all knew we'd die in the attempt. I rushed ahead now, praying to see a house. Thank God! As I rounded a bend, I saw a snow covered farmhouse in the trees, blue smoke from the chimney rising lazily into the still, late afternoon air. I dashed back to tell the others. The girls yelled with excitement, knowing we would be safe and a faint smile crossed Dad's lined and tired face. It didn't take us long to reach the house and I knocked on the door, which was opened by the smiling farmer's wife. In my best Russian I asked her if we could shelter for the night and she warmly welcomed us inside. The farmer had been attending to the animals in a byre a few metres from the house and hurried in, immediately inviting us to a meal and assuring us that we could stay overnight. In no time at all we were seated around the living room table with the couple's two children. The wife ladled out a hot nourishing broth from a large pot, and a plate of black bread was placed on the table. We all had second helpings before ending the meal with mugs of tea.

Then it was time to snuggle down around the stove in the living room, which was about four metres in size and very warm and cosy. The family slept on the platform upstairs, accessed by a ladder, where the smoke from the stove must have been a constant irritant, but perhaps they didn't notice it. We all fell into a deep sleep, totally exhausted after the problems and anxiety of the previous day and it seemed no time at all before the farmer woke us up as he climbed down the creaking ladder to go and feed the livestock. After breakfast, the wife gave us a pile of bread and cheese, as she could see we didn't have much food. Then it was time to leave this generous, friendly Russian couple who had undoubtedly saved our lives. I handed the farmer a packet of tobacco and he was delighted, thanking me profusely.

We had walked for about two hours when a woodsman stopped his horse and cart and invited us to climb aboard. He helped Dad to get up, pushing him onto the driver's bench and we made seats among the rolling logs and bales of straw. The kind man put a small tarpaulin across Dad's shoulder and goaded his docile horse into a steady trot. He told us he was on his way to his brothers, ten kilometres away and would drop us off there. His horse was very sure-footed considering the icy path and when we eventually stopped at our destination, I saw that the horse had canvas covering his shoes, so the animal was able to proceed safely even on ice-covered tracks. Later, over a hot drink, the woodsman's brother told us that Swieregorske was perhaps a week's journey away on foot, barring any blizzard white-out, in which case we would have to shelter however long it took to blow over. I asked him about the train situation, but he had no idea when rail traffic went to Tashkent. He did mention that the small country halt was now very busy, as it was being used as an embarkation point for Red Army troops going to the Eastern Front. Wounded soldiers were also brought there for transfer to hospitals in Tambov County.

We now started to make excellent progress in fine, dry, weather. Even Dad found the conditions suited him and for once was enthusiastic, talking about what he would do when we reached Tashkent. The girls told me that they had heard that a lot of Polish girls who had been in Siberia were headed for Rhodesia, to work in a clothing factory. If we reached Uzbekistan within two weeks or so, they felt there was a good chance of joining the group, or they could wait for the next batch of workers who wanted to head to Africa.

Once again the weather changed for the worse and we were confined to staying at a deserted farmer's survival hut for two days. There was plenty of wood there, so we just banked up the fire and lazed around, waiting for the storm to end. Two days later the Swieregorske station at last came into sight. We had heard trains passing for several kilometres approaching the halt, but were not prepared for what we saw as we walked up the ramp to the platform: before our very eyes was an apocalyptic vision of Dante's Inferno. There was a seething mass of Russian troops, civilians and row upon row of badly wounded Red Army soldiers laid out on the filthy platform. In the middle of this mayhem and screaming, officers yelled orders to the young soldiers jostling to get on trains already filled to capacity. Crying, barefoot, lost children wandered around looking for their parents. We walked along the narrow platform looking for a space to sit down but every nook and cranny was full of people.

To our horror we heard pitiful cries coming from the wounded soldiers. Many had severe head injuries, with arms and legs missing, the stumps covered in dirty bandages and their ragged uniforms covered in dried, encrusted blood. There didn't appear to be any doctors or nurses in attendance and nobody took any notice of their pleading for food and water. Helena and Salka suggested giving some a few sips of water but we didn't have any to spare. There definitely wouldn't be any sort of refreshments on our train if ever it arrived, so we would need all our water, bread and cheese. I came across a young mother crying hysterically. She told me that her coward of a husband had fought his way on to a train at the last second before it departed, in order to avoid a NKVD round-up of men for the Front, leaving her with her three children!

I asked a NKVD officer rushing by when the next passenger-train to Tashkent was due. He replied that all the trains were around twenty-four hours late, because German bombers had destroyed many of the rail-tracks. However, he'd just heard that luckily one was expected within the hour. Pointing to the hordes of civilians who were sitting expectantly on the floor, he said the train would never take them all. He added that several passenger trains had arrived already full of people trying to leave Russia. Hearing a train grinding and wheezing to a halt, I watched in disbelief as hundreds of wounded soldiers on makeshift stretchers were brought out of a hospital train. They joined the other poor creatures on the station floor and a few died within minutes of arrival.

The dead were left on the ground and panic-stricken people stumbled over them in a wild, crazy stampede to get a place on any train heading west. Soldiers with rifles tried to prevent them climbing on the hospital train, as it was returning for the next batch of wounded infantrymen. The frantic hordes were almost demented with fury and a small group who had managed to get aboard, were savagely thrown off onto the track by the soldiers, who hit them with rifle butts and kicked them off the train. They scrambled across the four tracks to safety, but one old man lay bleeding and unconscious on the rails near us. Suddenly, a huge goods wagon loaded with ammunition thundered towards him and he disappeared beneath its wheels. All that was left of him when the train finally passed was his brown fur hat, which had been blown to the side of the track. Merciful God, I pleaded, get us away from this hellish place somehow.

I returned to Dad and the girls and told them that train timetables didn't exist in this madhouse of a station. Nobody had any idea what was going on, but a NKVD officer had assured me a train to Tashkent was due within the hour. We were very fortunate as some people had been here

77

for days and as for the wounded and dying soldiers, their plight said it all: so many had paid the ultimate price for Stalin. Around twenty planes roared overhead, flying so low I could see the red stars on the underside of their wings. I asked the NKVD man where they were headed for. He glanced up and replied, 'Stalingrad', nodding pointedly to the piles of dead and dying soldiers.

Dad quietly sidled up to me, produced his bag of tobacco and suggested I bribe the officer to whom I had just spoken. I went up to him and showing him our best tobacco, and asked if he could arrange for us to get on the expected Tashkent train. The NKVD man looked hard at me with his wolfish eyes and nodded, grabbed the bag and told us to wait alongside him. A distant whistle announced the imminent arrival of our train. I watched in fascination as it approached, travelling very slowly, a huge cloud of steam billowing out from the rails beneath. The officer told me that the steam was injected down onto the rails in sub-zero weather, melting the ice coating the tracks, hence the very slow speed of all the trains in Russia in winter! We quickly climbed aboard, making sure that Dad had a nice seat and the girls found places throughout the battered coaches. I decided to stand in the corridor and said a prayer of thanks when our train to freedom slowly pulled out of Swieregorske.

CHAPTER 12
Famine in Uzbekistan

It was sheer Heaven leaving Swieregorske, after the horrendous scenes we encountered on the station. I wasn't worried that I may have to spend the journey in the cold corridor, reflectively looking out onto the bleak Kazakhstan countryside. Drawing in huge breaths of freezing air from the cracked windows, I exulted in my fortuitous escape from the Legion of the Damned. No doubt about it, at the eleventh hour I had crawled out of my grave before Stalin's evil cohorts had shovelled the black earth of the Volga Basin onto my shrivelled corpse. Now I was free and a new exciting challenge beckoned in Tashkent. I listened to the racing, clattering wheels, each kilometre taking me further away from Russia, hoping to be accepted by the army recruiting staff, despite being only sixteen. Nobody had any idea of where the army would be going to after the initial training period; some speculated that Stalin may change his mind and recall the Poles to fight alongside the Red Army. I resolved that if General Anders accepted me, I'd never go back to Russia, whatever dubious incentives were offered.

(Years later, I found out that Stalin needed more cannon fodder for the Eastern front, so he had stopped any more Poles leaving and in fact, we were the last train out of the Volga region). As Stalin ruthlessly controlled all military planning, he hadn't the slightest compunction about ordering his commanders to send literally hundreds of thousands of soldiers to their deaths in suicide attacks against overwhelming German forces. The Red Army soldiers were mown down in these futile assaults, which were repulsed with massive casualties. Any commander who questioned his orders and failed to direct these attacks was immediately demoted and sent to the front line. As an additional warning to any soldiers who hesitated, troops from ruthless NKVD rifle divisions were positioned at the rear of the attackers and mercilessly gunned down any conscripts who faltered or attempted to retreat during the advance.

We arrived at the border but had to sleep at the station as the lorries taking us to Tashkent weren't due until the morning and everybody, especially Dad and the girls, was exhausted. We huddled up on the draughty station floor and as usual, I was looking after our remaining half bag of tobacco, which I always used as a pillow. It was a dreadful shock to awake and discover that our precious tobacco had been stolen in the night! I was so tired I didn't hear the thief approach, so it was a bad loss and one we might regret in the future. Dad, as usual, was very philosophical about the theft and just said to forget it. Our ready supply had been very useful for bribing the guards in Russia, as they just smoked poor quality makhorka tobacco. I remember how grateful Dimitri was when I handed him a bagful in thanks for him letting me visit Mum during her last weeks and I had also given some to Anatoly, as a special 'thank you' gift before we left.

Everybody boarded the lorries later that morning for the final leg of our journey to Tashkent, arriving in mid-February 1942. We were to be billeted in farms outside the city before leaving for our new homes and everyone had compulsory check-ups by a military doctor at the Polish army barracks in Yangi-Yul, near Tashkent. I wasn't surprised to discover that I weighed barely six stones, such was the effect, on a fit young person, of the privations and starvation we had endured. Apart from the unsurprising weight loss, I was given a clean bill of health, so I was confident, that with good nourishing army food, I would eventually regain my previous body weight.

We quickly settled in at a kolkhoz (collective farm) outside the city. I found the Uzbekistani farmers very friendly and we easily overcame the language problem. In the meantime, I had met a Polish army chaplain and told him that I wanted to join up, but my age could be a problem. In no time at all, seeing my enthusiasm, he promised to put a good word in for me, as he knew all the Polish recruiting team. He did warn me that there were thousands of potential Polish recruits arriving daily, from all parts of Russia. Consequently, it would be several days before he would be able to discuss my case and hopefully, get me in. A week later, I received the news I'd been waiting so anxiously for. I went to the recruiting office, signed on and took the oath of allegiance: at last I was a fully-fledged soldier in the Second Polish Corps which later became known as 'Anders' Army'.

(Unfortunately for General Anders, not everything went according to his meticulously prepared plans. A certain officer on his staff named Sigismund Berling, who like Anders had been imprisoned in Moscow in 1939, had his own covert scheme to put into operation. During his time in the Lubianka prison, Berling had been 'persuaded 'by the NKVD to keep them continuously informed of the future plans, composition and relevant details of the Corps. One of Anders' officers suspected Berling was working for the NKVD and after a violent row, the traitor deserted and fled back to Russia. Stalin wasn't in the least perturbed and very quickly Berling was assigned to lead an army of 104,000 Poles and Russians, which fought alongside Konstantin Rokossovsky's Second Byelorussian Front Army all the way from Poland to Berlin. However the NKVD totally controlled Berling's army and in thanks for their service, the majority of his Polish soldiers were given a single, standard ticket to the Gulag in 1945 and Berling,his work for Stalin completed, quickly faded into obscurity).

There was a Russian garrison in Tashkent and I was amazed to see that the soldiers were wearing British and American uniforms; the hammer and sickle emblems on their caps being the only means of identification. Where on earth had they got them from? As usual, these conscripts looked thin and pale. I'd bet my last rouble that their superiors were very well fed and it wouldn't surprise me if they were also siphoning off the conscripts' rations for their own black market.

One day, I was walking along the tree-lined centre of Tashkent when a barely recognisable man came literally crawling towards me, dressed in filthy rags. His face was shrivelled with yellowish, parchment-like skin and his eyes bulged from their sockets. His stomach was bloated and distended and he was in the final stages of death by starvation. Pathetically looking up at me, he extended a filthy bony hand, in a last desperate attempt to live. I rummaged in my bag and gave him a piece of bread, which he grabbed and stuffed in his mouth. Moments later, he crawled away to a nearby lane, slumped to one wide and died. I returned to the farm and related my horrifying experience to the family: they confirmed that a famine had been raging in Uzbekistan and the adjoining Soviet Central Republic states of Turkmenistan, Kazakhstan, Tajikistan and Kirgistan since the early thirties, the same time-scale as the 'Great Famine' in the Ukraine. During our stay I saw dozens of similar wraith-like spectres, close to death, shuffling about the city. There was nothing that could be done for them. In despair, they had come to the city from once prosperous farming communities and as in the Ukraine, criminal gangs, encouraged by the NKVD, had stolen all their precious grain. Once again, Stalin, determined to punish the unfortunate peasants with hunger and starvation, wreaked a terrible revenge with callous disregard of the consequences for millions of poor people.

The Russian soldiers we met in the city always talked about the situation on the Eastern front, but as usual, were always wary of NKVD informants. The soldiers told us that the campaign of both sides was extremely fraught and uncertain, but they were positive that next year would be decisive, one way or the other. The Germans had experienced great difficulty with the severe weather conditions towards the end of 1941. They had been ill prepared for the sudden drop in temperatures in December, having unsuitable clothing for the conditions. In many cases, the fuel for the vehicles and tanks froze and the German supply lines were far too long, posing considerable difficulties. Although General Zhukov had staged a massive counter attack, the well-entrenched Nazis had held on. Our confidants seemed to think that if the Germans survived the winter, they could well make a determined push towards the Caucasus oil fields, which could be disastrous for Stalin and the entire Soviet industry.

The time had come for all new recruits to leave Tashkent for Iran, but we had to decide what to do about Dad in his billet on the farm, as his health was giving us cause for concern. Wlatka, Helena, Stefa and Salka wanted to leave Asia altogether and join a group of Polish girls who were going to work in a garment factory in Rhodesia. Their group also included Kristyna, Honorka's friend from the nursery in Oserki: she originally planned to stay with Honorka but at the last minute, she changed her mind and joined the others leaving Russia. It seemed a great idea for the girls to get away completely from being surrounded by soldiers in a continual war atmosphere. They promised to write and wished me luck in my new career. The farmer and his wife assured me that they would look after Dad, so that was a huge relief, especially as the girls wouldn't be with us much longer

The next day, Helena introduced me to Edith and Rosa from Radom, who had escaped from a munitions factory outside Krakow, called Zarcisco Kamienna. The girls had been delayed in Radom late one afternoon and were seized by militia setting up checkpoints for the night's curfew. Along with thirty other women, they were taken to a vast underground factory run by SS women guards. Conditions in this hell-on-earth were appalling and the life expectancy was only a few months at the most. The women slaves who were working there were a terrifying sight: the chemicals used in the manufacture of ammunition had turned their skin and hair green or orange and they looked like mad scarecrows. Edith and Rosa were put to work on machines for the production of shells. They had to stir the mercury in each shell with a metal rod every six seconds. That was 600 stirs an hour and a deadly 7,200 stirs on a twelve hour shift, standing up, with no break and almost fainting from hunger and weakness. The crafty SS guards would sneak up on the women and watch intently to see if they kept missing stirs after nine or so hours. Once the poor wretch hesitated through tiredness, or had become totally disorientated and stopped work, these sadistic harpies would give a screech of triumph and beat the prisoner senseless with leather whips.

Edith and Rosa had seen enough and decided to escape immediately, watching all the time for an opportunity. One night, the lights in the compound fused, which also short-circuited the electrified fences around the factory perimeter. The girls seized their chance, climbed over one of the lowest fences and ran across the railway lines. A munitions wagon was just starting to pull out of the factory and they climbed aboard. After many adventures, they finally reached Tashkent a month later. I congratulated them on their brave escape and wished them well in Rhodesia. Believe me, Edith and Rosa deserved every good fortune after their ordeal in the hell of Kamienna, where untold thousands of women must have been cruelly worked to death during the war.

The night before we left Tashkent, the local NKVD invited two hundred of us to a sumptuous meal at their barracks. Before the feast they even let us use the showers! The food served by the Russian mess staff was magnificent and having seen for myself the effect of the regional famine on the poor inhabitants, we were astonished at the lavish menu. It consisted of a superb goulash, with steaks, meat and a full range of vegetables and roast potatoes. To think we hadn't tasted meat for over two years! On the other hand, how many times had we seen the poor, starving people of Tashkent queuing for hours just to buy a precious loaf of bread? Believe me our lads took full advantage of the unlimited supplies of vodka, and all this at Stalin's expense! The next day, I awoke with a fearsome hangover, only feeling like strong coffee for breakfast, and then it was down to work. All our equipment was loaded onto lorries for transfer to the port and our journey across the Caspian Sea to Iran.

After the bitter cold of Russia we enjoyed the sunny weather and warm temperatures during the long and frequently bumpy ride across desert regions of Uzbekistan and Turkmenistan to the Caspian Sea port of Krasnovodsk. Our arrival at the port coincided with a local festival: there was a great atmosphere in the town, with singing, dancing and a huge feast of Bacchanalian proportions with an enormous metal bowl full of goulash and huge platefuls of lamb, chicken and boxes of fruit. We young soldiers really made the most of the fabulous banquet. (After our deprivations and starvation in Russia, I have never since wasted or thrown out one scrap of food in my homes in Neath). Our cups were continually replenished with excellent red wine and many of the lads joined in the dancing with local girls. Unfortunately the festivities ended abruptly for us, when the sergeants started ordering everybody in line to march to the docks.

A troop-ship lay at anchor and thousands of soldiers weighed down with huge rucksacks and weapons were queuing to board. The armour and lorries containing our stores and equipment were marshalled up wide gangways to a vast opening at the front of the vessel and were soon swallowed up in the cavernous interior. There was an ironic twist to our departure: each side of the gangplank, were two NKVD men, holding large bins. Every soldier was asked to put all his remaining money in the bins, as a 'donation' to the war effort. Anybody who refused was punched and ruthlessly searched. I put in all I had, as I didn't fancy a bashing from those animals. There was rampant inflation in the country anyway, so the money was virtually worthless and I hadn't been able to buy much in the shops. By the time boarding was complete, the NKVD thugs must have collected a few million roubles, so that sly fox Stalin made us pay for our meal after all!

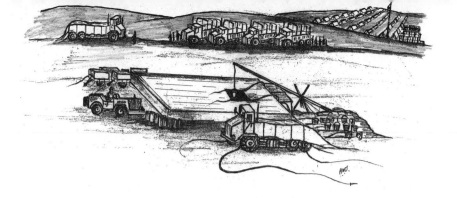

CHAPTER 13
The Forces Sweetheart

For the first time in my life I sailed on a ship and really enjoyed the experience. From Krasnovodsk it was luckily a fairly calm, uneventful five-day crossing of the vast Caspian Sea and I wasn't seasick. The lads who had sailed many times before had warned me that seasickness was a very nasty illness and suggested I stayed on the upper deck as much as possible. Apparently, down in the lower confines of a vessel in rough weather the sense of nausea is accentuated. Finally, the ship docked at the Iranian port of Pahlevi and it was a case of 'all hands on deck', starting the huge task of getting all the vehicles, hardware, stores and equipment unloaded. It took over a week to complete this long operation and then our lorries left Pahlevi docks for the journey to Kirkuk in Iraq.

Readers will by now be very much aware that any journey I have undertaken in my odyssey has been far from simple. Bearing this sad reality in mind, I became somewhat doubtful of our choice of vehicle and driver. The lorry looked about thirty years old, but since I wasn't familiar with the Gilan regional vehicle licensing laws, it was impossible to estimate its true age. The body was covered in bubbly rust patches and dents and resembled a relief map of the Himalayas. As expected, the tyres had probably not been changed for ages and on the two front tyres the treads were barely visible. I hoped at least the brakes were sound, otherwise it was surely going to be a nightmare trip for us. The windows, headlights and offside windscreen wiper were broken and it had deep lacerations along the body; evidence of previous encounters with other vehicles in night time journeys across the mountains. As our route to Kirkuk crossed the mountain range of Zamjan Province, things were not looking at all good for us reluctant passengers. Our driver then appeared, looking tired and dishevelled. He yawned repeatedly as he checked his instruments and we all had only one thought: had he slept at all after his previous trip? It certainly didn't appear to be the case.

The ancient engine coughed and spluttered into life and he roared off at high speed, driving exactly as I had feared. He tore through the desert terrain with complete disregard for our safety, determined to get his promised bonus for the round trip. He blazed around a series of gravity-defying hair-pin bends, laughing like a hyena as he climbed higher and higher, up to a snow-covered mountain pass at around three thousand metres. (I was certain that he'd earlier partaken of a few bottles of the local firewater to give himself confidence). Sure enough, it then started to snow. Now the driver's face was almost pressed against the windscreen, the one wiper valiantly trying to cope with the snow flurries. Suddenly, a massive behemoth-like wagon lurched out of the mist towards us, missing our vehicle by centimetres. Everyone automatically tensed, expecting the inevitable collision, but our wild-eyed driver yelled in triumph, as he obviously enjoyed the challenge of jousting with any on-coming traffic. We hung on in terror, looking out onto the plunging ravines as we were bumped and thrown from side to side because the lack of snow chains caused him to swerve and skid all over the road. In all this mayhem he was completely oblivious to the plight of his trapped passengers. Down the other side of the pass he roared, not taking his foot off the accelerator for a second, all of us praying that his brakes would hold, at least until we arrived at Kirkuk. Early that evening we screeched to a halt at our camp outside a small Iraqi village called Kinokin and we staggered out of that coffin on wheels, thankful to be alive.

We were to be based at Kinokin for a year and our first weeks of army life started with vigorous marching routines on the sandy flat ground. I found the drills physically very draining in these high temperatures, as I was still feeling weak. As we marched out into the desert, my legs felt like lead weights in the soft sand. However, I eventually became fitter and fully acclimatised to the conditions and the exercises were expanded to route marches over long distances, wearing full battle kit. Weapons training and target practice followed, so eventually we could strip and assemble our

Thompson machine-guns in pitch darkness. One day an engineer officer announced that lessons would be immediately commencing for soldiers who wanted to learn to drive. I jumped at this opportunity and was first in the queue the next day. Our instructor was first class and I soon got the hang of driving a jeep, simply by careering around the camp for hours on end. After three weeks, I felt supremely confident and the instructor, who was suitably impressed, said there would soon be a vacancy for a chauffeur to take officers around local towns and villages.

I also quickly picked up mechanical skills at classes held every afternoon and felt certain that I could eventually become an instructor as well as a chauffeur. My driving prowess got me out of a lot of the squaddies 'bull' attached to this training: as the officers decided that I would be their personal chauffeur, I began taking them around the area in my jeep. They treated me very well and it was the perfect antidote to the dreariness of the square-bashing. (Little did I know that I had unwittingly started in an army post that was to be hugely important in the remainder of my time in the services). Despite my youth, I was next given a very important assignment: they put me in overall charge of the transportation of cement to Kinokin, from a plant in Tel-Aviv. We took ten lorries for each journey, on a round trip of twelve hundred kilometres over the Tigris and Euphrates rivers and across the vast Sham and Al Hamad deserts, where mid-day temperatures of fifty degrees centigrade were common.

It took a week for each trip and luckily, there were two strategically placed garages on route. We always set off well before dawn, stopped mid-morning and then rested until 4.00 p.m., finishing each day at 7.00 p.m. It was imperative to rest during the hottest part of the day, so this necessitated a somewhat macabre ritual. Every serviceman on active duty carried a body bag made of canvas and lined with rubber and at the first halt in the day, this was placed over the camp bed in our tents. We then poured water from our truck tanks into the body bag, to a depth of several inches, and then lay in this 'bath' until it was time to start off again! I had often helped Dad with concreting on the farm at Rogozno, so I was able to supervise the mixing and laying of the concrete on our return. We always made a detour up to Baghdad on the return leg of our long, hot, journey as there was a transit camp there and we could have a well-earned break and snacks.

Joseph extreme left, Julian in centre with Polish Corps comrades at Kirkuk camp, Iraq, 1943.

I was sitting outside the camp offices one hot afternoon and noticed three soldiers strolling towards me. I looked hard at the middle one; could it be? Yes, it was my brother Joseph, I was certain. I jumped up and tried to attract his attention, but they were talking animatedly and walking away from me. I shouted after them, but the desert wind carried my voice away and they disappeared into the sea of tents. A week later I had severe toothache and had joined the queue outside the base dentists, for what I expected would be the usual appointment with fear. Joseph was in the queue! We embraced ecstatically. He looked fine and told me what had happened after he left Oserki with Martin, Edek and Tadek. Initially, they were all very keen on reaching Tashkent as quickly as possible and joining up. However, soon after arriving, his companions had second thoughts and told Joseph they had decided to return to Oserki. Martin especially was missing Honorka, who had remained behind to carry on working in the village nursery and Tadek and Edek probably had other plans. Maybe they decided that military life wasn't for them and had got carried away with the excitement of getting out of the logging camp. After Joseph enlisted, his unit left for Iraq immediately, so he was always a few months ahead of me. It was extremely providential that, having missed each other the previous week, we were re-united, so we promised to keep in touch.

Often on that long, very tiring journey to Tel-Aviv, in that sea of sand, blinding sun and brilliant blue sky, we followed strange mirages that floated tantalisingly ahead, before fading in an instant, in the shimmering heat haze. Although we stoically endured the searing, torpid, heat of each day, the nights were always a surprise: soon after dark the temperature dropped to freezing point. We gazed in wonder at the brilliance of the stars in their eternal firmament. They appeared close enough for us to reach out and touch. At dawn, we could see in the distance a silent, ghostly, camel train, wending its way across a trail that traders had used for centuries. Throughout our time in several desert camps, nobody was keen on night sentry duties, as by the time their watch ended the guards were chilled to the bone. Every day, six litres of water per person was the absolute minimum consumption to avoid dehydration, as any undue exposure to the sun in these temperatures could be fatal.

There were no showers at Kinokin, so we manufactured our own, standing in a wooden cubicle, the water being poured from a jerrycan onto the lucky recipient. After an arduous trip to Tel-Aviv, our shower was especially welcome. The desert air was so hot, that after using our shower, you were completely dry from head to toe in seconds! Tell me something; can you really fry an egg, on a steel sheet on the ground? Well, in the head-splitting mid-day temperatures in Kinokin, the answer was definitely yes!

The biggest problem in Iraq was the availability of fresh water, so it was decided to build our own permanent storage well. First a hole was dug in the sand to a depth of six metres and then lined with concrete. A section of the nearby Alfred River was damned with stones, so that the water flow could be controlled and river flotsam and jetsam carefully filtered to ensure the water was clear. Open-top lorries were sent to the river and two hundred large buckets would be filled with water. Back at the base, a line of soldiers passed along the buckets, which were poured into the well. To purify our new water supply we added a chemical and so this was enough fresh water for at least two months. A wooden top covered the well to keep out the all-pervading sand and the water was raised using a bucket and hoist. One big advantage of our new supply was that we could now fill our canvas water bottles every evening and hang them from bamboo tent poles. The water was deliciously chilled in the morning and a good start to any day! One pleasing result of my efforts to speedily complete the well was that I was promoted to lance corporal!

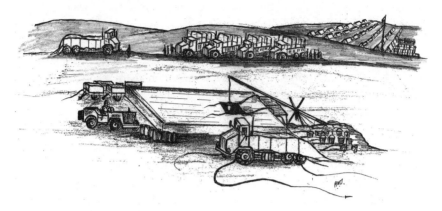

Nobody had any appetite for food in that continuously oppressive heat, so for breakfast, it was just tea and crackers. At lunch we usually had soup, potatoes, corned beef and bacon. The bacon came in tins that held enough for five men and in the evening, we just had tea or water. One constant irritation was the sand, which was whipped up into stinging clouds by the desert winds. The storms were often hurricane-strength and sometimes raged for days, virtually closing down the camp. The poor visibility made it impossible to drive and all the trucks and equipment had to be covered. Inevitably, the sand got into every single corner in a tent and often ruined our rations.

Although there were about a thousand men in Kinokin, very few were able to drive. Once again I was drafted in, to teach around a hundred soldiers the complexities of handling two-ton pick-up trucks. As most were total novices, it took a while for them to get used to driving in a desert environment. Their daily programme consisted of learning the various techniques necessary for this from me in the mornings, then in the afternoon they had lessons in mechanical maintenance. No driver could expect to survive in a hostile desert environment without being competent to carry out basic repairs: a breakdown in such conditions meant certain death. Anyway, their newly acquired skills would be very useful when they re-joined civvy life.

Now, although I was fully employed taking officers all over Iraq, another job entrusted to me was the organisation of the troops' summer concert.

I initially asked for volunteers to submit a variety of acts and we put together a creditable programme. For one of the items, I persuaded five lads to join me in singing 'Lilli Marlene' and a selection of Polish folk songs. Our stage consisted of two lorries placed back to back, with the sides let down, the truck headlamps ensured sufficient stage lighting and to create the full theatre atmosphere in the desert, we had an adequate sound system.

Vera Lynn

On a much more professional level, Vera Lynn, a popular British singer who was internationally known as 'The Forces Sweetheart' gave a memorable performance a month later. Vera was very well known to the troops, as she regularly broadcast on the BBC forces network. On the broadcasts she was always accompanied by Bert Ambrose's Orchestra and had been their singer for several years. She wasn't bothered one bit about our makeshift stage and like the true professional she was, enchanted the mass audience of several thousand. They gave Vera a tumultuous ovation at the end, cheering, whistling and shouting for encores. She duly obliged by again singing her wartime hits, 'The White Cliffs of Dover' and 'We'll meet again', with this time everybody humming along! It was a really exceptional, morale-boosting performance by a very talented singer. She was staying in Kirkuk, so after the concert, I drove her to the next engagement a few kilometres away, but one of our officers followed in his jeep, (probably to keep an eye on me!). Over the next few weeks, several groups from ENSA touring bases in the Middle East also gave concerts, which were well attended and greatly appreciated by the lads.

The final three months of our long stay at Kinokin concluded with exercises in the assembly of Anglesey and pontoon steel bridges, to ford rivers in the battles that lay ahead for the Polish divisions

CHAPTER 14
A Lucky Escape

A round this time, we heard that the Russians had achieved a momentous victory on the Eastern Front in late January 1943 at Stalingrad. (Its original name was Tsaretsyn, but in his customary self-effacing style, he had renamed the city years earlier after himself, 'Stalin' being translated as 'Man of Steel!). For over a year the odds were stacked against the Soviet defenders and it appeared that the fall of the city was inevitable. But in an epic, titanic battle fought in terrible sub-zero weather, the Red Army led by the redoubtable Generals Zhukov, Rokossovsky, Timoshenko and Vassily Chuikov, eventually encircled Field Marshall Friedrich Von Paulus' Sixth Army and took over two hundred thousand German soldiers prisoner. The city was situated on the East bank of the Volga and some thought it wasn't all that far from our village of Oserki but, if the Nazis had established bridgeheads all along the river, it was possible that Oserki could have been destroyed in nearly a year of bombing and shelling around Stalingrad.

The Red Army victory at Stalingrad was probably the most decisive in the war. At Leningrad, further north, the inhabitants endured a siege of the city by the German Army lasting for 871 days, until January 1944 and around a million died of starvation. So despite the heroic sacrifices by the citizens of both cities, in what was termed the Great Patriotic War, Stalin showed his gratitude by never visiting either. For the citizens of Leningrad, there was a bitter sequel: as they had survived the long siege, the city leaders decided that a degree of independence would be very beneficial and richly deserved Once word got to Stalin of their plans, he had all the officials immediately arrested and shot!

In March 1943 we began preparations to leave Iraq for Palestine. The departure from Kinokin was very well organised, bearing in mind the size of the base and the logistics. Now my efforts to train all those drivers nearly a year ago would come to fruition. We would need two hundred lorries and drivers for the seven-hundred kilometre journey to Jordan. At the end of this marathon, they would be very well trained and fully understand the importance of convoy discipline in desert conditions. What was more important was they would soon discover how the conditions could change very quickly from hot, sunny weather to blinding sandstorms that reduced visibility to a few metres. This journey would undoubtedly be a big challenge for the rookie drivers but I felt confident that they would cope with its demands. Every two hundred and fifty kilometres along the road, we would stop at strategically sited petrol stations to refuel and have showers and meals in the rest rooms.

In the early stages of our journey we by-passed Baghdad. For their amusement, some of the soldiers in the lorries threw small coins, called 'milshi', in the direction of beggars who always hung around at street corners throughout Iraq. One unfortunate, hoping to get more 'milshi', ran out in front of a lorry and was accidentally killed: not a nice experience for the young driver. After this distressing incident, the drivers were told never to stop for anything like this again, especially at night. In addition, at night, headlights were to be switched off, as armed thieves lurked outside cities and they would shoot at military lorries, then rob and kill the driver and occupants.

The countryside in Jordan consisted of arid desert scrubland, surrounded by black rocky cliffs. It was an incredible contrast to see green, beautifully cultivated fields after we crossed the Jordan River into Palestine. The Jewish farmers had built an irrigation system of canals in their fields, so a constant supply of fresh water was available for their crops. Our camp was at Bergigi, a small village two kilometres from Tel-Aviv and this was to be home for the next six months. The camp was situated just thirty metres from a river, but unfortunately the site was overwhelmed by the stench from animal intestines that had been dumped in the river by locals. The sickening smell permeated the whole area and drastic action was needed. We poured gallons of paraffin on to the mess, set fire to it and eventually the smell faded away. Heaven knows what effect the pollution had on the river water, as the locals used it for all their daily needs.

93

Luckily, we had ample supplies of water purification tablets but we were decidedly uneasy about the water quality, certainly for the first weeks of our stay.

Being so near to Tel-Aviv gave us many opportunities for dining in the many first class restaurants in the city. The proprietors got to know us very well so, to prevent unwanted intrusions by drunken soldiers, they kept the front doors locked and let us in at the back! One distinct advantage of the thousands of troops stationed in Palestine was the almost complete absence of crime which was so prevalent in other towns and cities in the Middle East.

Julian at the Polish Second Army Corps camp, Bergigi, Palestine 1943

One day, a large group of us decided to visit Jerusalem and Bethlehem; I drove the Polish chaplain and the others followed in lorries. Approaching Bethlehem, a very large flock of sheep filled the road and, trying to negotiate my way safely through the animals, which were totally oblivious of our need to pass them, I missed one by inches. The chaplain nearly died of shock. He most definitely didn't want to be in the same vehicle as this mad young driver, who appeared determined to ensure that his visit to the Holy Places would result in a sacrificial lamb being the most enduring memory! Most of our soldiers were devout Catholics and they considered it a privilege to see the deeply symbolic churches and shrines. We were especially impressed by the Russian Orthodox Church in Bethlehem, a building of outstanding architecture with a lavishly decorated interior of gold and marble. (How utterly tragic that Stalin and his morons had destroyed so many Christian churches in Russia).

All our soldiers in the sapper and engineer regiment, including me, had to take a crash course in bomb disposal and landmine clearance. The course would last three months and our instructors repeatedly emphasised the need for the utmost care when dealing with any explosives. This advice was really brought home to everyone when a fatal accident occurred. I had been invited to join three sergeants in their tent for lunch one day but declined, as I had other work to complete. A few minutes later there was a tremendous explosion that rocked the camp. The tent and the three poor sergeants were blown to pieces! A military investigation team concluded, after sifting through the wreckage, that they had been trying to remove the detonator from a mine that they had brought with them to defuse during their lunch break!

A few days later, after the investigation findings were announced, the three unfortunate men were given a funeral with full military honours at an open-air Mass attended by everyone at the base. Once again, I had cheated certain death by a whisker and I thanked God for protecting me. After this tragedy, I had to begin instructing fifty new recruits in the dangerous work of the wartime sapper. Believe me, after the explosion in the sergeants' tent no recruits have ever received a more intensive education!

CHAPTER 15
Pyramids and Pickpockets

September 1943, and preparations were made to leave Palestine. Our final base in the Middle East would be in Ismaillia in Egypt, on the Suez Canal. The base was a hundred kilometres from Bergigi and it would take all day for our snaking convoy to reach Ismaillia. This was the biggest camp we had been in and was two kilometres from the town, with thousands of tents stretching for miles into the desert. Our unit of five hundred troops was joining up with around two hundred thousand other Polish soldiers. On arrival at Ismaillia, we were warned that theft by locals had always been a problem in the camp and extra sentries were posted at night. The thieves took great risks to steal anything and weren't afraid of being shot at, but as there was a night time black-out in the camp, they often escaped.

I was on guard duty one night when one marauder slipped past me into a nearby tent and started searching for money and valuables. (Watches were always attractive to thieves as they could easily be sold in local markets or back streets). As the thief was busy ransacking the tent, the soldier who was billeted there unexpectedly returned and confronted the intruder. The robber pulled out a large curved dagger from his belt and the soldier, who was unarmed, shouted for assistance. I ran into the tent but the Arab had already fled empty-handed into the darkness, so I just fired a few bursts from my Thompson after him, but missed. After this incident we further increased the night patrols and there were no more robbery attempts.

A feature of life at Ismaillia was the daily visits from enterprising locals, who had liquor to sell. Believe me, this stuff was dynamite! They called the colourless liquid 'Arak', and it was so potent it made bootlegger's hooch taste like spring water! Any thirsty soldier downing a bottle in a few large gulps in temperatures of fifty degrees centigrade was slammed to the ground by its explosive potency. The effects of the Arak on an unsuspecting young soldier were so lethal that the traders were eventually banned from the camp. This didn't deter them one bit. All soldiers on guard duty carried pickaxe handles, not tommy guns during daytime patrols. The officers ordered us to take the basket of Arak off the salesman when we caught them, and smash every bottle! The first one who I encountered looked so poor that I relented; I didn't smash his Arak, just gave him a whack with the handle and sent him packing. My leniency was brought to my superiors pretty quickly, and I was told in no uncertain terms to smash all bottles of Arak in future, or be put on a charge. Sure enough one arrived a few days later, hoping we'd forgotten about destroying his stock. I grabbed the basket off him, and smashed twenty-four bottles, watching the volcanic contents drain into the desert sand. An expensive waste perhaps, but on the more positive side I saved a few guys from a brain-blasting hangover or even worse!

I met many young Polish lads who had been based in Britain before being posted to the Middle East and a lot of their friends were in the R.A.F. They proudly told me that there were now four Polish Squadrons in Bomber Command and ten Polish Fighter Squadrons. The fighter aces had bravely distinguished themselves during the desperate Battle of Britain. Another air force unit, the Polish Fighting Team, or 'Skalski's Circus' as they were called (after their squadron leader), had notable successes in dogfights with the Luftwaffe in the skies over Tunisia, during the Western Desert campaign. In the same theatre of war,' Popski's Private Army',(named after their General, Vladimir Peniakoff), was an unconventional Long Range Desert Group operating behind German lines. They caused havoc to the enemy by blowing up fuel depots prior to the final decisive Battle of El-Alamein, in 1943.

Now Hitler and his evil gang such as Goering, Goebbels and Himmler would be scuttling to their rat holes every night, as there were round-the-clock bombing raids on Germany, with the RAF night raids being supplemented by American daylight attacks. In an interesting postscript to the Poles' determination to do everything conceivably possible to assist the fight against Fascism, the Polish government-in-exile had ordered the entire Polish fleet of cruisers, battleships and submarines to sail to British ports on the eve of the outbreak of war. They now served alongside Britain's Royal Navy. A huge, sometimes forgotten achievement, which had enormous bearing on the course of the war, was the cracking of the German 'Enigma' code by a team of brilliant cryptographers which included Marian Rejevski, at the secret service establishment at Bletchley Park in the county of Gloucestershire.

Around this time, to my great surprise and delight, I received an unexpected award from our C.O. In my daily trips around cities and towns during the past year, I had clocked up 100,000 miles, so I was a recipient of the '100,000 miles Silver Wheel'. It was a silver, miniature jeep wheel and this award was much prized among the army chauffeurs. What, I wondered, would Stalin have made of my award? His army drivers and couriers were trapped on the Eastern Front, starved and worked until they were either blown up by shells or bombs while making hazardous deliveries, or shot by NKVD units operating behind Red Army lines. The NKVD were always on the look-out for deserters or 'defeatists' and these would be either summarily executed, or put in 'straf' or penal battalions, conducting suicide missions such as clearing minefields. (Years later, it transpired that a ruthless method of minefield clearance employed by Red Army battlefield commanders consisted of prisoners and even their own soldiers who had disobeyed orders, being driven in front of the assault teams with their legs shackled in irons).

A few days later, I received a letter from the Polish chaplain in Tashkent. He sadly informed me of Dad's recent death at the kolkhoz, saying that he had officiated at his funeral. Poor Dad; he had been grievously affected at the loss of Mum and never recovered. The horrible end to his beloved Anniela's life had completely broken him, and the combination of poor food, hard work and his war wounds hastened his departure form this terrible world. The chaplain said his body was interred in the local cemetery along with hundreds of Poles who had perished of cold and hunger on their journey to freedom from Siberia. I also received a letter from Wlatka expressing her sadness, but at least she and Salka were very happy, working in the garment factory in Rhodesia. She always had great skill at sewing and embroidery and when she was very young had even made all her dolls' clothes! The sedentary factory job was ideal for her, as her legs had been badly damaged by frostbite. Having at last established communication with them, I made arrangements for their future mail to be sent to me via army H.Q. at Ismaillia.

As the Egyptian capital Cairo was only seventy kilometres from Ismaillia, it was a great opportunity to see the Pyramids, Sphinx and any museums that were open, despite the war. Our visit was quite an experience. We had all of course seen pictures of them, but the sheer size of the Pharoanic monuments was amazing. We just couldn't believe that blocks of such size had been transported to the site by hundreds of slaves. Shades of the Volga really! One adventurous soldier decided to climb to the top and having gingerly surmounted the base block, he confidently climbed higher. Then suddenly, he made the mistake of looking down and his nerve completely failed him. He was stuck on the Pyramid wall like a novice mountaineer, too terrified to move up or down and he started wailing for help. We quickly contacted the police and they sent a local guide up to bring our intrepid alpinist down to prevent him having an unexpected souvenir of Egypt - a fractured skull!

Cairo was crowded with American GIs swarming all over the historic sites and they appeared to have plenty of money. Security in the Cairo streets was poor, and we had been warned not to go out alone. There had been several unpleasant incidents lately, when soldiers had been offered watches, perfume and other luxury items by unscrupulous street sellers. These traders persuaded solitary soldiers to follow them to 'view' the promised merchandise, but the journey invariably ended in a blind alley, where the unfortunates were robbed and killed by the seller's accomplices. Another target was soldiers' pay books, which listed the owner's army details and were highly prized by thieves: the information would be passed on to Fifth Columnists and the thief was paid twenty pounds, an absolute fortune at that time. Usually the serviceman later disappeared, and his body was found on a waste tip or in a river a few days later. Sometimes they were never seen again. As so many men were losing their pay books, orders were given that a false pocket was to be sewn on the outside of all uniforms and the wallet kept securely inside the tunic. Later, the problem became so acute that it was announced that if a soldier lost his pay book, he would be court-marshalled.

In January 1944, the main pre-occupation for everyone was to change the camouflage paint on our lorries, tanks and artillery from a sandy desert colour to green and black. This job took a week, as there was an enormous amount of equipment to be sprayed. In addition, camouflage netting to cover guns and command posts was prepared. All this frenzied activity pointed to the division being sent to Europe in the near future, but the destination and departure date were top secret.

The build up of troops continued, with new arrivals every day. There was precious time for relaxation now, and the vast camp was overflowing. One sunny morning, the entire force was ordered to turn out on the parade ground and there must have been nearly half a million troops of the Second Polish Corps, of all ranks. This indeed was a special day, as a group of the highest military top brass was to speak to us. We presented arms at the arrival of the visitors, as they walked in front of us. To our complete amazement, before us were assembled the American General Eisenhower, British Prime Minister Churchill, the British Field Marshall Montgomery and the Polish Generals Anders and Sikorski. They spoke in turn, congratulating us on the formation of our new Corps and Field Marshall Montgomery gave details of our forthcoming deployment in Italy. 'Monty' was already famous for his staggering victory at El Alamein in the Western Desert in 1943. This huge success, coupled with the Russian victory at Stalingrad, ensured that the tide of war had finally changed in favour of the Allies and the Soviets.

The leaders then bade farewell, with Churchill, who was just a few paces from me, giving his customary flamboyant 'V' for Victory sign to the cheering troops. After dismissal, we talked excitedly in groups about our new role and the danger of the approaching campaign in Italy.

CHAPTER 16
Convoy to Taranto

We were to leave for Italy immediately, linking up with a large force of Allied troops in General Alexander's Eighth Army. Our commanders had been planning the big move-out and the serious business was now beginning. It didn't take long to finalise arrangements for our departure, such was the organisation at our base. At dawn a week later, our huge convoy set out; a seemingly never-ending line of troop-filled trucks and lorries, tanks on low-loaders, artillery pieces, support equipment, stores and ancillary staff, moved slowly out of Ismaillia. Our route was across the Nile Delta to the large Mediterranean port of Alexandria. It took a day to cover the relatively small distance; such was the slow progress of the armour on dry, sandy roads with the leading vehicles keeping a watchful eye out for roadside mines. In late afternoon, we pulled into the huge parking lot at the dockside. Alexandria was the only deepwater harbour in the Mediterranean with sufficient draught and facilities to berth a large fleet. It was the main distribution port for Allied supplies in the Middle East and Northern Italy war theatres, but it was vulnerable to air attack.

We spent the days waiting for departure by exploring 'Alex' as it was affectionately known and our usual mode of transport was the battered, dusty, groaning trams. The city was no different from Cairo, with its hordes of beggars. Such was the problem of thieves here, we always travelled in a group of no less than eight people. If an attempt was made to steal from any of us, we all piled in and threw the thief off the tram; no matter at what speed it was travelling!

The vast fleet was eventually assembled for the crossing of the Mediterranean to the Italian port of Taranto. There were sixty troopships, guarded by six 'Bulldog Class' destroyers, to counteract German U-Boats which often patrolled this waterway and had enjoyed a good harvest of Allied shipping. It was rumoured, with good foundation, that the submarines lurked outside Alexandria harbour awaiting their hapless prey. The crossing of the Mediterranean took nine days, as the fleet only travelled at the speed of the slowest merchant ship, which in effect made the whole fleet susceptible to U-Boat attack. The overloaded supply ships zigzagged through the water at only twelve knots, the officers combing the sea for telltale submarine wakes and conning towers. But it wasn't the U-Boats that attacked us on our journey; it was German Stuka bombers based on the island of Crete, which had been in German hands since 1941.

The screaming Stukas dive-bombed the ships under cover of darkness and everybody was mobilised to man the anti-aircraft guns on the merchant ships. When the guns on the destroyers opened up as well, the noise was deafening. It was impossible to see the German planes but I soon got used to handling the guns. I followed the red tracer bullets of other gunners into the blackness, vainly hoping for a lucky hit. The battle raged for an hour and a half, the German pilots desperately trying to sink the troopships, and there must have been a large squadron attacking us. We shot down two planes in the melee but thankfully, no bombs hit any of the fleet.

The Sicilian port of Palermo had now been cleared of sunken ships after the Allied invasion in 1943, so it was used for a stopover for refuelling, replenishing the food stocks and taking on water. The last stage of the journey was through the Ionian Sea, finally rounding up the Gulf of Taranto to the port of the same name, where we arrived in January 1944. There were so many ships that it was only possible to berth a few at a time: the rest of the fleet lay at anchor in the Gulf, so a week was needed to complete the disembarkation. However, it took far longer than this for the lines of lorries, heavy armour, troops and equipment to be marshalled out of Taranto on to the road heading North. We by-passed the appalling ruins of once lovely Naples on our hundred and twenty kilometre slow journey to the town of Campo Basso in the Molise region, one of the many towns that were being used by the Allies for bases. The nearest large town to Campo Basso was Bari but the former Italian air base at Foggia nearby was now being used by the American and British air forces for operations in Northern Italy.

Campo Basso was to be one of our assembly areas for a build up of the British Eighth and Polish Second Corps armies as a prelude to an attack on the German stronghold on Monte Cassino, situated above the town of Cassino in the Abruzzi mountain range. A 1300 metre mountain soared above the town and on the summit had been built one of the most historic Benedictine Abbeys in Europe, which had contained, before the war, priceless manuscripts and treasures. These had been removed to Rome before the first battle and the monks had left the Abbey. Monte Cassino was to be a name that everybody in the Allied forces came to dread in early 1944: a name that was synonymous with death.

CHAPTER 17
The Battle of Monte Cassino

Field Marshall Albert Kesselring was Commander-in-chief of the German army in Northern Italy. He and the German High Command were fully aware of the Allies plans for an invasion of the beaches of Salerno and Anzio, which would lead to them swiftly reaching Rome and would bring the campaign in Italy to a decisive end. Kesselring conceived an ingenious defensive plan to thwart the Allies objectives. Detailed early German intelligence reports had given Kesselring ample time to ensure that the German defences in the Cassino Massif were virtually impregnable. The region, with its endless vista of inaccessible mountain ranges, plunging gorges and poor roads, was also criss-crossed with deep rivers. The Germans knew that progress would be very difficult for the Allies with these natural obstacles; difficulties they compounded by erecting several well-constructed defensive lines. The one at Cassino was called the Gustav Line and was defended by the elite German First Parachute Division and a unit of crack mountain troops, commanded by the very experienced Lieutenant-General Richard Heidrich.

General Alexander's Eighth Army and General Mark Clark's Fifth American Army landed at Salerno on September 9th 1943 and around five months later, after establishing positions around Monte Cassino, the first of three battles commenced on January 4th 1944. The Allied objective was to quickly break through the German defences and link up with another larger force which was coming ashore at Anzio on January 22nd 1944. This invasion was codenamed 'Operation Shingle'. However, the stiff German resistance prevented a swift Allied breakout from the beachhead and progress inland towards Cassino was very slow. The Allied troops already involved in the first battle at Monte Cassino soon found out that the German defences and the appalling weather made the campaign a nightmare of First World War dimensions. Another two battles followed all ending in failure, with little ground gained and an unacceptably horrendous loss of fifty two thousand Allied lives. The Polish Second Corps therefore, were to be the main assault force on the fourth attempt in early May 1944.

A seemingly insurmountable problem for the Allied assault troops was that their commanders had decided not to bomb the Monastery on the summit of the thirteen hundred-metre peak of Monte Cassino. They felt that the stronghold could be taken without recourse to destruction of the historic buildings. The German defenders on the summit had a bird's eye view of the surrounding valleys and every attack had been repulsed, despite months of Allied attempts. The route to the summit was a circuitous seven kilometres of narrow, worn tracks that were very exposed and had become increasingly pockmarked with shell holes. It was extremely difficult and costly in men's lives to maintain supplies and equipment to the units besieging the German defenders.

With no prospect of dislodging the Germans and alarmed at the heavy casualties, the New Zealand Lieutenant-General Freyberg went to Rome, to ask Pope Pius XII for permission to bomb the Abbey. This was granted and on February 5th American B17 'Flying Fortresses' dropped 2,500 tons of bombs, reducing the Monastery buildings to rubble. However, the ruins provided even better cover for the German defenders and so the stalemate went on. Arguments raged for decades over the necessity of carrying out this perceived act of cultural vandalism. Indeed, after the devastation of the historical site, which had stood so prominently in magnificent grandeur over the mountain region for fourteen centuries, Kesselring resolved that nothing would persuade him to carry out similar destruction to Rome, Florence, Pisa or Venice.

Campo Basso was situated at an altitude of four hundred metres and it took us days to get used to the mountain terrain and freezing temperatures after a year struggling in the desert heat of the Middle East. Everybody was feeling the cold and constant snow and some of the soldiers already at Campo Basso told us that it had been like this for weeks. The distant rumble of artillery echoed around the mountain panorama, which seemingly stretched for hundreds of miles into the distance. I looked around in awe at the gigantic snow-covered peaks. In peaceful times, the Molise region would have undoubtedly been a top skiing area; families would be coming to the slopes at weekends to enjoy the fun, but now everything had changed and goodness knows when any such sporting activities would be renewed. The mountains were truly magnificent, especially in the early morning on a fine day and at sunset; the setting sun's rays gave a cosy 'alpenglow' to the valley. When the mist lifted, I could see the distant glaciers glistening in their brooding silence. The mountains reigned supreme here, no matter what puny man in his war madness, was trying to do. I visualised the watching peaks gazing down in fascination and disdain at the daily, tragic performances on this stage of war.

There was a clinging, all-pervasive dampness to the air in this region. Often you couldn't see from one valley to another for days, as the fog and mist blotted out the visibility, and the bitter wind never seemed to abate at these altitudes. The roads were terrible for all types of transport, especially the armoured trucks and there was nothing we could do about it. Winter in the mountains, in the middle of a very difficult military campaign, was no laughing matter: everybody, from our commanders down to the foot soldiers, was dreading the approaching battle. We had heard disturbing accounts about the huge losses sustained by the Allies in the Cassino battles and now we Poles had been brought in to try and wrest the mountain summit from tenacious, well-entrenched, German defenders. We left Campo Basso a week later and moved to the town of Orantino, five kilometres from Campo. The sound of the guns and planes attacking Monte Cassino reverberated around the valleys and the artillery fire from the German defenders was continual.

The end of February brought even worse weather, with heavy snow a daily occurrence. The roads were very difficult for the trucks pulling the heavy weapons and there were long delays. After just one week in Orantino we were again on the move, this time to the town of Venafro. This was to be our final division assembly point for an attack on Monte Cassino – we at least knew that much. In their daily briefings, our commanders emphasised that after four long, desperate months of costly fighting, the mountain was as secure as ever for the Nazi defenders and it would be very difficult to dislodge them. Kesselring's defences were proving to be expertly positioned and any Allied progress or battle advantage had been repeatedly neutralised. Conditions were far from ideal for us in Venafro, with a risk of death or serious injury ever present, as the town was in range of the German artillery on the mountain and shells exploded continuously in the fields and on the roads, day and night. We sappers now came into our own after all those months of training in Egypt. To keep the military traffic on the move, we used bulldozers to repair the roads. The logistics for the approaching battle were enormous but, when combined with bad weather and constant German shelling of our supply lines, it couldn't be much harder.

One night, I was on guard duty and many of the boys had gone in to Venafro to enjoy themselves. Suddenly, a drunken soldier who I knew as Bishek, barged into my tent brandishing a rifle; he was completely out of control, screaming and cursing Stalin and all things Russian, saying that he wanted to shoot someone tonight! Luckily two other soldiers, hearing the uproar, stealthily crept up, grabbed the rifle and overpowered him, as he was too drunk to resist. We decided to hand him over to the Military Police stationed at Campo Basso that night and so I volunteered to take him in my jeep. Foolishly, I didn't handcuff him but let him sit alongside me. The route to Campo was over the mountains but the road was very icy, with a succession of hairpin bends. Dangerous enough conditions at any time, let alone accompanied by a violent, drunken prisoner. I made another mistake, as my Thompson gun was secured in its bracket alongside him! I was frantic when I realised this and drove along in sheer panic, constantly watching him out of the corner of my eye; terrified he would suddenly grab the gun. Luckily for me, he wasn't sufficiently alert to seize his chance. He could have easily grabbed the steering wheel, shot me and pushed my body over a cliff, then driven away before the alarm was raised in Venafro. When we arrived at the Military Police barracks in Campo, two M.P.s handcuffed Bishek and put him in the cells.

The police just couldn't believe the risk I'd taken, telling me I was very lucky to be still alive as this desperate prisoner would certainly have killed me if he'd had his wits about him. I stayed overnight at Campo, then left first thing the next morning, suitably chastened by my nasty experience. I thanked God all the time, on the way back to Venafro, for saving my life once more. I later learned that Bishek was tried and sentenced to four years in a military prison.

Towards the middle of April, orders came for our advance on Monte Cassino. Although the mountain was only a few kilometres away, I couldn't see it, as it was enveloped in mist and low cloud. Finally, despite the problems that had relentlessly dogged the Allies, it was now our turn for a fourth attempt on Monte Cassino. We were under the leadership of Lieutenant-General Oliver Leese of the British Eighth Army, with our new, determined Second Polish Corps led by General Wladyslaw Anders. The forces assembled in Leese's army were certainly an international mix, with soldiers from Great Britain, Palestine, Czechoslovakia, New Zealand, India, France, Morocco, South Africa and Greece. Anders' divisions comprised the First and Second Carpathian Brigade, the Fifth Wilenska Brigade, Sixth Lvov Brigade and the Second Armoured Brigade. Some of the Greek lads told us they would be caring for the mules kept in sheds at the base of the mountain. As it was virtually impossible for any vehicles to gain access to the upper reaches, we would be dependent on these docile animals for all our support supplies during the battle. It was to say the least, a very daunting prospect indeed.

In the morning, before we started preparations for the battle, thousands of officers and soldiers attended Mass in a field, as this was an important part of our daily routine in Italy. General Anders announced his 'Order of the Day' just before the battle, which ended with the exhortation, 'Trusting in the Justice of Divine Providence, we go forward with the sacred slogan in our hearts:

God! Country! Honour!'

To prepare for the Polish attack, we were ordered to drive our bulldozers in front of the mechanized units, repairing the roads as we went along. This was a very dangerous job, as the shelling was continuous and we were in range of the artillery on the mountain. The Germans had not laid any mines in this sector, but the in-coming shells were frightening. Jeeps towing trailers filled with ammunition followed our 'dozers, then came the big guns for the opening bombardment and finally the troops in lorries. Everyone was desperately praying that no shells would hit the convoy, as this would result in carnage before the battle even started. The narrow paths criss-crossing the mountain prevented access to large vehicles, so our supplies would have to be carried up by the mules.

On May 9th our Second Corps was firmly established two kilometres from the base of the mountain. At least one thousand six hundred guns would be used in the opening bombardment, on the night of the 10th. In addition, the Allies had two thousand tanks, three thousand planes, and numerically they outnumbered the Germans in a ratio of three to one, with one hundred and eight battalions compared to Field Marshall Kesselring and General Friedrich von Vietinghoff's fifty eight battalions. The attack, codenamed 'Operation Diadem', was about to begin. At 11.00 pm, the artillery started their opening salvos; the noise of the guns was deafening, even from two kilometres away, and the ground shook. The sky above the peaks was lit up with an orange glow and to us watching this awesome 'son-et-lumiere' of firepower, it seemed as though the whole mountainside was ablaze, such was the devastating power of the bombardment.

At dawn, waves of British and American bombers swarmed in from Foggia air base, pounding the German defences. Surely, we thought, nothing could withstand such an opening blitz. The earth shook continually, as the Polish conflagration steadily increased and unfortunately this had a very bad effect on some of the young soldiers, who were terrified of the overwhelming noise. I covered my ears and opened my mouth to prevent my eardrums from exploding. Such was the shock to the nervous systems of the lads that, in a few cases, their hair turned completely white overnight! Although it was early May, it was still very cold and so at night every soldier had a tot of rum. Some mornings, it was so cold that we started the lorry engines and warmed our hands on the bonnets. Joseph had told me days before that he would be in the first attack and I wished him well, with obvious misgivings.

Field Marshall Kesselring had been receiving continual reports of the devastating Allied bombardment, which certainly seemed to him to be the prelude of another attack. This was very strange, as recently there had been consistent intelligence reports of Canadian and American forces practising amphibious landings on beaches around Naples. The German High Command began to seriously think that the Allies had given up trying to break the Gustav Line. A stream of clever disinformation from the Allies and Italian resistance groups on the ground convinced the German High Command that these manoeuvres were a prelude to an imminent invasion of beaches at Civitavecchia, near Rome. To withstand the Allied attack, he despatched two divisions to Rome, weakening his defences around Cassino. The Allied deception was so successful that Kesselring's very able General von Vietinghoff was confident that the bombardment did not mean that a Fourth Battle was about to begin. Later in the day on May 11th, Kesselring began to have serious doubts about his enthusiasm in sending his reserves to Rome. Later, Vietinghoff telephoned to say that the Gustav Line defence forces were struggling to hold the line against unexpectedly heavy Allied attacks.

The 4th Indian Division of the British Army joined us in the first assault and after two days of bitter hand-to-hand fighting, little progress had been made. Our independent sapper platoon of fifty men stayed in the rear and when summoned by battle commanders, had to go in front of tank attacks in the mountain foothills to clear landmines. The tanks would eventually be dug in, firing up at the German defences. Invariably the tank shells would explode on the rocks and send shards of lethal rock fragments down onto our infantry, who were trying to establish positions on the heights. There was a ten man specialist bomb disposal unit working with us as well, defusing bombs on the roads before any tank advance. For both our units, it was extremely tense, dangerous work, under constant enemy fire: I dreaded to think what nightmarish encounters our infantry were having high up on the mountain. For the next two terrible days, they were desperately trying to cling on to hard–won sections and faced unrelenting, withering German fire. One of them later told me that the terrain higher up consisted of rocky escarpments and many Polish soldiers were unable to take adequate cover: they were mowed down by the enfilading fire of Nazi machine gunners in well-concealed, fortified dugouts. Dislodging the paratroopers was going to be very costly for the Corps soldiers and several assaults might be necessary

At night, our soldiers had to wear carpet slippers, as hob-nailed boots would clatter on the rocky ground and invite enemy fire. (Was this strange military innovation one of General Anders' brainwaves I wondered?). Groups of German prisoners were being led down the mountain, so some progress was being made. Medics were supervising the transfer of our wounded on mules and stretchers to the casualty station at the rear and the sad procession continued all day. A few shell-shocked soldiers followed, stumbling along the worn paths and a captain said there were many dead Polish troops on the mountain, the legacy of Monte Cassino. What a ghastly place!

The order was given to retreat lower down the mountain and re-group for another attempt after reconnaissance photos had been analysed by our Generals. I'd hoped we would be heading back a few kilometres for a rest, but we were told that we would be staying at the base of the mountain. Little did we know that Field Marshall Kesselring had seen for himself at dawn on the morning of 'Diadem', the devastation inflicted by the Allied gunfire on his Tenth Army and Fourteenth Corps, who, in his experienced view, had almost ceased to function. In fact he was sent a message from Vietinghoff suggesting that the time had come to give up the monastery. A radiogram was sent to the First Parachute Divisions' commander Kurt Landerlucke telling him to relinquish his position and start a retreat via the Senger Line at midnight.

My first glimpse of a war of attrition of such proportions was terrifying; the sheer hopelessness of our assault vividly brought home the difficulty we faced. Dad had often told us of his experiences against the Russians in the First World War before he was wounded and hospitalised. The reality of it to a new soldier like me was a new, unimagined nightmare. I don't think I slept at all during those two days and I'm sure everybody else was equally traumatised by their first experience of battle.

Again and again, the problem with Monte Cassino, evident since the first attempts back in January, was the sheer vastness of the Massif and the inaccessibility of the upper heights. The attacking forces' vehicles alone had great difficulty negotiating the sea of shell holes, deep bomb craters, mud, incessant freezing rain and lurking anti-personnel mines. (A British Eighth Army veteran 'Desert Rats' later conceded that in contrast to Monte Cassino, the Western desert battle of El Alamein was a picnic!).

To my horror, a message came to informing me that Joseph had been very badly injured in a German mortar attack and had been taken to the field hospital. Our second assault was scheduled to commence on May 17th, so we had just five short days to get re-organised. Preparations were intensified and perhaps staying at the base of the mountain did make sense, as the attack would be speedier with the heavy equipment in place. The advance units were soon positioned and this time we were resolute in our determination to succeed. Surely General Anders would solve the everlasting problem of how to subdue the German defenders occupying the sea of rubble on the summit? He and General Leese devised a plan to outflank the Germans, sending a unit of the French Expeditionary Force to do this. The manoeuvre succeeded in driving the German First Parachute Division out of their positions and they gradually retreated, leaving their wounded behind in the monastery ruins and many dead in the catacombs and wedged into cupboards, boxes and vestment drawers in the monastery.

The next day Colonel Lakinski, an artillery spotter, noticed a tattered white flag flying above the Monastery ruins. Lieutenant Kasimircz Gurbiel of the First Squadron, Twelfth Podolski Lancers Regiment, led a reconnaissance patrol up to the Monastery and reached the summit unopposed after the German evacuation. The Lancers regimental flag was raised over the Abbey ruins and the victory bugle call, 'Henjal mariacki', echoed in the mountain stillness. Such a waste of life on both sides! My stomach-churning night prior to the battle was now forgotten. Had I once again missed an appointment with death? Was the inevitable being delayed just a few weeks longer? Would I be buried in Italy along with so many of my comrades?

On the morning of May 20th, I took a party of officers in my jeep to inspect this charnel house of war. We looked at the mountain through field glasses. A pall of smoke like a Norse funeral pyre hung over the battlefield. Its slopes were littered with corpses from both sides of the fighting; tangled barbed wire, wrecked vehicles and the bloated cadavers of mules that had been hit by shells. The burial parties were now beginning their grim task, one that was to be repeated so many times in the battles that lay ahead for us in Italy. (It was later announced that in our one battle alone, eight hundred and sixty Polish troops had been killed and around three thousand wounded).

A final day was necessary to flush out snipers and round up Germans lost in the mountains in their hasty retreat. Then at last we headed back to Campo Basso.

Return to Monte Cassino. In late 1944, Julian's platoon returned to the battlefield. Of the original 50 sappers who fought in the fourth battle, only these 16 survived. Julian is standing on the truck at the right of the group

The town of Cassino and the Benedictine Abbey after the fourth and final battle - May 19th 1944

CHAPTER 18
The Final Battles in Italy - Part 1

The day after the battle of Monte Cassino, a party of our tired but euphoric troops went to Venafro to relax and unwind. The roads were relatively unscathed in this area, in comparison to the rubble-strewn ones we had been struggling with for so long at Cassino. Unfortunately, the Germans hadn't quite finished with us yet and there were a few unpleasant surprises awaiting unwary drivers, particularly in this area. Local German sympathisers (and there were a few of them) rigged steel wires across roads at night, especially on a section after a bend. Because our jeeps had the windscreens folded down when driving at night, an unsuspecting driver hitting this lethal trap would be decapitated! After several tragedies, effective measures were immediately introduced to combat this night-time menace: a five feet angle-iron post, curved at the top, was welded to the front of the vehicle in the middle below the bonnet and this protective arm would cut the deadly wires on contact.

At last! On June 6th 1944 came the historic, long-awaited news that the greatest military invasion in history had started, on the coast of Normandy, in France. Hitler now had two massive fronts to contend with and his much-vaunted 'Festung Europa' was to crumble before the Allied assault. Everyone was delighted with the momentous event and our celebrations were un-restrained. There were crowds of Italian troops in Venafro. After the Italian dictator Benito Mussolini and his Fascist followers had been removed from power by the King, the Italian army switched to the Allies. Seeing the somewhat strange colour of their uniforms and being able to speak Italian, I asked one which unit the uniforms represented. He told me that they were British standard khaki uniforms that had been dyed blue!

On returning to our base the C.O. informed us that we could have the next two days off, before our next clash with the Germans at Ancona. So once again, it was back down the mountains to Taranto for everybody. This visit gave us much longer to look around and we discovered that the town was divided into two areas, Old and New Taranto: being separated by a swing bridge over the port estuary. We'd heard a lot about the dreadful driving of some American troops in Italy. The roads around Taranto were especially dangerous, as these Americans, who always seemed to be drunk, roared along them at high speeds, smashing crazily into other vehicles and buildings. The M.P.s were always catching and arresting them and complaints from locals about damage inflicted on their parked cars or houses resulted in the miscreants, quite rightly, having to pay for repairs to vehicles and properties.

After an enjoyable two days in Taranto, it was back into the jeeps and up again to Venafro where we stayed for several weeks, until the next stage of our march North was finalised by General Anders and his officers. They gave orders for an advance to the coastal village of Porto Recconarti near Loreto. Here, preparations were made for a potentially decisive clash with a battle-hardened Waffen (armed) SS Division of fifty thousand soldiers, who were defending Ancona. This confrontation would take place in open countryside, one and a half kilometres from the town and as at Cassino. Fighting on the vast Marche plain outside Ancona was difficult and the Esino River was going to be the biggest obstacle; I always found it very frustrating that there so many well defended rivers all over Northern Italy.

Another problem facing armoured assault vehicles at Ancona was, as usual, the roads, which were like swamps: we spent days towing out tanks that had either sunk in the mud or broken down. I was in the forefront of attempts to free trapped vehicles as I was the only one who could handle a giant' Mack' American towing truck. This monster, which had been manufactured in Mack's huge plant in Kansas City Missouri, had a low loader for transporting bulldozers plus a heavy-duty winch and was vitally important for river crossings during assaults in Northern Italy. When seated in the machine I seemed to be twenty feet taller than even the tanks. This feeling of superiority was soon dispelled during battle, when I discovered that my prominent position made me a sitting duck for enemy machine guns! I fervently hoped it wouldn't break down in the next few weeks! To free twenty-ton tanks which had sunk in the squelchy, clinging mud or had slid uncontrollably into roadside ditches or fields, we used ropes as thick as a man's wrist, which were then attached to the towing winch on my vehicle. Establishing crossing points over the wide rivers was always a big problem. To cross relatively shallow water I used my truck to place sheets of steel mesh on the bed of the river, enabling tanks and guns to reach the far bank safely. If the rivers were too deep, our engineers assembled Anglesey bridges.

During one attempt to establish a bridgehead on the wide Esino River, I had a terrifying experience. Machine-gun fire poured down from the well-entrenched German Panzer defenders who were trying to kill me, blow up my vehicle and prevent the crossing. I was completely isolated, as all our men were taking cover, but when bullets started hitting my truck I jumped out and fled to the riverbank just in time. When the crossing was established later, I was shocked to discover a line of machine gun bullet holes dotted across the windscreen: thankfully, my name couldn't have been on one of them that day. The SS had sown landmines profusely in the Ancona battle area, so neutralising these was vital. After clearing a strip through the minefields, we marked the safe areas with white tapes, so they could be seen at night, and always put up warning notices. (The Nazis had a nasty habit of surreptitiously switching the white tapes to areas that hadn't been cleared and many men were killed by this despicable action).

The Waffen SS were very difficult opponents; they were efficient and highly trained, with a tough mind-set and never gave an inch, however desperate the battle situation had become. But hadn't Hitler told his forces to fight to the last bullet and the last man? At that stage in the war, he was giving wild orders from his bunker in the Chancellery in Berlin to phantom armies, who existed only in his deranged mind and had long been annihilated. The most fanatical Nazis were in the SS Totenkopf, or Death's Head units. These merciless killers were responsible for countless atrocities in Russia, the Occupied Countries and the horrendous Jewish ghetto clearances in Poland. After the war we discovered that they had staffed the concentration camps sited all over Europe. Captured German soldiers whom I met later told me that the ordinary Wehrmacht troops loathed and hated the SS.

The decent Wehrmacht soldiers must have been absolutely mortified when, months later, one of our intelligence officers told us of an appalling massacre in three mountain villages in the Apennines in late summer 1944. SS-Sturmbannfuhrer Walter Reder's 16th Reichsfuhrer–SS Division had retreated to the foothills of Monte Sole after their defeat at Bologna. His men now bore more resemblance to a dishevelled rabble than an elite SS fighting force. Only a few years ago, Reder himself had taken the salute at the passing-out ceremony for the division at the SS training centre at Bad Tolz. For many months, Reder had been receiving reliable intelligence reports confirming his long-held suspicions that the inhabitants of the Monte Sole communities had been sheltering and assisting the Italian partisans in the region. He and his officers decided that it was time to set an example to other villages in Northern Italy. They occupied and sealed off the villages of Marzabotto, Monzuna and Grissanda Morandi from September 29th to October 5th 1944. In what was the biggest massacre in wartime Italy, nine hundred and fifty five villagers (including over one hundred children and five priests) were slain. The murderers got away with their crime for decades because of extraordinary, unaccountable delays in the judiciary process; incredibly, vital documentation relating to the sordid crimes was 'lost' for fifty years!

As the years rolled on, there were no arrests or convictions apart from Reder himself, who was extradited to Naples in 1948 and sentenced to life imprisonment in the city fortress prison in 1951. In what became known as the 'forgotten massacre', the descendants of the murdered villagers must have suspected a huge, inexplicable government cover-up. Most of the SS officers were eventually convicted 'in absentia' but three, now in their eighties, escaped justice for sixty three years, being only found guilty, again 'in absentia', in January 2007! Knowing the reputation of the SS, I wasn't altogether surprised. During the battle of Monte Cassino a badly wounded SS trooper was being attended to by one of our dedicated medical orderlies. Suddenly, the German pulled a gun from inside his jacket and fired point blank at the medic, killing him instantly. One of our guys was so enraged at this horrific act of murder carried out on the unarmed orderly that he immediately pumped twenty rounds from his Thompson into the SS man.

On July 20th, a brave Wehrmacht officer tried to assassinate Hitler with a bomb hidden in his briefcase at his Wolf's Lair H.Q. at Rastenburg, in

East Prussia. Although the device exploded, Hitler was only stunned but, in the aftermath of the attempt, the Gestapo (Geheime Stats Polizei - State Security Police), hunted down hundreds of suspects in the military, many of whom were executed or forced to commit suicide. These included the renowned Field Marshall Erwin Rommel, who was highly respected for his military planning and resourcefulness by the Allies. What a waste of such a brilliant commander!

Throughout my service in the Polish army, I was always touched by the bonds of friendship and camaraderie that existed between the men, from soldiers to officers. This was always at it's strongest during particularly dangerous encounters with the enemy and we were always united in our determination, objectives and strength of purpose towards defeating Hitler. Despite years of training, nothing can prepare soldiers for the reality of war. We all depended on each other in the heat of battle and tears of relief or despair were always shed after successes or heavy losses. Everybody had their own method of dealing with this enormous stress and I believe every single one of us, including officers, was always terrified at the prospect of serious injury or death. All soldiers tried to assist in collecting and burying their dead comrades after battles. This harrowing duty was always deeply emotional, especially when friends had been killed and their bodies badly mutilated. Before a dignified burial, the soldier's identification discs were removed and his helmet hung from a cross, on which had been inscribed his name, regiment and date of death. A necessary duty perhaps, but one which no serviceman ever found easy.

There was just one event that gripped every single Polish soldier at this time: news came through on the radio in August of the uprising against the Nazis by the large Polish Underground Army in Warsaw, led by General Bor-Komorowski. The resistance had been planning and collecting weapons from various sources for a long time. As the all-conquering Red Army was virtually at the gates of Warsaw, the Russians encouraged the Armia Krajowa (A.K.) to take on the Germans, promising to advance towards the city and fight alongside the Poles. No help was given and instead, the Soviet General Konstantin Rokossovsky positioned his forces on the other side of the Vistula River and on Stalin's orders, ignored all requests, which eventually became desperate pleas from the embattled fighters. Stalin had already decided that the non-Communist

Polish resistance was going to be a big problem for the Russians after the war, so why not let the Germans finish them off? Churchill was alarmed at Stalin's evil subterfuge and arranged for the British Eighth Army to organise flights carrying food and arms from Italian air bases. Stalin instructed Rokossovsky to deny the Allies use of captured German air bases for re-fuelling and, combined with the heavy losses incurred from German anti-aircraft fire and in some cases also from Soviet fighters and guns, these relief flights were abandoned.

The brave Poles held out for sixty-three days and Bor-Komorowski finally surrendered on October 6th. The commander of the operation, SS Gruppenfuhrer Reinefarth, relishing having been given carte blanche by his adored Fuhrer to employ any methods to crush the insurrection, used artillery and flame-throwers to destroy the city block by block. Civilians trapped in upper storeys of burning buildings threw themselves out to escape being burned alive and were shot by Reinefarth's men. Convicts were then rounded up from Warsaw's jails and, along with Russian prisoners-of-war, were armed, put in uniform and assigned to the notorious Dirlewanger and Kaminski SS brigades, who let them run amok throughout the city. In two terrible days between 20,000 and 50,000 civilians were slaughtered in two districts by these killers, who were encouraged by Himmler to spare no one. Elderly residents, children and babies were cold bloodedly killed in an orgy of drink-fuelled sadism by these fiends against the Warsaw inhabitants. In an act of medieval barbarity, wounded soldiers of both sides and doctors and nurses in a large hospital were murdered. Horrifying sights were seen of bed ridden patients being thrown out of ward windows and some were impaled on bayonets and left as grotesque trophies on the hospital balconies. These bloody excesses appalled even other SS officers and the respected German Chief of Staff, General Heinz Guderian, pleaded with Hitler to stop the killings.

The exhausted Polish fighters attempted to flee from Warsaw by any escape route, even via the city's sewers, but the Nazis flooded the labyrinthine waterways, injected lethal gas or threw hand grenades down the manholes. The remnants of the insurrection were rounded up and later, 16,000 perished in Treblinka extermination camp. This was the second armed insurrection against the Nazis in Warsaw and cost the lives of 22,000 fighters and even more appallingly, 200,000 innocent civilians.

(A year earlier in 1943, brave Jewish fighters in the ghetto, knowing that all the inmates would shortly be sent to the gas chambers and the ghetto destroyed, revolted against their evil tormentors. They resisted the German attacks, led by SS-Gruppenfuhrer Jurgen Stroop for seven days, then succumbed to the remorseless firepower of their adversaries. The Jews had only a modest supply of light weapons and most were either shot or burned alive when the ghetto was torched. After this terrible event, the remaining ghetto buildings were razed to the ground).

We despaired at learning of the failure of the '44 uprising and my hatred of Stalin intensified. Rokossovsky's First ByeloRussian Front army could easily have come to the aid of the fighters, knowing full well that they could only hold out for a limited time. Another example of Stalin's scheming callousness; his complete disregard for the brutal Nazi suppression of the brave Warsaw inhabitants and the first part of his secret plans for the future of the country when the war ended.

After winning the battle for Ancona, we moved up the coast to the fishing villages of Catholica and Riccione, staying a few days before going up to Rimini. The town was a bleak wasteland of shattered buildings, rusting tanks and trucks, the inevitable wreckage of war. The frightened civilians, mainly old people, were huddled in basements beneath their collapsed homes. The Nazis had hidden booby-traps in many of the ruined buildings as a parting gift before vanishing, so it was another hair-raising job for us sappers. It took two weeks to find and dismantle hundreds of these deadly devices throughout Rimini, as they had been well hidden with typical Teutonic thoroughness.

Allied intelligence had warned of the possibility of a night time invasion of the Adriatic coast by German forces based in Yugoslavia. After these reports, we had to be extremely vigilant and increased nightly sentry patrols on the coast of Catholica and Riccione. Just as dawn broke one morning, a patrolling sentry raised the alarm after spotting a flotilla of boats off the coast. We rushed down to the beach and immediately poured a ferocious barrage of machine gun fire at the 'invasion fleet'. Many of the boats were sunk, but several were brought ashore by the in-coming tide. We were mystified to discover that there were no bodies of German troops on any of the boats. In fact they were fishing boats, with names such as 'Stella Maris': very puzzling indeed. Weeks later, a drunken local lad owned up to this escapade. He had of course heard of the possibility of a German invasion of Riccione or Catholica, so decided to play a trick on us. He crept down to the harbour at the dead of night, avoiding our sentries, and cut the ropes securing the entire Catholica fishing fleet! He then waited for the retreating tide to take them out to sea. A vigilant sentry seeing the approaching 'German armada', aroused the barracks and that's how two thirds of the Catholica fishing fleet were sunk. What happened to the local prankster? I've no idea, but he probably was grabbed by the outraged fisherman and joined their poor boats at the bottom of the Adriatic!

In November 1944, we moved inland to Cesena and the battle to take the town began, with intensive shelling from both sides. Early snow in the Cesena region prevented any ground attacks for three months, so we had to sit in our foxholes and trenches until the weather improved. We heard later that similar weather conditions were prevalent in the Ardennes forests of Belgium, where American forces were taken completely by surprise by a lightning Panzer break-through, which was eventually repulsed, but which gave the Americans a very nasty shock.

One day, I had another lucky escape when I was sheltering upstairs in a house in the suburbs of Cesena with some lads. A German shell hit the ground floor and, fortunately, the house didn't collapse and bury us. However, I wasn't so lucky at our base outside Ancona a few weeks later: somehow we carelessly forgot to cover our lorries with camouflage netting when they were parked. Sure enough, six German Messerschmitt fighters spotted these inviting targets and started strafing the vehicles and other stores. Two lorries burst into flames and I had to hit the deck as machine-gun bullets churned up the ground all around me in an untimely dance of death. My tommy gun was in the hut, so dodging the bullets I scrambled to get it, to at least return some fire at the planes. As I started off, another lorry was hit and exploded, throwing burning fuel over my face and hands. The pain was agonising and I crawled to the first-aid post for assistance. The medic injected me first, and then I was bandaged and taken to the military hospital, in Ancona.

CHAPTER 19
Hospital in Ancona

There were so many wounded soldiers on stretchers that initial medical assessments were made outside the emergency admittance entrance. My stretcher was placed alongside two badly wounded German soldiers and I protested about this, so they moved me across to the other side of the ambulance bay. Very shortly, a Polish doctor came to examine me, but told the staff to replace my stretcher back to its original place, saying, 'Put them together, they won't fight any more!' Before taking me down to the burns unit, the nurses covered my face and hands in a soothing blue jelly before bandaging them and over the next few weeks, I was given frequent blood transfusions. In the ward were nine young soldiers from all nationalities, including five members of a British tank crew. Their vehicle had sustained a direct hit during the battle for Ancona and had caught fire. They all had severe burns and were in such continuous agony that they couldn't bear sheets on their bodies, so special tents were suspended over their beds.

The worst example of injuries in the ward was self-inflicted. An infantryman in his forties carried out an extremely foolish act: he was feeling very cold in his room one evening, so he decided to light a fire. To make sure it lit immediately, he unscrewed the cap of an artillery shell and sprinkled the gunpowder over the wood, then struck a match. There was a blinding flash and the man ended up on the floor screaming with pain, his hair alight and his uniform charred and smouldering. Only very prompt action by his colleagues saved his life. As it was, he had potentially life threatening first degree burns and the doctors doubted if he would survive. Such was his overwhelming pain he called out to the poor nurses all night and drove us all crazy. I used to try to keep him quiet, feed him and later take him in a wheelchair around the hospital grounds and small garden area.

In my case, for the first five weeks of hospitalisation my mouth was so badly swollen that I could only swallow liquids using a straw. Even today, my mouth is still blistered and tender. The Polish nurses on the ward were really friendly and despite the total ban on alcohol, they often brought us bottles of wine, hidden under their capes! Because of the very poor health of so many of the soldiers in the ward, the Polish doctor recommended that we should sleep as long as we liked every day, as this extra rest would be very beneficial. Unfortunately, he omitted to inform our diligent ward matron of his order. The next day at 6.00 am, she arrived with her team and announced in her stentorian voice, 'Good morning! Sorry boys, wake up! We've got to make the beds!' We looked at her bleary-eyed in fury and disbelief, after the doctor's instructions only the previous day. Dave, one of the tank boys, whispered to me as we were having the beds changed, 'Never mind Julian, we'll get our own back tonight!' Every night, before 'light's out', the matron dispensed a tot of rum to each patient, or sometimes a bottle of Guinness. On that particular night it was rum, so after everybody had been served, we chatted to the matron to distract her, hid the bottle, then immediately she left the ward, Dave locked the door and we finished off the bottle in style!

As the weeks went by and I slowly improved, I was able to help the nurses by giving out meals, collecting dishes and feeding patients who were too ill to look after themselves. My bandages were thankfully removed in the middle of December, leaving an irritating itchy rash but apart from that, I was fully recovered. Christmas Day was a very happy occasion, with everything one could have wished for in the way of food and a great atmosphere in the ward and hospital. It was especially poignant when we later saw the deprivation of ordinary Italians, who had so little at Christmas and whose towns and homes were in ruins.

Queues of people waited outside wrecked churches for soup, coffee and bread on Christmas Day, which was served by cheerful nuns and helpers. Thankfully no families were unfed, but where the charity workers got their supplies from was a mystery to me, as all food was in short supply across Ancona. But I soon heard that our NAAFI lads were able to come up with sacks of freshly baked bread, tins of soup and coffee and Christmas goodies for the children!

After the festivities, the hospital authorities decided that I was sufficiently recovered to return to the transit camp outside Ancona. I was taken there in a jeep and produced my hospital discharge papers for the C.O, who said I had to wait for permission before rejoining the regiment at Cesena.

I hung around the camp for weeks, and some days, out of sheer boredom, went to the dingy cinema in Ancona. The flickering newsreel showed the progress of the war in Europe and on the Eastern Front. The announcer was hysterically ranting about the imminent downfall of Hitler. Graphic, grainy, footage showed Red Army soldiers and ex-inmates who looked like skeletons, at a recently liberated Nazi extermination camp in Eastern Poland, near Krakow. The camp was called Oswiecim, in German: Auschwitz. Thousands of frantic refugees packed the roads fleeing from the all-conquering Red Army. The announcer screamed that the noose was tightening around Hitler's scrawny neck and the Nazi Armageddon was imminent. By now the German army was in full retreat, with only the Hitler Youth and old men in cobbled together 'Volksturm' (Peoples storm) units trying to hold back the Soviet tanks. Totenkopf SS stalked the streets of the cities and towns, immediately shooting or hanging army deserters from trees or lampposts. The city of Lodz had also been liberated, but for the one hundred and seventy thousand Jews originally in the ghetto it was too late. The Nazis had been murdering the large Jewish ghetto population systematically for years and only eight hundred and fifty remained alive when the Russians arrived.

Things were certainly building up to the climax of the war. The tank armies of Zhukov and Konev were smashing their way towards the prize that Stalin coveted more than anything else: Berlin! What was not shown was that, in the wake of the Red Army came the NKVD, like swarms of brown rats, arresting and executing people in the 'liberated' cities and towns and filling trains with looted plant and equipment to rebuild the shattered Soviet industry. In the West, Eisenhower and Montgomery's forces were storming through Germany, with only fanatical Nazis putting up futile opposition. The announcer warned guardedly of the danger of a last-ditch Nazi redoubt being established in the Bavarian Alps by SS 'Werewolf' units. With a blaze of martial music the lights came up and I left the flea-pit of a cinema, confident that at last, Hitler's crimes were going to be devastatingly punished and it was retribution time for criminal organisations like the Gestapo, SS and SD (Sicherheits-Dienst, Security service) and Kripo (Kriminal Polizei).

I often came across Allied army deserters hanging around the cafes and bars in Ancona: many admitted that they just couldn't face another winter in the front line, or were suffering from battle fatigue or shell shock. They were hiding in bombed-out buildings all over the town, keeping a lookout for the Military Police, who continually caught them and returned them to their units for disciplinary action. Many lurked in caves in the Apennine Mountains and all drivers were warned never to attempt to travel on these mountain roads in daytime or especially at night. These really were desperate men and all had kept their weapons and had plenty of ammunition. Having fled from their units, they were always scavenging around Ancona for food just to stay alive. Starvation often reduced them to preying on military or sometimes civilian drivers. Their favourite trick was to stand on a deserted mountain road carrying a concealed gun, then flag down an approaching military vehicle ostensibly for a lift. When the unsuspecting driver stopped, they immediately opened fire, killed and robbed the soldier and after dumping his body in a ditch or throwing it over a cliff, drove off in the truck or jeep. I certainly avoided the Apennine region after hearing of so many army drivers who had been waylaid by these bandits, then robbed and murdered. One G.I. deserter called Lee from Austin, Texas, told me one evening over a few drinks of his unit's combat experience in January. He had been in the U.S. Texas 36th Division, which had attempted to cross the Rapido River, flowing through Cassino. The operation was ill conceived from the outset; being carried out in darkness, with thick fog surrounding the river. The assault boats were so heavy that it took eight men on each side to carry them for two miles, across marshy ground. Some GIs carrying the boats became disorientated in the dark and stumbled into minefields. Others got lost along the river banks in the fog and couldn't find the crossing point.

The Rapido River was thirty feet across and at least twelve feet deep. The swift-flowing milky waters were intensely cold, being fed from mountain glaciers further up the valley. When attempts were made to launch the boats they either immediately capsized in the raging water, drowning all the occupants or were sunk by sustained German mortar and machine gun fire. The American attack was decimated and hundreds of bodies floated down the river or were piled six feet high on the riverbanks. Lee was sure that the losses sustained by his 36th division were comparable to the first assault wave on the Easy Red sector of Omaha beach on D-Day. In his laconic Texan drawl he added, 'Ya know Jule, for the Krauts, (slang for Germans) it was just one helluva turkey shoot!' Lee had been pinned down on the riverbank totally isolated from the main group. Such was the confusion and panic that nobody seemed to be in charge and most of the officers had been killed. He decided that the only hope of survival was to creep away from the river under cover of the fog. Waiting until daylight would be a fatal mistake as the Germans would easily pick off the remaining attackers huddled on the grassy banks. He made his way back to Ancona and persuaded a local family to take him in. A few days later he got hold of civilian clothes, left the home and found shelter in a bombed building in the suburbs.

He finally told me that the British also endured horrendous losses in January, on a similarly ill fated attempt to cross the Garigliano river near Mondragone. Again, like the abortive Texan assault, it was carried out in darkness and fog, with resultant disastrous consequences. After his very distressing, sad story, Lee downed his bourbon and said, 'Well Jule, I'm gonna hit the hay. So long pal.' We shook hands and he made his way back to his hideout, somewhere in Ancona. (After the war, I found out that in Italy, in 1944, one thousand Allied soldiers were deserting every month).

CHAPTER 20
The Final Battles in Italy - Part 2

A t long last, in early March permission came through for me to rejoin my unit at Cesena. The Germans still hadn't relinquished their hold on several areas around Cesena and there was constant shelling from them. This continued on a daily basis as we later progressed North to the town of Forli. What a welcome I received at the camp: everyone was fussing over me and it was great to be back among my buddies. They had thoughtfully been storing up my extra rations and had bought a range of 'welcome home' treats! These goodies included a thousand cigarettes, for each week of my hospitalisation and about fifty tins of tobacco! The cigarettes only cost two lire in the NAAFI shop, so no wonder I had such a stock. Add to this stash twenty tubes of toothpaste and ten bars of soap and it was a fabulous surprise from my comrades. I sold a lot of the tobacco to buy wine, so we had a very boozy reunion! In addition, the lads had arranged for a local lady to wash and iron my tunic, so I was eventually resplendent in a pristine uniform as well!

Before the next offensive, a few of us drove down to Naples for a few days. I hadn't realised how much I missed the camaraderie of the unit, having been enclosed in a hospital environment for so long. When we returned to Cesena, I had an informal chat with the C.O. to decide how I felt about resuming full duties; I told him that I was really looking forward to carrying on as before, with chauffeuring and collecting army rations. Within a few weeks I was getting around Cesena in my trusty jeep once more and between duties I used to visit the local 'Café Cantonnierra'. One day over a coffee, the friendly proprietor told me he had a problem: before the arrival of the war on his doorstep, he always used to collect barrels of wine for his restaurant from local farms. Unfortunately, because of the fuel shortages in Italy, he was now unable to do this and wondered if I could help him. I said I would be happy to oblige and started to go to the farms during my lunch break and collected several barrels of wine on each visit. In return, the café owner would give me a barrel every week, which was soon demolished by the lads back at the barracks. One day, our C.O. was passing a farm and saw me loading the last few barrels into the jeep. He stopped and asked what was going on. I decided to tell him the truth, as he would have found out later anyway. On hearing of my little 'arrangement' with the café owner and the farmers, he just laughed and said, 'Well done Julian', so I later dutifully gave him twenty litres of best red!

Things now started to move quickly on the battlefront and I really enjoyed being back into action with the Corps once again. On and on our units pushed, meeting little opposition from the fleeing Germans. All the troops were excited; everyone aware that this was surely the last big advance and the end of the war was in sight. Reports on the army radio continually kept us briefed on the progress of the Soviet and American armies in Germany: the end of the so-called 'Thousand Year Reich' was fast approaching. In Berlin, Antonov and Chuikovs' assault forces were blasting their way towards the Chancellery and Reichstag, with orders to fight their way in regardless of losses and plant the Red Flag triumphantly on the pinnacle of the Reichstag, signalling total victory. In the west, Simpson's Ninth and Hodge's First Army spearheads were roaring down the autobahns towards the city before they were inexplicably stopped by Eisenhower and halted at the Elbe river. (This decision was to have far-reaching consequences for the Allies and the German people for half a century).

Our swift progress made it difficult to see exactly where the front line was. As we continued on the Milan road to Forli, we sometimes had to shelter from our own fighter-planes as they hunted down retreating Germans. We covered our lorries with large Union flags, but often the airmen gave us a few bursts from their cannon before realising their mistake. The pilots then waggled their planes' wings in abject apology before seeking other targets. The spearhead of the advance occasionally seemed to waver and then move in a fairly straight line. All the time, our job was to be in the forefront of the infantry, continually checking for anti-personnel mines on the roads. Occasionally, when we were at the rear, I could get my bearings in relation to the front positions by watching our advancing shell bursts. In this way, we approached Imola and there were no problems; passing through a nice town, which for a change hadn't been destroyed. Our tanks had been crashing ahead as the weather was dry and it was the best surface for them for a long time. At least we sappers didn't have to creep forward in front of them any longer. This was a huge relief, as it was obvious that the war was going to end soon and everyone was intent on survival.

On arriving at the city of Bologna, which was completely destroyed, we were told that the Polish Corps would push on to Milan and the British and Americans to Padua and Venice, to clear up pockets of resistance from fanatical Nazis who still refused to surrender. There was however, one final very nasty surprise awaiting us from the Germans: as our platoon rounded a bend in the road outside Bologna, Germans hidden in the roadside ditches opened up on us in a last-ditch attack. A fierce firefight ensued, lasting for an hour and a half and I reckon I killed at least two dozen Germans. This skirmish proved to be our last contact with the enemy. On April 21st Bologna fell, with General Anders getting a nice souvenir: the Panzer regimental flag!

On May 7th Germany surrendered and the war was over. It now seemed very strange that the artillery had finally ceased. The constant rumble had been our sonorous background throughout the long Italian campaign and the stillness did take some getting used to.

At last, after seven long years, the guns in Europe were silent.

CHAPTER 21
Dances in Senegallia

Everybody was ecstatic that the long, bitter war had finally ended. We held parties in the camp mess every night and why not? A week after the cessation of hostilities, four of us decided to go to Milan. Mussolini and his mistress Clara Petacci had been captured at Dongo, above Lake Como, whilst trying to reach Switzerland. They were then executed with other Fascists by Communist partisans on April 28th 1945 and their bodies displayed in the city's Piazzale Loreto. Victory celebrations were still in full swing in the city, which was packed with thousands of Communist resistance fighters. They had come down with their supporters from their mountain strongholds in Lombardy, and the atmosphere was highly charged. It certainly looked as if we'd definitely picked the wrong day to sightsee in Milan! Many of them disturbingly carried guns and knives, were drinking heavily and singing Communist revolutionary songs at the top of their voices. That was quite enough for me, after experiencing at first hand Stalin's oppression and cruelty, from the perspective of one of his slave workers. First I turned off the jeep's engine, in case the drunken baying mob got completely out of control and turned the vehicle over, or even worse attacked us. Spotting a gap in the crowd, I gunned the engine and we roared out of the square and back down the highway to Imola. Whew! Another lucky escape!

Accommodation for our troops in Italy after the war was always a problem. As I could speak Italian, the C.O. asked me to see what I could do about it. I decided to make a start immediately: if I were successful in persuading locals to put up our soldiers, it would solve an on-going difficulty for our officers. I was always surprised how harsh the winters could be in Northern Italy although, compared with Russia, they were fairly mild! So if accommodation could be sorted out now, there should be no difficulties next winter. An added bonus was that good relations would be established with the people of Imola. I went around the town with another soldier, knocking on doors, street by street. Sometimes the Italians were friendly and co-operative and on other occasions, openly sullen and resentful. Anyway, whatever the reaction, I was determined to find out how many people lived in a house and if there were any spare rooms. Certainly if the women had children and their husbands had been killed, or were unaccounted for, the generous accommodation allowances would be very welcome. In the aftermath of the war, there were acute shortages of all goods and essential materials throughout the length and breadth of Italy and many other countries. On one memorable occasion, in answer to my knocking, the door of a small house in the suburbs was slowly opened, to reveal a young couple. They shyly told me that they had got married the previous day, so I quickly told them I'd return next week!

At the beginning of August, we had to leave Imola and head down to the coastal town of Senegallia, sandwiched between Pescara and Ancona. This was to be our base for the next ten months, fulfilling our role as part of the Allied occupation force in Italy. Being a small town, it seemed as though the war had passed it by, as it was relatively undamaged when compared with many other areas. Our accommodation was in a large villa that had previously belonged to a town official. The townspeople were friendly and welcoming, probably hoping that our arrival might generate income for the shops, and especially the bars! Some were so hungry they hung around the camp hoping for leftovers from our meals. As usual in the early days after our arrival, I was kept busy collecting weekly rations for our troops, both in Senegallia and Pescara. I often passed the neutral state of San Marino near Rimini, where tax-free luxury goods and spirits could be obtained. In many towns in Italy such goods could only be obtained on the flourishing black market. The state had probably done very well during the war years, but like neutral Switzerland, they must have encountered diverse problems, with both Allied and Axis soldiers crossing their borders, as well as a profusion of well-organised, lucrative smuggling in the mountains.

There were five soldiers in our villa who aroused my suspicions: they spoke Polish with a strong German accent and I was certain they were Germans, who had somehow inveigled their way into the villa, masquerading as bona fide Polish soldiers. I registered my concerns to a senior officer, but he was adamant they were Polish. A few days later, they didn't appear at breakfast. A few of us checked their room, but it was empty and they must have left in the dead of night. Senegallia station was just across the street from the villa and wearing Polish uniforms, it would have been easy for them to catch a night train to Rome, then a connection to the German border. After that embarrassing episode, any newcomers to the regiment were very carefully vetted: it was very much a case of bolting the villa door, after the impersonators had left!

At night we patrolled the town in three pick-up trucks, collecting drunken soldiers from the bars and it was quite usual to return to base with around thirty soldiers collapsed in the back of the trucks. The number of arrests never seemed to decrease, as the drink was cheap. Now that the war had ended, there was a huge upsurge in heavy drinking among all ranks. But the following evening, they all came sauntering back to the bars in large groups, regardless of the state they had been in the previous night!

The next assignment for yours truly? Setting up a monthly dance for the hundreds of troops based in Senegallia. As the summer progressed, it was still warm well into the night, so I suggested the dances take place in a local park. We had a spacious venue, an army dance band, hundreds of young men, but no girls! I solved this by putting up posters all around the town, advertising the forthcoming dance, hoping to encourage young single girls and couples to come along. To back up my promotion, I persuaded friends to knock on doors and tell the girls about the event, assuring them and especially their very protective parents, that they would be well looked after. In addition, they would be collected from their homes in a lorry and returned safely when the dance finished at midnight. Needless to say, the dances were a storming success and everybody was disappointed when they ended in October. So for the remainder of our stay in Senegallia, the locals knew me as 'Juliano'!

The long cold winter months of 1945 were a huge anti-climax for the lads, as it was back to the boredom of drinking in the Mess and town bars. How they missed the dances and especially the extra-curricular activities of those long, balmy summer evenings! In retrospect, after

I was demobbed, instead of becoming a construction worker, I should have made a career as a dance impresario! We made up for the absence of the dances by enjoying our first post-war Christmas, but everybody's thoughts were focussed on their towns and villages in Poland and especially the plight of elderly relatives, under Soviet occupation. They must have been enduring great hardship and there were probably severe shortages of food and fuel.

Soon after the dances ended, I was put in charge of all transport for the regiment for the remainder of our stay. At the beginning of the New Year of 1946, there was a large surplus of lorries and trucks in Italy; with hundreds of vehicles parked up on any spare land in the area. The powers-that-be decided that some would be sent to Germany and the remainder taken to a scrap yard at Monza (now a venue on the Formula One race calendar). Two or three times a week, twenty lorries and trucks were driven to the scrap yard. I always brought up the rear in a five-tonner and another back-up lorry came to transport the drivers back down to Senegallia. Wily local entrepreneurs always bought the scrapped vehicles; they must have made a fortune, especially during the post-war steel shortages.

Things were becoming more relaxed in Italy for us and consequently, we took full advantage of the hospitality extended to all servicemen at the celebrated Eighth Army 'Alexander Club' in Rome. All food, drinks and cigarettes were free and there were always scores of friendly American G.I.s there. We had a very special affinity for an Italian beer called 'Peroni', so there was always a nice fat keg of 'Peroni' sitting on the bar awaiting our arrival. Needless to say it was soon emptied and replaced! Now at last my command of the English language began to improve, as the U.S. soldiers insisted we conversed in English and I could teach them a few useful Italian phrases or choice swear words! The American generosity knew no bounds, as I discovered on one journey to Rome to collect rations for fifty of our men. The American quartermaster gave my request slip only a cursory glance, but when I arrived back at Senegallia I discovered that sufficient supplies for one hundred and fifty men had been loaded onto my lorry while I was having a few cups of cappuccino! I drove back and forth to Rome weekly for about three months and had great fun with the G.I.s who spent their allowances extravagantly, with no thought of saving for the future.

Many were permanently in debt to either their buddies, card-schools or the many shady gambling operations or black marketeers throughout Rome. The bars and enticing delights of the cities bordellos were irresistible and they always returned broke and consequently distinctly unsatisfied! Some would even sell their uniforms to get money, but one extremely novel way of raising funds was by selling a jeep! This operation was undertaken in great secrecy, via unscrupulous local operators, and the millions of lire obtained topped up the GI's kitty for another few months. M.P.s were deputed to track down stolen jeeps and they recovered several. We were sure that the local new 'owners' would be incandescent with rage when their prize acquisitions were taken back to the barracks: I'm certain that they spent weeks scouring Rome trying to find their 'business partners' and get their money back. I queried the advisability of such a risky transaction with a tough Marine sergeant, but he laughingly told me, 'Well, now ya know Jule why the name 'jeep' is short for General Purpose Vehicle!'

At the end of May 1946, arrangements were made for the scaling down of our base in Senegallia. One last duty for my jeep and I was to go from Imola down to the port of Naples, to discuss the cargo arrangements for next week's departure with the Port Authorities. Finally it was back up to Rome, on my very last duty as a courier, taking important documents to the Army H.Q. I was also curious to see the Piazza Venezia, where a few years earlier Mussolini yelled to his adoring Fascist supporters, 'Polonia e liquidate!' (Poland is finished!). Really, Mr Duce? I don't think so. You and Clara are dead and buried, but Poland is very much alive and kicking! As I drove across the square a riot started, with about two thousand screaming Italians, challenging a small group of American GIs. Suddenly reinforcements arrived, packed into jeeps and armed to the teeth. They slowly and skilfully manoeuvred their vehicles towards the mob, which soon retreated. I had no idea what it was all about and didn't care much, as in a week I'd be far away from Rome on the Med. I delivered the documents to H.Q., stayed overnight in Montevedro, then returned to Senegallia for the last time.

Tell me, why is it that whenever I visit an Italian city to do some innocent sightseeing I seem to provoke riots and unrest?!

CHAPTER 22
Peril on the Sea

For the previous weeks, all the goods and materials that were no longer needed at Senegallia had been packed into twenty two large crates for shipment with us to the port of Helensburgh, on the Clyde River near Glasgow. As I had never been to Great Britain, I was looking forward to seeing a country that had been ruthlessly bombed by the Germans, but had eventually triumphed. My final job in Italy was to supervise the transport of our crates by lorry to the railway station, where they were put on board two freight cars for the journey to the docks at Naples. So it was finally 'arrivaderci Italia' for two hundred very tired Polish soldiers. As our train pulled into Naples, we were shocked at the scenes of devastation: the people had endured so much during the war and there had been reports of starvation and many deaths. It was going to take years for the town to recover, so there would be very difficult times ahead. I sincerely hoped that things would improve before next winter, otherwise the outlook for the inhabitants was grim.

A large troopship lay at anchor awaiting our arrival and cranes soon loaded the crates onto the deck. There was an additional cargo for this trip, as six hundred Waffen SS prisoners were being kept in the hold and we would be guarding them during the weeklong journey. We had strict orders not to fraternise with them, but in fact they were subdued and co-operative. A few days into the voyage, as we were sailing through the Straits of Gibraltar, the weather changed for the worse. The sky darkened, the sea swelled and the winds gradually increased to hurricane velocity, accompanied by heavy rain, thunder and lightning. The ship rolled violently from side to side, being smashed by the twenty to thirty foot waves. At the height of the storm, I was alarmed to hear the ship's structure creaking and shuddering and began to wonder if it was going to break up. Having survived so many brushes with death these past five years, I didn't fancy ending up at the bottom of the Med! Believe me, everyone on that ship was praying, including the German prisoners, many of who were Catholics from Bavaria.

On the third day, the winds finally abated and the terrifying storm ended. Thank God! I had visions of emulating St. Paul and being shipwrecked on the Gibraltar coast! Later, the captain admitted that we had been very lucky: he had expected the ship to break up, as the hull was welded, not bolted! Nearly all the prisoners were violently seasick, as were some of the seamen, but somehow I wasn't affected. Maybe because I'd mysteriously lost my usual large appetite! There were no more alarms as the ship steadily sailed up the Atlantic coast to the English Channel, continuing up the west coast of Britain, finally arriving at Helensburgh, on the vast Clyde river. We watched silently as the big ship slowly inched up to its berth and looked in disbelief at the devastated dock area, warehouses and buildings. Clydebank was dreadfully damaged, with bomb craters everywhere and terraces of houses had been destroyed. Glasgow's city centre and industrial areas had also suffered considerably. A seaman told me that in the incessant raids of 1941 the Luftwaffe had virtually obliterated many British ports especially Bristol, Southampton, Cardiff, Swansea and Liverpool.

In Glasgow, a huge reconstruction programme had started with hundreds of Glaswegians working around the clock to repair the shattered infrastructure. Watching their labours from the upper deck of our ship, our Second Mate told me this brought back vivid memories; he had sailed from Liverpool many times in the darkest days of the war on merchant ships as part of the North Atlantic convoys. They often linked up in mid-Atlantic with American ships sailing from Halifax, Nova Scotia, taking much needed supplies and military equipment to Russia. Every trip was fraught with grave danger, either from the weather or lethal German U-Boats. On arrival at the Arctic ports of Murmansk or Archangel for the first time, the merchant's crew had been amazed to see that the cargo was unloaded with great skill by burly Russian women stevedores. Both ports were lit with powerful arc lights that pierced the Arctic gloom and enabled the work to carry on twenty-four hours a day. (At last! Now

I knew where the U.S. and British uniforms worn by the Red Army conscripts in Tashkent had come from!).

Serenading our arrival on the quayside was the local Salvation Army band and Women's Voluntary Service helpers were distributing sandwiches, cakes and tea: but only for us troops! Welcome to Scotland! Soldiers from a Highland regiment arrived to escort the German prisoners to lorries, which would take them to a prisoner-of-war camp near Glasgow. We left the dockers to unload the crates and I returned later to check that everything was in order. To my shock, there were two crates missing! I dashed to the harbour-master's office and showed my cargo manifest proving that twenty-two crates had been loaded at Naples. He went to see the dockers' foreman and eventually our crates were located, having been deposited outside another warehouse.

My first base in Britain was to be in the south of the country at a large U.S. base called Foxley, fifteen kilometres from the market town of Hereford on the Welsh borders. We were issued with rail passes and each given four pounds in sterling for expenses and having heard so much about Britain, we enjoyed the long journey south. The damage wrought in Britain was considerable, as like poor Poland, the country had felt the full wrath of the Nazis. In 1944 Hitler, enraged that the tide of war was lapping at the doors of his lair, gave orders to launch his much vaunted 'secret weapons' from the rocket base at Peenemunde, on the Baltic coast. V1 and V2 rockets rained down on London and south coastal towns, killing many civilians and terrorising the population.

On arrival at Hereford, our freight cars and passenger compartments were shunted into a siding, then later continued to the small halt at Foxley. Lorries were waiting to take us to the camp, which was idyllically set in the Herefordshire countryside and surrounded by five quaintly named hamlets. After Russia, the Middle East and Italy, the English countryside was a delight; it was so peaceful, with rolling green hills and fields. The past terrible war seemed an eternity away.

The huge camp was run by the Americans and held thousands of soldiers. It had been an important assembly point for the Normandy landings in 1944. Before settling in at Foxley, I supervised the unloading and stripping down of our crates, which contained NAAFI equipment, stores, tinned food, and other catering bits and pieces. When this was finished, I was given a nice present of three bottles of whisky! The lads were really impressed with conditions at Foxley and in fact many of our contingent of two hundred eventually joined the British army as career soldiers. I was warmly welcomed by the C.O., Colonel Browne, and shown to a beautifully appointed private room. I really liked the Colonel, but he was promoted and left soon afterwards. Now this really was sheer luxury, after some of the damp, miserable, places I'd stayed at in the Middle East and Italy. This little palace was to be my home for the next two months and it was going to be a very lazy existence indeed. I was officially exempt from the usual camp duties and there were no dawn inspections by regimental sergeant majors! I could get up when I liked and really luxuriated in my surroundings. I didn't neglect the hectic social life either and on most weekends joined the other lads for the customary pub-crawls in Hereford. Aware that I had plenty of time on my hands, the lads used to get me to write letters to their former pals, and even girlfriends, back in Italy. I had a standard letter for them extolling the virtues of life in Britain and as overseas letter censorship was now considerably relaxed, I didn't have to keep explaining to my comrades why such and such a letter had been returned.

All too soon my sojourn at Foxley came to an end and in August 1946 I drove west to the small market town of Abergavenny in South Wales, a part of the country that was eventually to have enormous significance for me.

Abergavenny Castle

CHAPTER 23
Abergavenny

A bergavenny Castle is situated on a spur overlooking the meandering river Usk and dates from the tenth century. Like many castles, it has a dark history of wars, treachery and massacres. If Stalin had ever come to Britain, (God forbid) it would have been the perfect accommodation for him, chained up in the deepest dungeon of course! I stayed in two rooms in the castle, travelling daily in a jeep (what else?) to the army camp outside Abergavenny. After the small-town appearance of Foxley, it was a tiny camp, with just fifty British and ten Polish soldiers. After settling in at my new home, I was introduced to the C.O., Colonel Mathews, an Arnhem veteran and we discussed the future duty rosters. In Abergavenny and district, I would be on permanent call, chauffeuring at least ten regimental officers on their visits to prisoner-of-war camps in South Wales. The largest was at Chepstow, with others in Brecon and Monmouth. All these camps were very secure and there had been no successful escapes from them during the war. (We had all heard of a dramatic escape from the Island Camp Farm at Merthyr Mawr, near Bridgend. On the night of March 10th-11th 1945, sixty nine German prisoners, mostly fanatical SS men, escaped via a tunnel which ran from the nearest hut to the perimeter fence. All were recaptured in the next weeks, after a huge manhunt covering most of Wales and England).

When I was given the keys to my car, I was speechless: it was a gleaming, gunmetal grey, left-hand drive American Ford V8 limousine, with a plush interior and a host of unbelievable extras to match! Hardly the sort of car to be seen around in post-war Britain! I'd wager a year's salary that Stalin, Beria, Molotov, Kaganovitch and the other criminals had never seen such a car, let alone been chauffeured to and from their Moscow dachas in one. Their Zyl cars looked more like tanks and any poor Muscovite who came too close to them, trying to peer into the darkened interiors was given one warning only, then shot immediately by the bodyguards! To complete my transformation, I was measured for a new uniform, with the obligatory regimental tie and brown leather driving gloves which had to be worn at all times. What a come up in the world for the lad from Rogozno!

Of course in quiet Abergavenny, the local girls had already noticed my dazzling American 'wheels' and immaculate appearance! Perhaps by then they had already labelled me the Polish toff from the castle! One weekend, there was an out of town 'hop' that I heard several were keen on going to, but had no transport. Their knight in shining armour, in the person of me and my glittering steed, duly made arrangements to take five of them to the gig and a few days later I received a bottle of Scotch as a 'thank you' present. Unfortunately, somebody reported me and from then on I was only allowed to use the limo for army business. So it was a definite relegation to the jeep and assorted Bedford and Ford trucks for any social junketing!

With the castle used only for my accommodation, I had meals in the camp mess; there was an outstanding German cook there and the food was wonderful. On a typical day, I would arrive for breakfast before picking up the duty officer and planning the day's visits, being paid a daily allowance for meals at pubs or cafes. Sometimes for a change, I would pull into a camp like Sennybridge or Brecon at mid-day and have a quick word with the sentry, who would point me in the direction of the mess. I would always enjoy a hearty meal and later pocket the allowance! Most days I would drop my passenger at the camp office and if I had three or four hours to kill, meet up with the guards and drink endless cups of coffee, exchanging war experiences with them. In my case, they were stunned by all my adventures since 1940!

A lasting memory of my sojourn as a base chauffeur was the officer's insistence that I sat alongside them at restaurants, a gesture I greatly appreciated. One day, an over-zealous sergeant with a distinctly unpleasant manner, booked me for obstruction outside Abergavenny. I was extremely concerned about this as, if I was charged it might well prejudice my future as a chauffeur, a job I loved. I decided to let the C.O.

know immediately and left an explanatory note on his desk. He soon took action, reprimanding the sergeant and I heard nothing more. Colonel Mathews later told me, when I was taking him out on business, that he had given the sergeant a furious tongue-lashing and reduced him to a whimpering, apologetic, wreck.

One evening over a drink in the Mess, I asked Colonel Mathews what had gone wrong at the catastrophic Allied airborne assault at Arnhem in Holland in September '44. His craggy face changed, becoming serious and for a moment I regretted my intrusive question. He stood up and walked slowly across the Mess floor to the large windows looking towards the Pen-y-Fan and Fan-Hir mountains. He said nothing for a few minutes, pensively re-visiting in his memory the events that turned into one of the biggest Allied disasters in the war. Eventually he started relating his personal experiences in Holland, after his Red Devil paratroop unit had missed the D.Z. (drop zone) on September 17th 1944, because of high winds that deposited the men at Uden, near S'Hertogenbosch, ten kilometres from the planned assembly point for a march towards the town of Apeldorn, then on to Arnhem, to reinforce the British 1st Airborne Division units defending the bridge over the Neder Rijn river at Arnhem. The American 101st and 82nd Airborne Divisions were to secure vital canal bridges and the bridges over the Maas river and the Waal river at Nijmegen. Holding all these bridges was imperative to assist the arrival of armoured units from the recently captured port of Antwerp via the Scheldt estuary. Unknown to the invasion force a division of the 10th SS Panzer were already in the area, watching the arrival of the paratroops and they were soon in action, killing hundreds of helpless Allied soldiers as they descended in utter chaos and confusion. Along with hundreds of British men the Colonel had been trapped on the outskirts of Oosterbeek, several kilometres from Arnhem. The British First Polish Parachute Brigade under Major General Sosabowski was delayed by two days by bad weather whilst trying to assist the entrenched British at Oosterbeek. An attempt by the Poles to cross the Waal river using rubber boats at night ended in disaster. The Germans spotted Sosabowski's men launching these hopelessly unsuitable flimsy craft, then when the soldiers had paddled halfway across the very wide Waal, lit up the river with flares and massacred the entire force. After days of heavy fighting in the woods and open country around Oosterbeek the Colonel's unit knew it was a lost cause. The Hartenstein Hotel near the town was their last ditch refuge and became a hospital for the mounting casualties who had to be left when the remainder of the Red Devils successfully crossed the Waal at night, but only 2000 men out of 11,000 soldiers and glider pilots survived the carnage at Oosterbeek. The remnants of Colonel Frost's Second Battalion of the First Parachute Brigade at the vital Arnhem Bridge held out for three days and eventually surrendered with just 100 men alive. I listened to this catalogue of disaster enthralled and saddened, but tentatively asked the Colonel what, in his opinion were the serious mistakes at Arnhem. Many things it appeared. Firstly, many British and American commanders thought that Montgomery's plan was too daring and ambitious. Whilst believing that the strangely named 'Operation Market Garden' could end the war by the end of 1944, the plans were dependent upon surprise and speedy armoured support for the airborne troops. The American Commander-in-chief Dwight Eisenhower and his Generals Bradley and Patton were amazed at the audacity of Montgomery's plan and saw many problems, especially the weather, and the paramount importance of holding the Arnhem and Nijmegan bridges until tanks and artillery arrived. Monty crucially asserted that although Dutch Resistance intelligence had warned London of Panzer units in the Arnhem area, which were resting and re-grouping after returning from Normandy, they wouldn't pose any threat. Indeed the American Lieutenant - General Browning after spending days surveying the maps, logistics and planning his attack advised Montgomery that in his opinion it was definitely a case of the assault being: 'a bridge too far!' In an unbelievable stroke of bad luck, an American glider which crashed outside Eindhoven, was found by the Germans to contain all the plans for the operation! Battlefield communications were confused as the British field radios failed to work outside Arnhem. There were delays in sending reinforcements and the D.Z.s (drop zones) were too far from Arnhem with many gliders crashing into the Waal river. Lastly Colonel Mathews vigorously maintained that many of the officers in the whole dreadful business at Arnhem, were too inexperienced to handle an operation of such complexity and which was fraught with danger from the outset. I thanked the Colonel for sharing his private thoughts and overall misgivings with me.

He declined a further drink and slowly walked out of the Mess, leaving me dazed by what he had told me. Arnhem was yet another example of wars brutality and to think that until the Colonel's disclosures, I was convinced that Monte Cassino was the ultimate in a pointless waste of young lives.

In fact, the ultimate cruel harvest of 'Market Garden' in the Autumn of 1944 was British, American, Polish, Dutch and German lives.

A few weeks later, just before Christmas, the obnoxious sergeant who had slyly booked me a few months earlier in Abergavenny sheepishly approached me. After apologising for his previous attitude and behaviour, he asked me whether I could take him to a friend's farm in the Rhondda valley, in South Wales, to collect his Christmas turkey and a goose. I was at first understandably very reluctant to help him out, but eventually relented. He explained that every year, the farmer supplied the poultry for the sergeant's Christmas family dinner and he went to collect the birds in his car. Unfortunately, because of the petrol restrictions in force, he wouldn't be able to go and so he had come cap in hand to me. We collected the turkey and goose a few days later and over the Christmas period, I gradually got to know the sergeant. Afterwards I was a frequent guest at the farm and had many enjoyable meals. So, one initially very reluctant good turn led to many others being reciprocated!

There were two duty officers I occasionally met on my rounds, who certainly puzzled me. To begin with, on one visit to their base, I heard them speaking exceptional Russian to each other. I was naturally curious to find where they had learned the language and also where they had been during the war, but no matter how nonchalantly I tried to engage them in conversation and elicit this innocent information, I always drew a blank. These guys had been very thoroughly trained and easily avoided unwelcome questions. I concluded that they were, or had been, spies, working in a shadowy intelligence unit in the Russian zone in Berlin. Whatever their mysterious background had been, they made me the strongest coffee I've ever tasted and thinking back, in doing so, cleverly ensured I would avoid their table in the mess in future!

CHAPTER 24
Eighteen Lives?

All good things come to an end and in the first week of November, Colonel Mathews asked to see me before I left Abergavenny for Pembroke, in West Wales. During our very cordial conversation, he asked me to consider switching over to the British Army: he said all his officers and staff had been very impressed with my punctuality and dedication during my stay. He said they found my overall demeanour excellent and he was, in effect, asking me to start on the road to eventually becoming an officer in the British Army. I was very flattered by his pleasing comments and assertion that I was officer material. He assured me that my rank of Lance Corporal would be retained and the move would be a very positive one in my future career.

Internationally, the current situation was decidedly ominous, as the Russians were constantly stopping and demanding to search military and civilian vehicles travelling through their occupation zone, causing long delays. Normal life for Berliners was deteriorating rapidly in the Russian zone and the C.O. feared greatly for the civilian population. He emphasised that very soon action would have to be taken by the U.S., Britain and France to prevent a catastrophic collapse of civilian life. Starvation on a large and hitherto unprecedented scale could be the end result if the Russians sealed vital access routes for food supplies from the west via road, river and air. He had assurances from the highest level that the western Allies would not stand by and let such a calamitous situation develop. Armed conflict with the Russians, who had many armoured divisions already in place in the eastern sector of Berlin, was therefore possible.

Prophetic words indeed; on June 18th 1948, the Soviets closed all access routes to Berlin by road, river and air. Disregarding this Russian wilful obstruction and intransigence, a decision was made by the three Allied countries controlling the western zone, the U.S., Britain and France, to deliver supplies to the two Berlin airfields at Tempelhof and Gatow. Initially, the logistics of an air corridor or bridge from Britain and America to Berlin seemed insurmountable, such was the daily tonnage required to feed the two and a half million Berliners. Despite an initial shortage of C12 and C14 transport planes, the number of flights was steadily increased, as aircraft and pilots were sent from many sympathetic countries, to assist what by now had become known as 'The Berlin Airlift'.

The lifeline from the west continued for 324 days and 'Operation Vittles' from the U.S.A., and 'Operation Plain Fare' from Britain and France, sent 2,300,000 tons of food and goods. An incredible total of 278,000 flights were made from June 21st 1948 until May 11th 1949. On one day alone, at the height of the airlift, 1,398 flights landed at Tempelhof, Gatow and the new airfield at Tegel. The transport planes delivered 12,000 tons of coal and supplies in this twenty-four hour period! Gatow airfield was especially dangerous for pilots of the lumbering transporters, as it was adjacent to the Havel River, and fog was a constant hazard. The Tegel airfield and landing strips were built in an incredible forty nine days by a small team of British and U.S. engineers and civilian volunteers!

On May 11th 1949, Stalin gave in to the staggering accomplishment of the Allies in maintaining life and hope for the inhabitants of the city and all roads, rail and river access routes were re-opened. Finally, to make absolutely certain that the Berliners would not be in the same dire position if Stalin again imposed a blockade on the city, the shipments of supplies continued until late September 1949, thus ensuring there would be no shortages of essentials in the 1950 winter. A memorial to the 76 airmen who died in this incredible mercy mission stands at Tempelhof Airport.

Before I left, the Colonel asked me to make one last trip to Foxley suggesting that I be taken there by a trainee chauffeur from the base driving pool. He thought this would be an excellent opportunity for the lad, whom he said was very keen, to gain distance chauffeuring experience. I said I would give him a few tips and it would be nice to meet up again with the staff at Foxley. The next day I met my young chauffeur. He was confidently, almost brashly, sitting at the controls of my lovely Ford, revving the engine excruciatingly loudly. He seemed to be very impatient to leave and barely acknowledged me. This was his big chance to show how he could drive and he intended to enjoy himself. Clearly, he didn't need any advice from me and intended to show me how my Ford could really be 'encouraged'. The powerful limousine roared off and he painfully crashed through the gears. As soon as we reached the outskirts of Abergavenny, he floored the accelerator and soon reached a hundred m.p.h.! I immediately remembered those maniac American drivers we had encountered in Taranto, but this guy, even if he wasn't drunk like them, was in another league.

The road from Abergavenny to Hereford has a succession of dangerous bends and none of our drivers liked it, especially at night. He ignored my frantic yells to slow down and drove even faster. I had both feet welded to the floor, as I braced myself for the inevitable crash. Sure enough, attempting to straighten up after a deadly bend, he lost it completely. The back of the car swung wildly as he fought to regain control, the engine screaming at maximum revs. Too late! He smashed into a roadside tree with a sickening bang! I was showered with glass and had cuts to my face and arms, but having my legs firmly clamped to the floor saved me from a headlong windscreen dive to oblivion (no seatbelts in those days!). My 'expert' driver was in a sorry state: he was moaning, barely conscious and covered in blood. Somehow I managed to extricate myself from the wreckage and flagged down two passing cars. I asked one driver to go back to the barracks and tell them what had happened and the other man helped me to pull the injured driver out and place him on the grass verge at the side of the road. Two jeeps quickly arrived from the base, followed by an ambulance for the dazed and shocked 'chauffeur.' I looked in horror at the state of my beautiful Ford: it was a write-off and unrecognisable from the car I cherished so dearly. The soldier was taken to Nevile Hall hospital and I was driven back to the castle. I telephoned Foxley later, telling them I'd be staying at the castle for a few weeks to recover. I'll openly admit that not being in control, I found the incident more terrifying than being under attack in Italy!!

After this alarming episode, the camp authorities rigorously clamped down on the driving pool. After I had recovered from my luckily superficial injuries, I was put in charge of re-training the drivers. When the injured soldier came out of hospital, his very short career as an army chauffeur was suspended and he was later court-marshalled. Once again, in my short adventure–strewn life, I'd eluded the bony hand of the 'Grim Reaper', who always seemed to be hovering around me! In fact, by now I must have been well into my second allotment of nine lives!

Pembroke Castle

CHAPTER 25
Pembroke

The town of Pembroke is dominated by a magnificent Norman castle. This is a splendid example of an edifice that has successfully withstood the ravages of the centuries. Pembroke Dock on Milford Sound was the base for the large Sunderland flying boats, which buzzed continuously around the harbour. There is a vast parade ground at the castle and when I arrived, hundreds of National Service recruits were being indoctrinated into the finer arts of dreary 'square-bashing'.

Behind the imposing façade of the castle was the Penarth Barracks, where I would live for the next six months. My duties involved the transportation of goods and rations from the Lion Barracks stores, the other side of the town, to camps around Pembrokeshire, especially the vast one at Manorbier. On Sundays, I had to take troops to the morning Mass at the Catholic Church. It was definitely going to be a busy time, servicing the camps, but driving a less lugubrious five-tonner was a rude awakening for me. There was one advantage to the lorry: the cab was completely enclosed and warm in comparison to a draughty jeep, but there were no heaters then in military vehicles.

The army H.Q. in Pembroke was in a large former Town Hall and all the operations were planned there. This was to be my jumping-off point for forays into the lovely Pembrokeshire countryside. Later, in early January, I would be helping to establish a training camp on the island of Anglesey, in North Wales. After all my experience at Abergavenny, I found the daily ration distribution trips easy and enjoyed seeing new faces.

The 1947 winter was the worst in living memory, affecting all of Europe and I dreaded to think what conditions would be like in Poland and Germany. The radio frequently mentioned the thousands of starving, displaced people, existing in appalling conditions and for whom the victory against Nazism had really changed nothing. There was almost continuous snow in Pembrokeshire and penetrating frosts; Russia re-visited for me, I suppose! Despite the weather, arrangements were being made for Anglesey. There would eventually be two hundred recruits based there who would arrive by train, so the canteen and stores had to be set up prior to their arrival and our cooks also had to be taken there. We put chains on the lorry tyres and I was confident the five tonners would cope. There were twenty lorries in the convoy and as usual I was the pathfinder. The local policemen did advise us not to travel, but it was vital that the base be prepared. It took all day to reach Anglesey, in very bad road conditions. At one point the snow drifts were five feet deep and I think everybody thought we'd have to turn back. Thinking fast, I employed a unique method of dealing with the drifts: I simply turned my lorry around, making the heavy steel rear bumper into a snow plough and kept reversing back and fore until I forced a gap wide enough for the rest of the convoy to squeeze through. I always did have a flair for ingenuity! Remember how quickly I became a skilled lumberjack in the Volga forests?

We unloaded everything at Anglesey then slept in the bare barracks, which were warmed with a gas heater. The cooks worked all night getting the kitchen prepared for the new intake and in the morning, after a hearty breakfast, we started back down. Conditions hadn't improved, but I decided to take a chance. If the lorries kept closely together, as on the journey up, it should be okay for everybody. Thankfully, we safely negotiated the frozen, deserted route south, with the convoy drivers concentrating very hard and paying meticulous care and attention throughout the slow journey. On arriving at the Lion barracks, I discovered we were one lorry short: I had no alternative but to go back immediately. Luckily, before I set out, a telephone call came from RAF Valley. Apparently the driver had been very slow at the back of the convoy and with poor visibility and the winter gloom, had taken a wrong turning and ended up there! Believe me; he had the biggest telling off in his life, first from me and later the C.O. He'd carelessly broken the convoy golden rule and become separated and lost. He had been very lucky indeed to find the Valley base as he did, otherwise in those conditions, his careless action could have cost him his life.

Some days I would go down to Pembroke Dock harbour and catch a film at the cinema. The limited on-screen offerings there attracted large audiences of bored soldiers, but it helped to pass an evening, or I sometimes went to an afternoon showing. It was also great fun watching the huge Sunderland flying boats taking off and landing in the harbour: they were very graceful planes and reminded me of a mechanical version of the flocks of cranes flying around Kamionka. The switchboard operator in the harbour office was a friendly Polish lad named Wladek, but a complete mystery. He always joined us for the Masses on Sunday mornings and I would often call in for a chat on my visits to the harbour. He was definitely a strange character and very secretive in his behaviour. Whatever time of the day or night I called in, he was always there! I never did find out where this chap lived in Pembroke and he was always very evasive if he thought I was trying to find out any of his secrets and especially his living quarters in the town. In the end, I remained convinced that he lived in that tiny office twenty four hours a day and saved up his allowance for his future plans! He would have been the ideal recruit for my two spies in Abergavenny, don't you think?

The local exercises continued as increasing numbers of troops arrived. We used to take them to the large Ministry of Defence training area at Castlemartin, a short ride away on the coast. Castlemartin was a tank and artillery training centre and is still in use today. In fact, during the Cold War era, it was used to train German Panzer units who were part of the North Atlantic Defence Force. At Pembroke, I seemed to be doing more driving than in Abergavenny or in the Middle East for that matter, and this continued up to my departure at the end of April 1947. There was great emphasis in the post-war army on sporting activities: I travelled all over Wales and up to the English border, taking army teams competing in a diverse range of sports, from rugby and football, to athletics and boxing tournaments. Finally, to complete my pleasant stay in Pembroke I was awarded my second 'One hundred thousand miles Silver Wheel'!

CHAPTER 26
Llandeilo and a Surprise Meeting

The time had come to decide about my future in the army, so I met a career officer to discuss this. Like the C.O. at Abergavenny, I think he was initially hopeful that I would stay on. Again he suggested that if I wished, he could easily arrange a transfer to the British Army. I firmly told him that my mind was made up; I wished to leave and requested that he prepare the necessary arrangements and paperwork. A week later, along with two hundred other Polish lads, I made my way to Pembroke train station. Our destination was York, where the Army had its clothing stores. All servicemen who were to be de-mobbed had to go there to collect civilian clothes, but we were allowed to keep our uniforms. We had to complete this long trek and return in a day, but the stores covered an area of a least a mile. It took hours to distribute our civvy clothes, as there must have been more than a thousand Polish ex-soldiers queuing up. We eventually returned to Pembroke, all very tired, in the early hours. We had all received the standard 'demob.' money and discussed what we intended to do with it. In addition we were given ten-year Government War Bonds, which would be a very nice windfall when we eventually redeemed them.

A few days later, fifty of us were given rail passes and told to report to the local railway station. Our destination in South Wales was to be the town of Llandeilo. Unfortunately, being totally unfamiliar with Welsh place names, we got on the wrong train and ended up in Llanelli! The stationmaster found this very funny but promised to get us to our correct destination, despite the fact that there were no more trains, as it was Sunday. He contacted the local newspaper (the Carmarthen Journal) delivery driver, who soon arrived at the station in his large van. The stationmaster also telephoned the staff of our hostel in Llandeilo, informing them of our late arrival and that now that our mode of transport had changed, there would be no need for our group to be met at Llandeilo station. All fifty of us somehow squeezed into that van, including three of us alongside the driver in the front and we shakily set off from Llanelli.

Llandeilo is a small market town set in rural Carmarthenshire, about twenty kilometres from Carmarthen. Our accommodation was a hostel in an old converted manor house. It had been the H.Q. for the celebrated Land Army during the war and had also housed German P.O.W.s who had been working on the many farms in Carmarthenshire. When we arrived, we were somewhat disconcerted to see that there were still four Germans there, but they left the next day, so we made ourselves at home. We were to work for the post-war Agricultural Committee. This government body had been established to reclaim unproductive marshland into land suitable for growing produce. Food was in short supply in Britain, as elsewhere in Europe in the post-war years. All families had been issued with ration cards for their weekly groceries and shortages were common in a variety of foods. The Carmarthen area was the exception and the food was plentiful and of excellent quality. The large downstairs hall in the manor had been fitted with fifty cubicles, each holding four lads. Besides being very comfortable, it was really the only accommodation we could afford, as we didn't have much money.

The next day, we were taken in lorries belonging to the Government Land Drainage Authority to nearby fields. They were surrounded by high thick hedges and were marshy and waterlogged, as it seemed to rain a lot in these parts, probably due to the proximity of the nearby Black Mountain range. Well-fed cows ambled lazily around the fields in a truly pastoral scene, but their hooves had sunk deep into the boggy ground, creating hundreds of water-filled holes. Our job was to install a drainage system in the fields, allowing them to dry out in preparation for growing vegetables. The foreman showed us how to mark out the field and dig ditches, ready for the laying of drainage pipes. It was such a far cry from the swamps of the Volga, so very long ago, but now we had plentiful food, good companionship and friendly, helpful, local supervisors.

The size of an average field was five acres and the procedure for positioning the network of pipes consisted of digging a ditch with an old rope-driven excavator to a depth of two feet. The six inch terracotta pipes were then laid with a gap of half an inch between each pipe, for the length of the field. Ditches were dug by hand at an angle to the central pipe and three inch pipes laid along these. There were three or four large pipes laid in the average field and the additional pipes ensured the field was fully covered. Finally, a ditch was dug around the perimeter, but it was essential for this ditch to have a deep base and narrow top to prevent subsidence. Six weeks after the drainage pipes had been sunk, the field had completely dried out and was ready for ploughing! The whole procedure, though complicated at first, became second nature to us. So much so, that our speed increased and as we were being paid piecework rates, our wages soared from seven pounds a week, to twenty pounds: a staggering sum in post-war Britain!

We had other opportunities for making money while at Llandeilo, doing private work on days off and at weekends. The problem of the water held in the low-lying fields affected everybody who lived off the land in Carmarthenshire. Many farmers had seen how successfully we laid drainage systems and the speed at which the fields became ready for cultivation. They ordered the pipes from Carmarthen, then recruited as many of us as they could to solve the drainage problem in their fields. Another essential farm job they needed us for was annual hedge maintenance. The hedges were first trimmed and then one side was chopped with billhooks and bent over. This section of hedge was then clipped firmly into the ground using wooden V shaped forks, thus eradicating dead leaves and establishing new growth for the next year. The usual farm labourer rate for this type of work in 1947 was two and six (25p) an hour, but because the farmers knew we were exceptionally good workers, they paid us double the rate, five shillings (50p).

As the weeks went by, we did every conceivable type of farm work, including harvesting and even concreting, so my efforts in the blistering heat in Kinokin did come in useful after all! The meals we received at the farms were substantial, considering the average family's food ration at that time. The gammon steaks alone were amazing, and I often thought that the table of food regularly set for us was sufficient for a week! Later during our stay in Carmarthenshire we progressed from farms near villages, such as the wonderfully named Bethlehem, Carmel and Salem, to the large forest areas. The delightful village of Trap, overlooked by Carreg Cennen Castle is about eight kilometres from Llandeilo, in the foothills of the Black Mountains. Here the work was tree planting, which was slow and methodical work. We used tractors for the line digging and believe me, planting between five hundred and one thousand trees a day is very hard work. In fact around this time, I started making serious enquiries about a job in the construction industry. But in the depths of rural Carmarthenshire only farm labouring was on offer, so I decided to stick it out and move away in the future.

The Mass centre for Llandeilo was at Cefngolau House, and was run by three friendly Carmelite priests: Fathers Malachy Lynch, Walsh and Hegarty. They lived in the lodge at the entrance to the private Tregib college (now a thriving comprehensive school). Father Lynch was a veritable titan in the Carmelite Order, who became world famous as the Abbot of Aylesford Carmelite Priory in Kent. As time went by during my stay in Llandeilo, I became acquainted with local families and young people: I often walked along the road after Mass with Antonio and Adelina Fornari and their three children. A few weeks later, they invited me to their home for Sunday tea and eventually I fell in love with their middle daughter Anita!

There was quite a selection of farms up for sale in the Llandeilo area after the war, as families moved away. They were very reasonably priced indeed. For example, a 100 acre site could be bought for £1,000 and a much larger farm wouldn't be much more than £1,500. It was a very tempting proposition for us ex-soldiers, but there was no way we could have raised even the deposit. One day, a message came from the foreman: the owner of a 350 acre farm at Llandovery called Glyn-Hir farm needed two labourers, so he assigned me and a lad called Stefan to do the job. We were dropped off early the next day and immediately realised this would be a long hard slog for the two of us. The work entailed digging ditches around the boundary of a large field by hand! There didn't appear to be much serviceable machinery, and what there was needed urgent attention. I was kept very busy at Glyn-Hir, sorting out and repairing what equipment I could, as well as working with Stefan on the field.

The first weekend, we noticed the owner arrive and decided to introduce ourselves. Stefan knocked at the farmhouse door and to our disbelief it was opened by none other than General Anders!! To say we were astonished would be a complete understatement. The General called out to his wife, 'Two of my boys are here!' He ushered us into the house and introduced his wife, Irene. Steaming mugs of tea and home-made cakes were quickly served up by Irene and as we tucked into our tea the General asked us details of our regiment, what battles we had been involved in and numerous other questions. In a more serious vein, he apologised to us, saying that the situation in Poland at present was completely unacceptable. He said that he had been trying for a very long time to get cast-iron assurances from the Soviets that any Polish soldiers returning home would be allowed to settle and re-integrate into their communities. Polish Army Intelligence had learned that Stalin had enslaved entire nations such as the Tartars, Kalmuks and Chechens after the war, even sending decorated former Red Army fighters, (some of whom had fought from Stalingrad to Berlin) to the Gulag!

He patiently explained that the outcome of three conferences between the Soviet and Allied leaders had been a disaster for Poland. Stalin had easily duped the Americans, but Churchill was fully aware of the consequences that would follow their capitulation to Stalin's vociferous demands. The U.S.A. never believed that 'Uncle Joe', their wartime ally, was planning world domination, even as Soviet and captured German scientists frantically attempted to perfect an atomic bomb at a secret base in Russia. British intelligence had in fact received astonishing information from a spy in Moscow, stating that Stalin had conceived a diabolical plan to position Soviet submarines from the coast of Alaska down the western seaboard of Canada and the U.S.A., thus blockading supplies to North America and eventually crippling the country. A likely riposte to this frightening scenario would be the Allies targeting nuclear missiles at Soviet cities

General Anders pointed out that the Allied Conference at Yalta had effectively put the final seal on Poland's future. Article Five of the so-called Yalta Agreement for instance, gave the Soviet Union half of Poland's pre-war territory! Although the American President, Roosevelt, knew of the brutal Soviet deportations, collectivization and famines, he naively expected Stalinist Russia to become democratic! In effect, the General grimly told us, our sacrifices had all been in vain. He finally told us that he was attending an important meeting in London the next day, so thanking them both for their hospitality we left the farm. Over the next few days, Stefan and I talked dispiritedly about the General's stark assessment of the future of the Polish nation. So many had died: in the RAF, on the battlefields, in the tragic Warsaw uprisings, as well as the three million Polish Jews who died in the Nazi gas-chambers, the countless civilians and the millions of ghosts in the Gulag. What freedom did our people have now in Poland? Precious little it appeared. So many, many questions for us, the lucky survivors.

Two weeks later, General Anders returned. He immediately came across the fields to see the completion of our work and again invited us back to the farmhouse for tea. We talked about our future plans and then it was time for us to leave Glyn-Hir and the General and his wife for good. We shook hands at the door and as we were going out through the farmyard, the General called out, 'Thank you boys. Good luck!' We shouted in return, 'Goodbye General. God Bless!' Then with tears in our eyes, we walked back up the road.

END OF PART ONE

PART TWO

CHAPTER 27
Antonietta

Antonietta Giovanna Louisa Fornari was the second child of Adele and Antonio Fornari. Her grandparents were Giovanni and Adele Casali and the family lived in the mountain village of Morfasso, in the Piacenza region of Northern Italy. When Antonio Fornari was just eighteen he fought in the Great War. He had to be evacuated from the front line after a bullet pierced his right leg: the injury never healed and he endured the pain and discomfort for the rest of his life.

Like so many young Italians of his generation, Antonio realised that there was no future in a small mountain village where, apart from agricultural labouring and seasonal vineyard work, job opportunities were very limited. To find gainful employment, young men headed for the large cities such as Rome, Venice, Turin, Naples and Milan. Unfortunately, the worldwide Depression triggered by the cataclysmic Wall Street Crash in 1929 caused many of the larger Italian manufacturing companies to cease trading. Their capital reserves had been seriously depleted during the Great War, and many banks had collapsed worldwide, leaving millions of small savers destitute and relying on charity and soup kitchens.

Following the lead taken by thousands of Italian families, Antonio left Morfasso in 1929 and travelled by train and ferry to Great Britain. Many families settled in the small towns and mining villages of South Wales, quickly seizing opportunities for starting businesses in the service sector; opening cafes, fish and chip restaurants, ice cream parlours and later, hotels. They worshipped as families at the local Catholic churches and their businesses prospered in spite of the depression, often becoming the hub of communities. The entrepreneurs worked slavishly around the clock and quickly developed a strong rapport with the locals; the cafes and restaurants becoming a byword for first class, reasonably priced food and dedicated service.

As he had a few contacts in Swansea, Antonio decided to try his luck in the seaside town in late 1929 and was helped with accommodation by the established Rabaiotti and Bertosi café owners, who found him a room at the White Swan public house in High Street. In addition, Antonio was kindly given a job by Signor Bertosi selling ice cream from a large basket on the front of his bicycle. He would ring the bell to announce his arrival in streets across the town, steadily building up his weekly customers. For years after the 1926 General Strike there was mass unemployment in Britain; an entire generation of young men had perished in the Great War and every business was susceptible to failure and bankruptcy.

This uncertainty made Antonio even more determined to succeed, as his aim was eventually to own his own family business, so he started looking for a site for a café in Swansea. Alongside the terminus waiting room and office of the Mumbles train in Rutland Place, he noticed an empty building that he decided would be an ideal spot. The position was perfect and he was sure it had considerable potential because the road was always busy with docks workers, 'Coastlines' Shipping Company, Mumbles train Terminus staff, drivers, conductors, regular train passengers and most importantly for the Fornaris there were no catering facilities at the train terminus. Antonio relished the challenge of starting up from scratch and was very confident he would eventually be successful. He simply named his new business 'The Café'.

Throughout all these deliberations he was in constant touch with his parents back home in Morfasso and especially with a certain young lady named Adele, to whom he proposed on a later visit. A few months later, in a ceremony attended by the villagers, they were married in Morfasso church and came to Swansea in 1930. Adele and Antonio's first married home together was above the café, which by now had built up a regular clientele, particularly the early shift dock workers and the drivers, inspectors and passengers of the Mumbles train.

In 1932 their first child, Caterina (known as Rina) was born, followed in 1933 by Antonietta, who was known as Anita. The last of the sisters, Maria was born in 1937. The two eldest girls attended the nearby St. David's primary school and the family went to the adjoining church. Although the café was thriving throughout the late 1930s, a cold wind of fear and uncertainty was blowing from Germany and Italy. This fear intensified as the world rolled inexorably towards the Second World War. In the summer months of 1939, local attitudes to Italian people generally, and Italian business owners in particular, changed markedly for the worse. On September 3rd 1939, after Hitler's failure to reply to the British Government's ultimatum regarding the German invasion of Poland, war was declared.

Upon the outbreak of war, the atmosphere and local attitude towards Italian shop and café owners deteriorated alarmingly. Organised gangs of thugs hung around outside Italian businesses all over Swansea. Veiled threats and taunts began to increase, terrifying the owners, their wives and young children. Shops and cafes were now regularly attacked in what were termed 'spontaneous' (meaning organised) demonstrations. Scrawled crude messages and telephone calls accused the Italians of being Fascist sympathisers and of 'milking' local economies. Boycotts of the businesses were encouraged across Britain to drive out or bankrupt the immigrants. The Italians strongly denied these rumours, but at the outbreak of war the government decided to intern all Italians in Britain for the duration of the conflict. As in Nazi Germany, in the evil 'Kristallnacht' pogroms against the Jews in 1936, this announcement led to increasingly violent attacks on café or shop frontages by gangs armed with stones and bricks.

CRASH! The café upstairs bedroom window shattered as a well-aimed brick thumped onto the bed, centimetres from the three sleeping children! Antonio and Adele rushed into the room in horror expecting the worst. By a miracle the missile had missed its target, but if it had been a petrol bomb the entire family would have been trapped and died before they could escape. The parents cuddled and reassured the children, who were terrified, crying and shaking with fear. Antonio and Adele decided that they were going to leave Swansea immediately, as the next unprovoked attack could be fatal. First thing in the morning, on hearing of the children's lucky escape, Italian and Welsh friends rallied around and boarded up the café windows, effectively closing down the business.

As many local policemen had been patrons of the café, they soon arrived to see what help they could give. They advised Antonio to go to the town council to request that the family be taken to a safer area of South Wales. There was another, more sinister reason for the family to leave Swansea immediately: the policemen knew that arrangements were in hand to intern all foreigners across Britain, under a secret directive listed as '18B.' If the family delayed their departure for even a week longer, it was certain that Antonio would be arrested, so it was imperative they left within a few days. The policemen told Antonio that Swansea town council would organise transport for the family to a safe, small market town in Carmarthenshire called Llandeilo, which neither Adele nor Antonio had heard of, nor could pronounce!

(Across the length and breadth of the British Isles the round-ups of suspected aliens were carried out. To illustrate the devastating result of these arrests, I would like readers to dwell on the effect of such actions to the families of hard working Italians in Wales, when the head of a highly regarded local family business was taken away in dawn raids by determined policemen, without any prior warning. In one case in Neath, a young lad, Dorino Moruzzi, returned from a refreshing morning swim at the local Gnoll Park lake on June 11th in 1940, to find that the M.C.Cafe in Orchard Street, where he lived with his brother Remo was being searched by the police. There was no sign of his father and so Dorino, who was extremely frightened and bewildered, asked a burly policeman what had happened to him. He was abruptly told that his father had been arrested and interned and as he was being held at the local police station, the lad couldn't see him. Dorino's uncle Pietro Moruzzi who owned the popular 'Cosy Café' had also been arrested by Neath policemen and his premises searched for evidence of his involvement with Fascist, or anti-British organisations. Remo Muruzzi, Dorino's brother, luckily wasn't in Neath during this distressing time and later Dorino went to live with relatives in Aberdare. Shops and cafés were 'taken over', or rather stolen by local opportunists and the remaining family members left destitute, being constantly insulted and ridiculed by street gangs. Anyway, under new draconian laws introduced, the wives and family members of business detainees were forbidden to trade in their former premises for two years, or live less than five miles from the coast. Marietta Moruzzi somehow managed to overcome a devastating personal loss earlier during these times of great hardship and courageously took up the reins of the 'M.C. Cafe after the two years had elapsed. The sequel to the internment of the boy's father is described in the next chapter).

A letter from the council informed Antonio that the family would not be allowed to take any household belongings with them to their new destination. The young couple strongly protested, but nothing could be done about this order, which even the police couldn't revoke. With heavy hearts, the following day the family boarded a lorry provided by the council and left Swansea. Antonio knew that they now had lost everything, as the war invalidated any compensation payment from their small business insurance. During the journey the lorry driver reassured Adele and Antonio that the area they were being taken to was a peaceful farming community. He said Llandeilo was untouched by the war and would be perfect for bringing up the children.

As later events unfolded, going to Llandeilo was a blessing in disguise for the Fornari's. Antonio would have been arrested as an ' undesirable alien' by the Swansea police and, along with hundreds of other Italian men, taken to Liverpool, then by ferry to a squalid camp on the Isle of Man. During their internment the men were held incommunicado and their loved ones weren't told of their whereabouts, or ultimate destination, which was St. John's, Newfoundland, Canada.

Author's note: At this juncture in the narrative, it is important for readers to understand that the future of the Fornari family changed forever after an event which took place a few months after their arrival in Llandeilo. To illustrate this, it is necessary to 'fast forward' the narrative to explain what happened on the afternoon of July 2nd 1940 and the devastating consequences.

Maria and Anita rushed into their house in Llandeilo to tell their parents to go to the Post Office immediately, to receive a telephone call. A friend from the Rhondda Valley was on the line with grave, shocking news for Adele and Antonio: a ship taking thousands of internees from Liverpool to Canada had been torpedoed and sunk off Southern Ireland! There were no details available at present, but it was feared that many lives had been lost. The young couple broke down, completely, utterly devastated and bewildered at the terrible news. Adele and Antonio went home and gently told the children what had happened. The next numbing days were spent trying to find out if any of their friends had lost their husbands, uncles or brothers. Families across Britain were distraught, desperately clinging to hope that they weren't amongst the untimely bereaved victims. As the days dragged on, the full scale of the tragedy became sadly apparent, further emphasising just how lucky Antonio had been. They frantically kept trying to batter down the wall of silence put up by the British government over the disaster, desperately needing answers to many questions such as what was the name of the vessel? How had so many died? Surely it was flying a flag signifying it was carrying men to internment in Canada? Did it have a destroyer escort? How long did it take to sink? Did the ship have sufficient emergency equipment? Most importantly, did any of Adele and Antonio's relatives survive?

It took weeks, if not months, for some of these questions to be answered. Sixty-seven years later, mystery still surrounds some of the events that occurred on that terrible day in 1940. In the next chapter, I have attempted to answer some of these searching questions.

CHAPTER 28
The S.S. Arandora Star: 1927-1940

In September 1939, shortly after the outbreak of war, the British government decided to intern thousands of foreigners living and working in Great Britain. The British Prime Minister, Winston Churchill, was paranoid about potential Fifth Columnists in Britain and in reply to a question in Parliament about the status of the foreigners, many of whom had been born in the Britain roared, 'Collar the lot! Around 8,000 men were detained across England, Wales and Scotland over the next few months. They were taken to several holding centres and arrangements were made with the Manx government to send them to the Isle of Man, where they were kept in prison camps. Many Scots-Italians were completely innocent and had been born and brought up in Scotland, but they were rounded up and joined the other nationalities, in what had become an alien, or spy phobia, whipped up by the rabid right wing British press.

Negotiations with the Canadian government in 1939 resulted in a large internment camp being set up at Pettawawa near the capital Ottawa. Other prisoner-of-war camps across Canada were already holding captured Germans and later on, detainees would be also sent on the long voyage to Australia. In late June 1940, 1,300 detainees were brought by ferry from the Isle of Man to Liverpool docks. They comprised 734 Italians, 479 German and Austrian nationals and 87 German P.O.W.s guarded by 200 British soldiers. They were then escorted aboard a London-based 15,000, 500 tonne former cruise liner, the Arandora Star, part of a three ship group leased to the British government by the Blue Star company for use as troop, prisoner-of-war and internee transportation. The ship had been built in the Cammel Laird and Co. shipyard in Birkenhead in 1927 and had been re-fitted to luxury standard for pre-war Mediterranean and Caribbean cruises.

The Arandora Star had been working around the clock for the military for most of June, assisting with the retreat of British troops from Norway. Along with a flotilla of other ships, she sailed up the fjord towards Narvik. The British Expeditionary Force had started to withdraw from Narvik and on June 4th the Arandora Star brought 1,600 officers and men of the RAF and some Polish and French troops back to the Britain. She returned to Norway on June 7th and brought a further 1,600 men to Glasgow, before sailing to Swansea to refuel and replenish stores and finally crossed the Channel to Brest, where she picked up hundreds of French refugees fleeing from the Germans, who by now were closing in on the Channel ports.

The liner was originally fitted with anti-submarine nets, but after extensive trials in the English Channel these were taken out: a decision that a month later had tragic consequences. She was painted wartime battleship grey, fitted with guns and the luxurious staterooms were reduced to basic cabins, sufficient to hold five prisoners. The vast ballroom accommodated the overflow from the cabins, but the facilities throughout the ship were very primitive, with insufficient toilets and wash basins; all the previous luxury fittings having been torn out on requisition. The portholes had been boarded up and in appearance the ship now took on a strong resemblance to an armed troop carrier. The prisoners and internees were locked in cabins in the lower decks and access to these areas was restricted. A double row of ten feet high barbed wire fences surrounded the lower decks and the internees' cabins were secured with barbed wire.

The ship's Master was 50 year old Captain Edgar Wallace Moulton, with a crew of 176. As the date of departure approached, Moulton was very anxious about several aspects of the voyage, particularly the lack of a destroyer escort during the 2,000 nautical mile journey to St. John's Newfoundland. He was a very experienced sea captain and aware that whilst the immediate weather forecast was very good, the calm seas meant that his ship would easily be spotted by enemy submarines. Another cause for his disquiet was that the liner was armed, carried no discernible Red Cross markings denoting its mission and could easily be mistaken for a cargo-carrying merchantman. Other potential shortcomings included insufficient life rafts and a reduction in the complement of lifeboats to one third of its cruise figure, so that more space was acquired for the prisoners. Soldiers patrolled the lower decks twenty four hours a day, ensuring no prisoners slipped overboard while the ship was docked at Liverpool. Moulton must have made strong representations to the Royal Navy requesting destroyer support, but failed to convince the senior Navy officers. As if that wasn't enough to provoke grave disquiet in Captain Moulton, the absence of the anti-submarine netting must also have grievously troubled him.

On June 30th, the Arandora Star slipped her moorings and sailed out of Liverpool Bay towards the Atlantic and Newfoundland. The first two days into the voyage were uneventful. The ship made steady progress at fifteen knots in the customary wartime convoy zigzag pattern in the calm Irish Sea, up the Northern Channel, passing the Mull of Kintyre and Rathlin Island and rounding the top of Northern Ireland. On the morning of July 2nd the ship had passed through Inishtrahull Sound, heading out towards the Atlantic Ocean. Its exact position was fifty six degrees north, ten degrees west.

On July 1st 1940, a German submarine U47 commanded by 32 year-old Lieutenant Kommander Gunter Prien, was returning to its base at Kiel in North Germany, after operations in the North Atlantic. The submarine needed urgent repairs and servicing, having survived several depth charge attacks from destroyers protecting the British Atlantic convoys. It had just one serviceable torpedo left, which had been damaged in the vessel's desperate flight from its pursuers and there was no ammunition left for the deck Bofors gun or machine guns.

Prien's submarine hadn't been as successful as usual on this mission and could easily have been sunk, but he wasn't the least bit concerned. In fact, he was still proudly enjoying his newly acquired fame as the submarine commander who sank the 32,000 tonne British battleship H.M.S. Royal Oak, on October 14th 1939. He had skilfully penetrated her anti-submarine nets at the entrance to her berth at Scapa Flow in the Orkneys. The battleship was hit by three torpedoes but catastrophically, the watertight compartments were not closed and she sank in just fifteen minutes, with the loss of over 800 lives. Prien received massive acclaim all over Germany for his submarine's success and safe escape back to Kiel, having dealt a huge blow to the morale of the Royal Navy and Great Britain early in the war. He was later decorated by Hitler with the Iron Cross.

On the morning of July 2nd 1940, U-47 was positioned approximately 95 kilometres west of Malin Head, Inshowen, in Southern Ireland. The visibility was excellent and the sea calm: ideal conditions for detecting enemy ships. Just before 7.00 a.m., Prien's second officer, who was manning the vessel's periscope, spotted a large ship approximately 3 kilometres in the distance. It was painted a merchantman's standard grey camouflage and travelling west without any destroyer or corvette escort. He called Prien, 'Take a look at that Commander. What a target and no escort!' Prien had a quick look at the distant vessel then made an instant decision. 'Right, we've only got one fish (torpedo) left. Let's make it count!' The second in command shouted on the intercom, 'Battle stations! Battle stations!'

The time was 7.05 a.m.

Suddenly, at 7.15a.m. the liner was struck by a direct hit from the single torpedo fired from U-47. The torpedo exploded on the starboard side and the engine room was immediately flooded to sea level; two officers and all men below were killed by the blast. The main turbines and emergency generators were put out of action and the ship's internal communications malfunctioned. Pandemonium swept through the ship, as most of the internees and prisoners were asleep in their berths when the torpedo struck. They had great difficulty climbing the ladders in the pitch darkness, as they rushed up on deck in their nightclothes to find out what had happened. There had been no lifeboat drill in the two days journey from Liverpool and many internees grabbed lifejackets from piles that the crew threw on the tilting decks. There were ninety life rafts on the upper deck and the crew and soldiers threw about forty into the water, urging the dazed passengers to jump into the water and cling onto them.

Captain Moulton, certain that the ship would quickly sink, instructed his Chief Officer Brown to send an S.O.S. to Malin Head radio station and then gave the order, 'Abandon ship!' He then told the officer commanding the soldiers to release all the internees from below decks immediately, but by now the lower decks were already underwater. Sadly, there were just fourteen lifeboats on the ship, barely adequate for a cruise complement of three hundred and thirty four passengers and the large crew. Of the original fourteen craft, one had been destroyed by the explosion, another couldn't be released from its davits and two were damaged during the attempts to launch them. Four lifeboats were eventually launched successfully, but only contained a small number of passengers. Seeing there was no chance of getting in a lifeboat, the crowds of panicking internees on the decks found planks of wood or oil drums, threw them overboard and jumped off the ship, swimming towards the timber and life rafts, hoping to cling on until help arrived. The ship's crew and soldiers did everything they could to help the people get off the ship; throwing ropes down the sides of the listing vessel followed by tables, benches and anything that could float. Unfortunately, several men desperately struggling in the water were hit by the heavy objects and drowned.

One group of internees successfully released one of the last lifeboats and pushed it into the seas, which were now all but engulfing the ship. Sailors steered the few lifeboats in the water, sailing well away from the ship to avoid the final vortex when she sank. The occupants watched in horror as Captain Moulton and his officers walked over the side as the waters came up to meet them. Men too terrified to jump stood on the upper decks holding onto the rails until the end came. In the terrible last moments, the main boiler exploded, breaking the vessel's back and accelerating her final journey to the bottom of the Atlantic. A huge patch of oil marked the vessel's final resting place and as the seas settled, the lifeboats came closer to pick up as many survivors as possible, who were now covered in bilge and fuel oil. The Arandora Star sank in just half an hour, at 7.45 a.m.

An R.A.F. Coastal Command Sunderland flying boat arrived at 9.30 a.m. and dropped emergency supplies in waterproof bags. It radioed one of the Canadian eastern seaboard ports to summon help and circled the disaster zone until the Canadian destroyer St. Laurent, commanded by Captain Harry G. de Wolf arrived at 2-30p.m. The St. Laurent quickly dispatched lifeboats to pick up the survivors, who by now had been in the water for seven hours and were suffering from hypothermia. The Canadian sailors efficiently dispensed blankets, hot drinks and food and treated any seriously ill survivors were in the destroyer's sick bay. It took five hours of desperate, unrelenting work by the destroyer's sailors to rescue 1000 passengers and recover the bodies of those who had drowned. Many survivors were too weak to even hold onto a rope, and time and again the Canadian rescuers had to jump into the sea and tie the men to ropes which they hauled into the rescue boats.

One Welsh survivor, Giovanni Rabaiotti of Tonyrefail, had quickly seized two deck chairs, tied them to his front and back with his belt and then jumped off the ship. He later told reporters when the St. Laurent arrived in Greenock, Scotland that he was surrounded on the upper deck by many men who were paralysed with fear: he begged them to jump and hold onto any piece of timber in the water, but they stayed and drowned. Aldo Sterlini of Tenby was rescued after seven hours in the water and he recalled the despair and fear that gripped so many, who were either too terrified to jump off the ship, or couldn't swim.

Two Swansea men, Giuseppe Pelosi and Angelo Greco, also had a fortuitous escape from a watery end to their young lives. For some strange reason Giuseppe always carried around with him in his jacket pocket the stub of a candle and one match. His family used to tease him, wondering what on earth he kept the candle for. He always replied: 'You never know, one day it might come in useful.' He was certainly right, as on July 2nd 1940, that tiny candle saved two men from certain death.

When the ship was plunged into darkness after the initial explosion, he and Angelo desperately tried to claw their way up to the upper deck, stumbling and falling in fear and blind panic in the impenetrable blackness, as they felt the vessel tilting beneath them, knowing they had only minutes to escape. Suddenly, Giuseppe clearly heard the voice of his recently deceased mother calling out 'Giuseppe, the candle! the candle!' He grabbed the candle from his coat, lit it with the one match he had and in the weak, spluttering light, they saw ahead of them a ladder to the upper deck! The two lads quickly scaled the ladder, ran to the ship's railings and jumped into the sea. Luckily an empty life raft was within reach and they dragged themselves aboard to await rescue!

Several survivors spoke with admiration of the valiant efforts made by a

German P.O.W. who saved many lives single-handedly. He superhumanly righted a lifeboat that had capsized and helped the frightened passengers back into the vessel. Alas, he failed to save himself, being so exhausted by his Herculean efforts that he drowned in the last moments of the liner.

The eventual casualty figures for the tragedy were realised at eight hundred and five men. Captain Moulton, twelve officers and forty two crew members of the Arandora Star all perished, along with thirty seven of the military guard, four hundred and eighty seven Italians and two hundred and forty three Germans.

Gunter Prien's success was greeted with unmitigated delight in Germany. The 'Berliner Zeitung' depicted a photo of the ill-fated ship on its front page with the gloating banner headline: 'Prien's prey!' Nazi Propaganda Minister Joseph Goebbels made sure no mention was made of the circumstances of the sinking in relation to the internees, prisoners and the ship's mission to Canada. Prien was later promoted to submarine Flotilla Kommander and further decorated. Captain Moulton was posthumously honoured with the Lloyd's of London War Bravery medal.

In maritime tragedies involving large loss of life, wild, unsubstantiated stories sometimes persist, suggesting that passengers fought each other like trapped beasts, in panic and desperation, trying to secure a place in the few serviceable lifeboats. To prevent any such unfounded rumours spreading about passenger behaviour in the last minutes of the Arandora Star's demise, four survivors - three English and one Italian, recuperating in Mearnskirk Hospital near Greenock, signed a deposition stating that any suggestions of uncivilised behaviour by passengers and crew were totally without foundation.

Just three weeks after the disaster, the survivors who were fit enough to travel were shipped off to camps in Australia. As a result of the tragedy, government policy was changed and all future internees were kept in camps on the British mainland.

Every year on July 2nd, a dwindling group of survivors attend a service of Remembrance in the Italian church in London. In 1962, a chapel was built in Bardi, Northern Italy, as a lasting memorial to those who perished. Later a street in the town was named Via Arandora Star. In another sad episode to the tragedy, the body of Dorino Moruzzi's father, Ernesto, was washed up on rocks near the port of Bodden, in County Donegal and later discovered by the local priest. Ernesto's body was identified by a letter found in his wallet, which had survived immersion in the sea and disintegration, as the wallet had been firmly pressed against his chest by his jacket. The address of the Neath Conservative Club was on the letter and these important artefacts of the disaster were later returned to the Moruzzi family by the priest at Bodden.

At midday on July 2nd 2005, exactly sixty five years after the tragedy, a granite memorial plaque was unveiled by local man, Donald McNeil, at a moving ceremony at Leum a' Bhirair, on the cliffs of the Inner Hebridean island of Colonsay, the nearest island to the ecumenical pilgrimage centre of Iona. A week after the ship foundered, Donald, who was twelve, pulled the body of Giuseppe Delgrosso from the sea.

The monument is inscribed:

Sacred to the memory of Giuseppe Delgrosso
And more than 800 others
Who perished with 'Arandora Star'
July 2nd 1940

Fo sgail do sgiathen falaich mi- Psalm 17, vs. 8

Dynevor Castle, Llandeilo

CHAPTER 29
The Fornari family in Llandeilo
1940-1954

On 7th June 1940 the family sadly left their home and business in Swansea first thing in the morning, travelling west in the council lorry to Carmarthenshire. They looked in amazement as they passed through the small compact villages in this beautiful, peaceful and unspoilt part of Wales. For many kilometres in every direction there were acres of ripened corn and verdant fields. Farmers and seasonal labourers were busy cutting and stacking hay, making the most of the late summer fine weather and strong sunshine. After the busy streets of Swansea, there was noticeably less traffic on these winding country lanes and narrow roads. The occasional horse-drawn cart loaded with freshly cut hay slowed down the lorry, but it soon crossed the Towy river into the market town of Llandeilo, stopping in the small square surrounded by the very narrow streets of the town. Many of the houses were imposing Victorian listed buildings, decorated in pastel shades. Antonio helped Adele and the girls to dismount, unloaded the few cases and bags and thanked the driver, who went off to the nearby Ship café for a snack before returning to Swansea.

Swansea officials had arranged accommodation for the family above a small grocery store in Carmarthen Street. As they were in need of provisions, Adele and Antonio went into the shop and introduced themselves to a Mrs Megan Williams, who was expecting them. She rented the premises from Llandeilo District Council and explained that her husband Wally was serving with the British Army in Burma. The Council

171

had arranged for the Fornari's to rent the two small upstairs rooms and a tiny attic. She pointed out that the vacant rooms had neither beds nor furniture, but she was expecting a delivery from the Council the next day. Antonio and Adele replied that they were so relieved to have a roof over their heads that they were quite happy to sleep on the floorboards the first night! It was such good fortune to have found rooms with a very friendly, helpful landlady. There was a gas stove, gas lighting and a coal fire in one room, so Adele decided that it would be the kitchen-cum-living room. Everybody would sleep in the other room and the parents felt that once the beds and furniture arrived, it would be adequate accommodation until Antonio found a job. A few years later the girls all slept in a double bed in the tiny attic, but for now these arrangements were quite satisfactory and as promised, the furniture arrived in a large red 'General Deliveries' van the next day.

Being tired after all the trauma of the last week, everybody slept soundly and after breakfast the next morning, they walked around the town to get their bearings. The children were very excited and considered it a great adventure, a world away from the recurring danger in Swansea. A very large parkland area named Penlan Park was situated very near the shop and extended for many kilometres up a steep grassy hill and down to the river, which they later learned was named the Towy. The children were fascinated on seeing hundreds of sheep, which had been coaxed into a large pen by several lively sheep dogs. Antonio asked a burly, weather-beaten farmer standing alongside the pen what was going on. The farmer looked him up and down, didn't reply and then turned away, scrutinizing and tapping the scrambling, restless mound of sheep with a long stick. Megan met the Fornari's when they returned for lunch and explained that Mart Day was every Monday and the farmers from outlying areas brought their livestock to be auctioned in the cattle mart in town. The other big event held each week in Llandeilo was Market Day, which was every Saturday. Again, farmers and locals who had smallholdings came to the town to sell their produce in the market.

There was no Catholic Church as such in Llandeilo, but in the early weeks of their arrival, Masses were held every Sunday at either Tregib private college or alternatively the Castle, King's Head and Victoria public houses. The host of the latter was a Catholic and later Anita made her First Holy Communion at the 'Vic'. In the early days, they were surprised to discover they were the largest family in the congregation of just twenty, and after the service Antonio introduced Adele and the girls to Father Lynch of the Carmelite Order. Later, walking around the town they discovered that St. Teilo's (the saint that Llandeilo is named after) Church of England building was very strangely positioned. The busy main road bi-sected the graveyard so the church and one part of the graveyard were situated on the left-hand side of the road and the rest of the burial ground was on the right-hand side! (In fact the bodies of several young soldiers from Llandeilo are interred there).

One day, they noticed a group of soldiers in khaki uniforms standing outside a large building in the town, called Bradford House. The soldiers spoke very loudly in a strange accent and later Megan told the children that they were a company of American soldiers who were based in the house. Very early every morning, the GIs marched out of the town to a camp nearby, singing lustily at the top of their voices, to the extreme annoyance of the sleeping locals. Megan also informed the family that Italian P.O.W.s worked as labourers on a number of farms in West Wales, long after the war ended.

The most pressing urgency for Antonio was finding a job to keep the family in food, lighting and fuel, but he wasn't offered any work. The only casual work in the area was on farms, but all employment opportunities had ended with the outbreak of war. Fortunately, Adele was employed twice a week at the small 'Ship' café across the road owned by the Thomas' and occasionally she did a few more days if the café was busy. With winter fast approaching, Antonio used to collect bundles of twigs from the park to build up a stock of fuel for the family. However, being unable to carry heavy loads because of his war injury, he hid his cache of twigs under a park bench and the children carried them back to the shop after school.

The children's education was the next priority and they were enrolled in the local National or primary school. At first they were made to feel very unwelcome by the local schoolchildren. This very unpleasant situation did thankfully change, as the locals became used to the newcomers and friendships slowly developed. The headmaster was a Mr.Price, known to the children behind his back as 'Boss' Price. When he was out of earshot, they regularly sang a mischievous ditty in the playground, which went like this:

'Boss Price, pudding rice, goes to church on Sundays, to ask the Lord to give him strength, to smack the kids on Mondays!'

The family's small savings started to dwindle without a breadwinner's income, so the girls did anything to help out. Anita went to the Bridge Farm dairy every day at 5.00 p.m. for the local butcher Mr Lewis, to collect a jug of milk which had just come from one of the fat dairy cows and was still warm! Lewis paid the girl four pennies (4d) a trip but expected her to go on this errand in all weathers. Maria and Rina helped her out if she was unwell, as the family needed every penny to buy necessities. Additional weekly income came from 'Auntie Megan', as the children called her: she often came up with suggestions for work for Antonio, but in her heart knew that any 'foreigner' was going to find it very difficult getting any sort of job in Llandeilo's very close- knit community. From time to time, Rina also helped out at the Ship café at busy times such as Mart and Market days. Each weekend, Megan sent the children around the town with groceries that local pensioners had ordered a day earlier, paying each child just six pennies (6d). This was a paltry sum by any standard, but any money was welcome to the Fornari's in those bleak times. (For instance, a loaf of bread was two and a half pennies!).

A few weeks later, a large group of young evacuees arrived in Llandeilo from Croydon in Surrey. Nuns of the Sisters of Charity Order cared for the 'vacees' (as they were known). The nuns had huge white headdresses that looked like billowing ships' sails and these fascinated the Llandeilo children. One of the Sisters told Adele that the Germans were expected to start bombing Britain very soon, with London and the South Coast areas becoming obvious targets; hence the children's enforced evacuation to Wales. Author's Note: (During an interview for this book, I was informed by Shirley Moruzzi, (nee Stevens), that she and another young girl named Edna Doughty, also from Neath and their families were 'vacees' in Llandeilo. They arrived just before the Luftwaffe raids in 1941 and stayed on a farm on the outskirts of the town, near Fairfach. Anita and Rina were totally unaware of the existence of another two Welsh families who were based in the town until I informed them. Incidentally, the young girl's fathers carried on their jobs during the week and visited the children each weekend, until both families returned to Neath after the German bombing campaign ended in 1943).

The Dynevor country manor, estate and castle ruin outside the town were always a magnet for the children. They loved roaming around the large gardens, playing in the castle ruins and collecting baskets of fruit such as blackberries, gooseberries, redcurrants, hazelnuts, apples and pears. Adele made the soft fruit into delicious tarts and the hazelnuts were dried at home and when later separated from the husks, were very tasty and nutritious. One day they came face to face with a wild deer, which seemed as surprised as they were and vanished immediately into the trees! They often met Lady Dynevor as she strolled around the estate and town: she was tall, striking, refined lady, who took a keen interest in the children. Being a Governor of the National school, she was always asking them about their school activities and progress and telling them the history of Dynevor castle and estate. Above all, Lady Dynevor was very sympathetic and astutely aware of the girl's poor clothes and straightened circumstances at home. Once a year, as was her generous caring nature, she arranged for the pupils to enjoy a half-day off and treated the entire school to a visit to the cinema. If Adele needed vegetables or salads, the estate gardener dug them for the children, but they had to pay a modest amount for the bag of greens.

A strange gentleman, well into his eighties, called Mr Fenn, was the Dynevor estate lodge keeper. He sat in his tiny cubby hole at the lodge entrance surrounded by curious sheep, busily knitting all day (Anita is convinced he was knitting woolly jumpers!). Lord Dynevor, on the other hand, wasn't as approachable as his wife: he invariably stayed in the family home and the only time people saw him in Llandeilo was when he rode through the town. However each Boxing Day, as Master of the Llandeilo and District Hunt, he sat imperiously on his mount outside the historic Cawdor Arms, dressed in his finest hunting attire, enjoying a celebratory 'stirrup' cup before the chase began.

The Fornari's enjoyed their first modest Christmas in Llandeilo, and seeing that there was an opportunity to make extra pocket money, the girls went around the town knocking on doors and wishing the occupants 'Happy New Year!' They told their father Antonio that they intended calling on Mr Hughes the newsagent and coal supplier. Antonio, knowing Hughes' reputation, was decidedly dubious and he couldn't see Hughes dispensing any festive largesse. Dad was quite right! Instead of giving the poor children a few pennies for their good wishes, Hughes gave them old postcards, which had been on his shelves for years! When the disappointed children took the postcards home, Antonio was furious and, knowing full well Hughes' proclivity for stinginess he decided to teach him a lesson. He got the children to send the postcards back to Hughes, without a message and hopefully Hughes had to pay for the postage as well! The local shoe shop owner gave the children brown shoe laces in lieu of money when they did errands, but in contrast to Hughes' cards, the laces always came in useful.

After this incident, Hughes decided that he would make it up to the Fornari's by offering Antonio a job. He was well aware of the family's destitution and Antonio's failure to find work, so having a vacancy for a coal deliveryman he asked Antonio if he wanted the arduous position. Antonio had no option but to accept, as by now his previously respected position as head of the family had become increasingly eroded through a year of unemployment. It was a large delivery round and Antonio's day began at the railway depot at 8.00 a.m., shovelling coal from the trucks into hessian sacks, weighing the sacks and loading them onto the delivery lorry. Antonio found the work terribly difficult, lifting the 50 kilo sacks from the lorry onto his back, trying desperately not to stumble. His injured leg often gave way because of the weight of the coal, throwing him to the ground and, being unable to lift the sack, he often had to drag it through wet, muddy streets to the house. On arrival at customer's houses, he had to hump the sacks down the back gardens, emptying them into the coal bins situated there.

Deliveries to farms were always an ordeal, as he had to carry the coal down flights of steps into a large bunker. His day's work ended at 5 p.m. and Antonio would arrive home absolutely exhausted; as black as a chimney sweep; every bone in his slight frame aching and his injured leg throbbing with pain. (During active service in the First World War, a bullet had penetrated his leg, leaving a hole, which suppurated continuously). There was no bathroom in the flat so Adele heated water on the coal fire and poured it into a zinc bath in the living room. After his bath, Adele put fresh bandages on his injured leg and often the children witnessed the distressing sight of their Dad crying with pain. Despite his suffering, it was important for Antonio to keep the job and so he worked for Hughes for four long backbreaking years. What was Antonio's weekly remuneration for this slavery? Just four pounds, and Hughes made him pay for every gramme of coal he took home to the family!

The German bombing campaign of Great Britain started in late 1940. The key targets were seaports across the country, including Cardiff and Swansea. During these attacks, the family could see the reddened sky above Swansea in the distance and hear the exploding bombs and the defensive anti-aircraft guns. Some nights, Antonio walked up South bank Hill in the blackout, to watch the raids. There were forty-four Luftwaffe raids on the port from 1940-1943, inflicting death and enormous destruction, with 1,238 civilians killed or wounded, the heaviest raids being in February 1941. A searchlight unit was based outside Llandeilo and every night the children looked out from the attic window, watching the ghostly fingers of the powerful beams waving around the sky, vainly trying to pinpoint bombers. The oil storage tanks at Milford Haven were destroyed in a devastating raid and burned for three weeks, with the smell of the wind-born, acrid, fumes hanging over the Pembrokeshire and Carmarthenshire regions.

The next step in the children's education was progressing from the National school to the senior or Grammar school at Rhosmaen. Maria and Anita went there, but Rina left at fourteen to commence a secretarial course at the commercial college in Ammanford. All the local farmers' children who attended the school spoke Welsh as their first language, so before starting classes, Maria and Anita tried to learn a few words. 'Auntie Megan', like most Llandeilo people, was a fluent speaker and was able to give them lessons, but they did find the language very difficult to master. In 1948, after completing their schooling at Rhosmaen, Maria and Anita also enrolled at the college to study book-keeping and shorthand typing: it proved to be an excellent course and shortly after passing their exams, both girls were successfully employed.

Terrible News! April 23rd 1947. The village of Mumbles is in mourning! The Fornaris and the Llandeilo community were deeply shocked on hearing that a ship called the 'Samtampa', on route to Newport from Middlesborough with 39 seamen on board, had been sheltering in the Bristol Channel, attempting to ride out one of the worst spring storms in living memory. Due to near - Hurricane force winds and raging seas, the ship's anchor cables had snapped and it was driven onto rocks at Sker Point, near the resort of Porthcawl, breaking up into three sections. The

Mumbles Lifeboat, 'Edward, Prince of Wales', with a crew of 7 men under Coxwain Phillip Gammon was immediately launched in mountainous seas and slowly struggled to Sker Point, bravely attempting to assist the stricken ship, but it too succumbed to the appalling conditions and there were no survivors from the 'Samtampa' or the lifeboat crew.

The Fornaris had made many friends among Mumbles people who regularly patronised their café at the terminus at Rutland Street, while awaiting their train and Antonio was especially affected by the tragedy. Although 47 lives seemed insignificant compared to the huge loss of life on the 'Arandora Star' seven years earlier, the enormity of the event in the lives of both the Mumbles and Swansea communities was unparalleled.

Anita obtained a post in the office at Fairfach creamery, which adjoined the L.M.S. railway line. She used to travel to Fairfach by bus during the week, but it was a twenty minute walk on Sundays, when there was no bus service. Farmers brought milk from all over Carmarthenshire to Fairfach and the steel churns were unloaded onto the railway platform. The milk was weighed and tested, then poured into a large stainless steel tank and piped onto a milk tanker for transfer to cities in England. Maria was also very fortunate in being employed by the civil engineering firm of Costain in Llandeilo. A few weeks later, hundreds of Irish labourers arrived, having been hired by Costain for drainage work and for building a large pumping station outside the town.

Rina, in the meantime, was gainfully employed in Carmarthen at the offices of the Gwili Farmers Union. A few months later, Gwili decided to open a branch in Llandeilo, but employment was only offered to Welsh speakers and Rina was dismissed. Antonio was very upset at this injustice and said bitterly, 'Don't worry Rina, they'll soon cop it!' A year later, due to lack of business, the Gwili Union closed! Soon after this shock, Rina secured a clerical position with the established auctioneering firm of Thomas and Philips: their speciality was furniture and antiques and Rina was kept very busy collating items to be auctioned in the town market. In addition, the company acted as agents for farm sales, so she visited the properties, taking inventories of animals and equipment prior to future auction or disposal.

Considering their traumatic flight from Swansea, their destitution and

Antonio's initial fruitless attempts to find work, the Fornari's had slowly started to successfully integrate into the Llandeilo community. Above all, the family had managed to survive the bleak war years. Like everybody else in the town, although they went through periods of elation and agonising disappointment as the conflict raged, Antonio and Adele were confident that the family would have a stable future.

CHAPTER 30
Council worker: 1947-1954

After the hostel officially closed in 1947, I decided to stay in Llandeilo; pretty sure that there would be regular work. Accommodation was my first priority, so I rented a large house in Carmarthen Street, which I shared with Florien Busko (one of the lads previously at the hostel) who now worked as manager of the local cinema. Florien paid ten shillings a week rent but because I did odd jobs around the house, I was charged seven and six. Around this time, our landlord Mr Edwards, who lived in Hill House, a large property in the town, sold his declining coal business in Ammanford to Ernie Hughes the local newsagent; an action he later regretted. In the meantime, I was asked by the Carmarthen Agricultural War Committee to supervise twelve former hostel lads in more drainage work in the area. The committee's offices were in Lammas Street Carmarthen and the depot at Glangwilli, so there were fair distances to travel for this work.

Soon after the drainage work was completed, I was employed (initially on a temporary basis) at Langley's timber yard in Llandeilo. The family also had a sweet shop in Carmarthen Street. The work at the yard consisted of cutting up trees into pit props of varying sizes, which were sent to Coventry and then on to mines in the Black Country. (After my experiences in Russia, any reader would have thought that this was the last work I needed, whatever the wages were!). As things turned out at Langley's, my 'temporary' position lasted a year. By sheer hard work, I increased production in the yard by fifty per cent, so my wages were doubled!

During my time at Langley's, a certain Mr Jones (who was a manager at Llandeilo District Council of Works department) always passed our house in Carmarthen Street on his way to work. He was well aware by that time of my skills, my reputation for honesty and capacity for hard work. Seeing I was home one day, he called and asked if I would like to work for the council in the civil engineering department. I considered this offer carefully and eventually decided to accept, as it would provide me with an excellent salary, pension, security and long term prospects. The next day I went to the council offices for an interview with Mr Evans, the head of works who immediately agreed to take me on. I returned to Langley's and handed in my notice: Langley was naturally very disappointed as after all, as he told me several times, he was losing his best and most reliable worker.

Cayo was the first village earmarked for my introduction to council civil engineering work. In common with many of the outlying small hamlets and villages in Carmarthenshire, there was no mains water supply; it was drawn from springs by householders for all their washing and drinking needs, but the council decided that this system had to be modernised. Engineers built a large tank outside Cayo and the underground spring was located using a water-diving rod. Pressure pumps were then installed in the tank, to pump water in copper pipes up to the houses. Next on the list for modernisation of their water supplies were the many farms and houses around Llandovery. This was a huge task for the council and necessitated the workmen shovelling lorry loads of gravel from the river Towy for use on the sites, as well as the tons of cement needed for the house footings. A separate tank was installed at each farm for the water distribution to the farmhouse and fields. The farmers were always extremely generous to us workers, and every week I returned home with a large juicy ham and other succulent delicacies to share with Florian.

The children's play facilities at the village of Brynamman were non-existent, so the Council decided that a new playground and park had to be built from scratch. I started this operation by bringing materials from the council depot using a Ferguson tractor and trailer. On site I drove the tractor during the ground preparatory work, using the back shovel to spread a layer of earth and hard core base. Within just two months, a fine new play park was installed with swings and roundabouts, to the delight of the Brynamman children and their parents.

In 1948, council houses were urgently needed in Llandeilo and district so this was a priority for our team. Over the next two years, fifty houses were built on the outskirts of Trap, Salem, Cayo, Bethlehem, Cwmgorse Ammanford and Gwaun-cae-Gurwen. To get much-needed extra cash, I did garden work and odd jobs for wealthy locals, who paid very well. On passing through Bethlehem one day in late November 1952, I noticed a very long queue outside the Post Office. I slowed the van down and asked a villager what was the queue for: after all, the war had ended seven years earlier and I thought queuing was (apart from the January Sales in the Llandeilo and Carmarthen shops) very much a thing of the past. The local told me that Christmas cards franked with 'Bethlehem' were in huge demand and sent all over the world. Why didn't we have a village called Bethlehem in Polish Ukraine? I could have set up a Post Office and made a fortune, but then of course friend Stalin would have wanted not just his cut, but the shop as well!

By now, Anita Fornari and I were seeing each other regularly. As I explained in Chapter 26, I attended Mass with the family each Sunday and often joined them for meals. Twice a week, Anita and I we went to the small cinema in Llandeilo and it became our regular haunt. The cinema was situated on Carmarthen Street, opposite the now defunct slaughterhouse. (On top of the wall of the slaughterhouse, a wartime air raid siren still stands 'on duty' to this day!). On our first visit to the cinema, we were intrigued by the entrance to the auditorium, which was accessed by a walk along a gloomy passageway, then up a flight of stairs to the tiny box office. My house-mate Florian was the ticket seller and when he finished that duty, ran up another flight of stairs to the pokey projection room to start the evening's entertainment. I had mistakenly assumed the he was the manager for the premises, but in fact he was a very busy 'jack of all trade's and the place couldn't function without him doing almost everything. The cinema's capacity was two hundred, but there was a problem in wet weather as the roof leaked and the patrons often departed wetter than when they arrived! Actually, Anita and I were given VIP treatment at the cinema. Florian arranged with the usherettes that we would always be shown to the best seats in the house, definitely a tangible expression of his gratitude to me for securing a lower rent for him from our landlord.

As I began to get to know the family, I realised just how unhappy Antonio was with his coal delivery job; sometimes I was in their flat when he staggered in, filthy dirty and worn out. I felt really sorry for him and Adele, as the situation was hardly conducive to a happy relationship, but he had no choice. Eventually I told him that I'd ask Mr Jones if there were any impending vacancies for labourers with the council. To the family's great delight he was offered a job shortly afterwards and he triumphantly gave his notice to Hughes, starting with the council a week later.

AT LAST! AT LAST! STALIN IS DEAD!

March 4th 1953 is a date I'll never forget! The B.B.C. broadcast the pleasing news as soon as the shaken Politburo released it to the world. The evil monster that destroyed my parents and countless other poor souls died alone in his Kremlin apartment. Cause of death? Heart failure! I don't believe that for one second. All information relating to the cause and the circumstances of Stalin's death was very carefully scrutinised and vetted before a worldwide announcement was made, days after his departure from his bloody life. I imagined Beria and the others crouched in the shadows of St Basil's Cathedral, the flickering candles illuminating their pasty faces as they watched thousands of Muscovites filing past his black draped catafalque. They were already whispering, plotting and positioning themselves to be his successor, even as they hovered over his embalmed corpse.

In the hours after his death they had ingratiated themselves by offering crocodile tear-like commiserations to his daughter Svetlana, while at the same time trying to decide which of them was going to make the first move. Beria had a very strong hand as he controlled the security apparatus but hadn't Stalin made so many enemies in the military, like Marshall's Zhukov and Timoshenko? (Stalin knew that Timoshenko's grandparents were Jews and being virulently anti-Semitic, intended to eliminate the great wartime general when an opportunity arose). The military commanders must have been making contacts with their former colleagues and possibly discussing a lightning coup. I enjoyed all the fake information given by the Soviet authorities, knowing that not a single word was to be believed.

Days later, I relished listening to a radio transmission of his funeral service, laughing my head off as I heard the false grotesque eulogies given by successive toadies and sycophants. These fawning creeps had only one thing on their evil minds: survival in the coming months, as the inevitable secret police hunts and arrests started. I fervently hoped that Stalin's black soul was burning in the depths of hell along with Hitler's: a lovely thought! I later learned that his body was interred in a wall of the Kremlin overlooking Red Square with just a simple inscription of his name and dates. I can think of a better epitaph for the murderer. Try this one:

'Here lies the body of Josef Stalin,
Succeeded by Khrushchev and his sidekick Bulganin.
His ghost will wander the Gulag plains.
(I wish I'd have buried his evil remains).
Grab all his gold, and then food will be cheaper,
Torch his dacha; push his Zyl into the Dnieper.
(Pity Svetlana, her Dad was a monster,
She'll get a one –way ticket to San Francisco!)
I'm glad he's kicked it, truth to tell,
A message from his victims?
Burn in Hell!'

Like it? I hope so. (Incidentally I am often asked who, in my opinion was the worst of the twin evils: Stalin or Hitler. I can answer that tricky conundrum by replying that Hitler, to the best of my knowledge, only killed his enemies!).

Well after that unexpected, but very enjoyable interlude, it was back to the much more mundane things such as council work. I made sure that Antonio worked in my team so I could help him get used to the work. He had slaved for Hughes since 1941, six years before I arrived in Llandeilo, so he deserved an easier job. We worked together happily for a further six years in Llandeilo and I especially remember going with him and a group of farmers to watch Queen Elizabeth's Coronation on one of the very few televisions in Llandeilo in the 'Vic' pub. (In those days it was considered totally inappropriate for women to go into public houses).

A few months later, Antonio confided in me that he wanted to move back with the family to Swansea and open another cafe. I had of course heard again and again about their flight from Swansea in 1940 and Antonio's lucky escape from the Arandora Star tragedy. After their success there in the late Thirties, I saw no reason why the young family shouldn't prosper again. He started making contact with Italian business owners, seeking their advice as to the post-war potential for a café in the town. Antonio met a Mr Monterossi who owned the 'Express' café in Neath, but he strongly advised against setting up in Swansea a second time: the town centre was in the process of extensive reconstruction following the war, so Monterossi suggested Antonio and Adele should look elsewhere.

Monterossi felt a better prospect for a business was the town of Neath, situated twelve kilometres from Swansea, despite there already being a plethora of cafés and restaurants in the town. Antonio made enquiries and decided to rent the established 'Model' fish restaurant in Windsor Road, which was being run by Pietro Moruzzi and his family. He also rented a house in the nearby Ropewalk Road. (I later discovered that the name 'Ropewalk' derived from the steel cable linking the Gnoll and Greenway collieries tramway. Dating back to the 1880s, it carried coal drams to R.S. Jones the overseas coal exporter, at the busy docks and wharf on the River Neath).

Ah ha! Beria's gone now; he died on December 22nd. Cause of death? Heart failure! What, again? A plausible reason? Possibly. The given reason, or the real reason? Strange that the two Party-controlled Soviet newspapers just can't get anything right: Pravda means Truth, Isvestia means News, but between the two of them, their black-bordered 'tributes' were neither news nor truth, as the latter just didn't exist in Soviet Russia. The cause of his death was accepted by the gullible masses as 'heart failure'. Dare a young ambitious Pravda or Isvestia editor print the real cause of his timely demise? If he even hinted at the cause of Beria's death, he would have been dragged from his dingy flat in the dead of night, bundled into a prison van and delivered at high speed to the Lubianka jail. After quickly descending to the deepest torture chamber, the editor would be viciously beaten, executed with a single shot to the back of the head, then his body dropped through a trapdoor or slid down a ramp into the icy Moscva river (the usual 'departure gate' for 'Terror' victims). A nice afternoon tea for the fishes! Yes, VERY good news for them! Now we hopefully have a trio of mass murderers toasting nicely in the deepest, hottest abyss of Hell: Hitler, Stalin and Beria. Lovely!

(A final thought for readers at the death of this monster: if Stalin's hands were dripping with blood, then Beria would have been soaked in the gory stuff up to his armpits!)

Antonio had already informed me that there was a lot of house-building taking place in Neath, Swansea and the surrounding districts and that I would definitely be taken on by any of several building contractors, once they saw my reference from Mr Evans in Llandeilo. I told Mr Evans of my decision to move to Neath: he was extremely disappointed and was so determined to retain my services if we returned to Llandeilo at a later date, that he kept my 'cards' for six months. (In fact, eventually realising later that I would not be returning to Carmarthenshire, he brought the documents to my home in Neath in person!).

Unfortunately, before we left Llandeilo in the autumn of 1954, a dark menacing shadow of fear, outrage and disbelief covered the entire Carmarthenshire region, as two similar, grisly events unfolded before the eyes of the shocked communities.

CHAPTER 31
Prosecution Witness

On 16th October 1953, the owner of a farm near St. Clears, Carmarthen was mystified at the strange and abrupt disappearance from the adjoining Killining farm of his neighbour, farmer John Harries, who was 67 and his wife Phoebe, 54. The cows hadn't been milked for days, so he had quickly contacted friends to rectify this, before contacting the police. He telephoned a Sergeant Albert Phillips at Llandeilo police station to register his concern. The sergeant and a constable Jones immediately drove over to St. Clears to investigate, where they were met by the neighbouring farmer and together they walked around the deserted buildings.

The worried man explained that he knew the couple very well and such behaviour was totally out of character. He emphasised to the police officers that John and Phoebe were very conscientious, hardworking farmers and if for instance, they had decided to go away for a short break, they would have made careful arrangements for feeding the animals, milking the cows and general farm duties. One of the locals had told him that the couple had attended a Harvest Festival service at St Clears Methodist chapel earlier in the week, before their disappearance.

The farmer told the policemen that the couple's nephew, Ronald Harries, who was 24, helped his uncle and aunt as well as looking after his own farm at Cadno, near St. Clears. The officers immediately went to see Harries, who nonchalantly explained that he had taken Phoebe and John to St. Clears station a day earlier, as they were going to London for a well-earned holiday. The policemen didn't believe him and returned to Llandeilo police station where they began making further enquiries, contacting the railway station to ask the two staff there if they recalled seeing the couple earlier in the week. They said that only six passengers had caught the London train on October 15th and the Harries's, whom they knew, definitely didn't board the train. By now, Sergeant Phillips was certain that a terrible crime had been committed and immediately contacted Scotland Yard. Three detectives arrived at Llandeilo the next day and started a minute examination of the missing couple's farm and outbuildings.

I always met Albert Phillips for a pint at the Vic. each week and he kept me informed about the progress of the investigation. He said that detectives had made a potentially significant discovery at Ronald Harries's farm at Cadno: during a meticulous search of the farmhouse they found a cheque for nine pounds made out to Harries. The co-signatories were John and Phoebe Harries, but the original amount, which was for wages due to Ronald, had been changed from nine pounds to nine hundred and ninety pounds!

Ronald was arrested on suspicion of murdering his relatives and taken to Llandeilo police station. Hundreds of police officers were then drafted in from all over Wales to find the bodies of Phoebe and John, which Scotland Yard officers were convinced had been buried on the land at Ronald's farm at Cadno. This was going to be a huge undertaking, as there were many acres of kale fields. As the days went by, no sign of the bodies was found, and the search was intensified. My friend the sergeant told me that he was confident he would find the couples grave. When I asked him why he thought he would be successful when the police had so far failed to pinpoint the burial site, he waved his blackthorn walking stick saying; 'I'll find the spot Julian, tomorrow, at first light'.

The sergeant came to see me when I returned from work; he was waving his trusty blackthorn and had a huge grin on his face. To my amazement he announced, 'Found 'em Julian, just as I thought, in one of the furthest fields!' He had arrived at the site, which had been marked off, just after dawn and well before the police search parties arrived. Scanning the fields with powerful binoculars, he noticed a mound of fresh earth a few metres in from the perimeter of a field which hadn't been dug over by the searchers. Walking up to the mound, he prodded the soft earth with his stick and felt it hit a buried object. When the search parties arrived, he told them to dig up the mound and soon the bodies of John and Phoebe were brought to the surface. To their horror the police saw that the couple had been battered to death with a blunt instrument. Harries was charged with the couple's murder. His trial took place at Glamorgan Assizes at Carmarthen and after eight days he was found guilty by Mr Justice Havers and on March 16th sentenced to death. A week later, Ronald Thomas Edward Harries was hanged at Swansea prison.

Unfortunately within a few months the good people of Llandeilo were horrified, and the town rocked to its very foundations, to learn of another murder investigation: this time, it concerned someone from their own community, and I would become a prosecution witness at the trial.

One day in early September 1953, I was contacted by the Carmarthen Agricultural committee to supervise drainage work at Cefn Hendre farm, at Cwmdu outside Llandeilo. The committee sent five lads from the hostel to join me at Cwmdu and as usual, I plotted the area to be drained with an Ordnance Survey map. Cefn Hendre was a hill farm of one hundred and seventy acres. The present owners, two Polish ex-soldiers, had sold the large flock of sheep on acquisition, preferring to concentrate on milk sales from the fifteen cows. The milk was sent for processing to the nearby Cwmdu dairy, then on to Fairfach distribution centre. The two farmers lived in a new bungalow; perhaps they had other ideas for the land when it was drained and had dried out. The work proceeded quickly enough as the weather was excellent and I gradually got to know the two Poles.

The bigger of the two was Michial Onufrejczk, aged 60 from Warsaw and his slight, quiet partner was Stanislaw Sycut from Wroclaw, who was 56. Onufrejczk cut a distinguished figure, with a determined military bearing and full white beard and there was no doubt who was the boss in their farming enterprise. He told me had been a warrant officer in the Second Polish Corps and had distinguished himself during the ferocious battle at Monte Cassino, being later awarded the Polish equivalent of the Victoria Cross. He proudly showed me his medals and I later learned that he was a judo expert. Unfortunately, his arrogant bearing frequently betrayed itself and some days I heard him speak very harshly to Sycut; swearing and taunting his partner as the poor man struggled with the farm work. I always had the feeling that Sycut was afraid of Onufrejczk and as a sequence of chilling events evolved, my initial assessment of their working relationship sadly proved to be correct.

Although I was very busy helping the Fornari's with their imminent move to Neath, I did agree to help the Poles with the hay one weekend. They had a fairly serviceable combine harvester, but like so many farms in Carmarthenshire, some of the other machinery had broken down, so there was more work for me! Even the hay loader was out of action, so we had to pitchfork the hay onto stacks in the fields: a very laborious method. (I couldn't understand why they hadn't had the machine serviced and repaired well before harvest time). One afternoon, when I was in the shed trying to repair some of the equipment, I heard Onufrejczk shouting at poor Sycut, telling him he was useless and accusing him of being a liability in their partnership.

I expressed my disquiet to Sergeant Phillips over a drink later that week. He told me that on May 15th, Stanislaw Sycut had come to the Llandeilo police station to complain that he had been beaten up by Onufrejczk; sustaining a cut forehead and a gashed leg. Phillips went to see Onufrejczk with an interpreter and the Pole admitted there had been a confrontation but promised it wouldn't happen again. After this, he probably terrorised Sycut even more and the situation further deteriorated when Onufrejczk told Sycut that he wanted to buy him out and dissolve the partnership. He kept trying to get his partner to agree on a sum which would give Onufrejczk ownership of the farm. (Onufrejczk knew exactly what he was doing, as we'd all heard that recently an ex-Polish soldier had bought a farm nearby for just four hundred pounds!).

A week after we had finished the hay, Sycut came to see me at my house: he told me he was terrified of Onufrejczk. Even worse, after yet another row over Sycut's contribution to their partnership, Onufrejczk caught him by the throat and half strangled him. After this fright, Sycut decided to dissolve their partnership and buy out Onufrejczk. He couldn't speak, read nor write English and needed my help, so he asked me to go to Grassbrook solicitors in Rhosmaen Street with him, in order that I could act as interpreter. We arranged an appointment for noon the next Saturday, December 13th, but Sycut was delayed and didn't arrive until 12.50 and as the office closed at 1.00 p.m. we made another appointment for the next Saturday, again at midday.

That week, I was so pre-occupied with the arrangements for our accommodation in Neath, and the setting up of the restaurant that I forgot the appointment arranged with the solicitor for the Saturday. As a series of terrible events unfolded, I regretted my lapse, but it was too late. My friend Sergeant Phillips called around a week later to give me some disquieting news: the Cwmdu postmistress had told him of her concern that Stanislaw Sycut, a regular customer, hadn't collected his Polish newspaper for over a week. In addition, the local grocer had told her that he still had Sycut's ration card. I was immediately greatly alarmed and told the sergeant that he should go to the farm and offered to join him as interpreter. I had mentioned to Phillips on several occasions about the rows I'd heard between the partners and the bullying manner of Onufrejczk.

On arrival, the sergeant asked Onufrejczk, through me, where Sycut was, as it had been reported that he had failed to collect his papers from the Post Office. He confidently replied that Sycut had gone to London, and said he hadn't heard from him. I immediately challenged this, telling him, 'That's because you've killed him!' He looked furious, didn't answer and shut the door. We returned to Llandeilo and throughout the journey discussed what might have happened to Sycut. Sergeant Phillips said he'd wait a few more days in case Stanislaw did return from London, but if he failed to return, a full crime investigation would be mounted. Anyway, we both agreed that it was a very strange coincidence that a year earlier, Ronald Harries had also told the police that his relatives had gone to London! Had Onufrejczk copied Harries' plan and also fabricated a similar tale to account for his partner's sudden disappearance?

Two days later, Onufrejczk came to my house. He asked me if I could lend him one hundred pounds, saying that he wanted to go to London to find Sycut. I told him I didn't believe him and anyway I didn't have a hundred pounds. I could see he was very worried and again I challenged his story, making it clear that I believed he'd murdered Sycut. With that, I told him he'd never get away with the crime and shut the door in his face. I immediately told Albert Phillips about this visit and he disclosed a very interesting piece of information. Aware that Sycut was going to sever their partnership, Onufrejczk had confided in one of his Polish colleagues that in a few months, Sycut might well have raised sufficient funds to buy him out, leaving Onufrejczk with nothing. At this, Onufrejczk raged that before such an eventuality took place, 'Sycut will be rotting under the hedges, even if I go to prison for it!' He also made a veiled threat that Sycut's daughter, who lived in Russia, would suffer the consequences.

Around this time, Sycut had visited the local blacksmith to have new shoes fitted to one of their horses. The blacksmith had noted the date of the transaction, December 14th 1954. He was very surprised to receive a visit from Onufrejczk a week later, who asked him to confirm that Sycut had in fact been at the smithies on December 17th. He requested that the date should be changed in the daybook to that date, and appeared very anxious. The blacksmith refused to do this, so Onufrejczk lost his temper and left abruptly. Later, as the murder investigation proceeded the blacksmith informed the police of this strange request.

Onufrejczk was arrested on suspicion of murder, a charge he denied, protesting his innocence. He then concocted a fantastic tale of how three Polish men arrived by car at the farm one night, dragged Sycut out, and he had never heard from him again! In a subsequent interrogation, Onufrejczk confidently said that he hadn't harmed Sycut and declared that he believed that Sycud was a Communist. As in the Harries case, hundreds of officers descended on Cefn Hendre farm. The forensic scientist assisting the investigation had found several hundred bloodspots on the walls of the farmhouse and a bloody handprint on a dresser. When challenged about this gruesome discovery, Onufrejczk insisted that Sycut had cut his fingers on the hay baling machine a day before going to London and that the blood on the walls came from rabbits that he had cut up in the kitchen. This was of course fabricated nonsense and I told the sergeant later that day that the baling machine was broken and hadn't therefore been used during the hay harvesting.

After a lengthy, detailed search of the farm and outbuildings, a huge operation commenced to dig up the fields to find the remains of Stanislaw Sycut. Scotland Yard officers were positive that the partners had quarrelled and in a fit of rage, using his superior strength, Onufrejczk had bludgeoned Sycut to death and buried his body in a field. The search for the body began on February 9th 1954 and continued unabated until February 27th. Not only Capel Hendre farm was searched, but also some neighbouring farms and in total fifty square kilometres was covered by the police teams. No trace was found of Sycut's body, so Onufrejczk was charged with his partner's murder based upon the existing evidence. (I was certain that he had buried Sycut's body beneath a tree, as this would have made it almost impossible for the police to find).

The first hearing took place in the tiny nineteenth century Shire Hall next to the police station in Llandeilo, presided over by Director of Public Prosecutions, Mr W.L. Mars-Jones. Twenty witnesses had been assembled and during the course of the hearing they stayed at the One Ton public house, opposite the courtroom. My close working connections with the deceased and his alleged killer meant I was to be a key prosecution witness. The hearing was held over several days and the presiding judge eventually informed the court that there was a prosecution case to answer. Details of the date of the forthcoming trial at Swansea Assizes were later circulated.

In the meantime, we had left Llandeilo and settled in Neath, where I had started work with Jones Brothers, a local building firm. I was contacted by the Swansea Assizes officers and told to attend the first day of the trial on September 14th 1954. As I would be on duty for the entire trial, I booked a room at a local bed and breakfast house as my travel and subsistence expenses would be covered by the authority. The courtroom was vast in comparison to the one in Llandeilo and the public had been queuing for hours to get a seat on the opening day, for what was going to be one of the most eagerly anticipated murder trials held in Wales. The national and local newspapers had all sent reporters and Pathe News and the BBC were broadcasting daily bulletins on the trial. The national press trailed the story as 'The murder without a body!'

There was added piquant expectancy and intrigue to the proceedings, as the circumstances of the murder bizarrely appeared to replicate those of the 1953 Harries crime. Two Polish interpreters were on hand to translate prosecution and defence questions and the responses of the accused and the other Polish witnesses. As is customary in all court cases, the first day began with a series of lengthy submissions from prosecution and defence barristers. I took the stand the next day. The defence barrister was from London and had a pronounced Cockney accent, which I found very difficult to understand. Perhaps he couldn't follow my Polish accent either and our altercations became quite funny for the packed courtroom, so we eventually had to compromise by both speaking slowly! I was in the witness box for most of the day telling the court how I had worked with the former partners. I also related that I had heard raised voices and arguments, and gave details of my conversation with Onufrejczk when he came to my house hoping to borrow the hundred pounds.

The trial lasted sixteen days, resulting in Michial Onufrejczk being found guilty of the murder of Stanislaw Sycut based on the circumstantial evidence available. Because no body had been found, Onufrejczk was sentenced to twenty years imprisonment, but was released after ten years. He returned to Wales and went to live in Penygroes, near Ammanford. Six months later, he returned to Llandeilo: if he was hoping to be rehabilitated and accepted once more into the community, he was very much mistaken. He stayed at the Vic. pub for two days, but during his brief sojourn in Llandeilo the community shunned him. Because Sycut's body was never found, and as Onufrejczk steadfastly refused to say where he had hidden it throughout his lengthy interrogation and trial, all sorts of rumours persisted. Even today, over fifty years later, many locals are convinced that Onufrejczk had chopped up Stanislaw's body and fed it to the pigs. I can categorically refute this rumour, as quite simply there weren't any pigs at Cefn Hendre farm!

So ended two dreadful years for the inhabitants of Carmarthenshire and especially Llandeilo. In a way, I was relieved that my new environment and job at Neath would help me to forget the trauma of those two terrible events, in which I unwittingly became so deeply involved.

CHAPTER 32
Neath and the Model Restaurant
1954-1965

Having been travelling back and forth to Swansea during the trial, I felt confident that was the last I had seen of the inside of a court of law for a very long time. Well, not quite, as with so many of my life's interesting previous encounters, I should really known better and not assumed anything! A few weeks later, as I was coming to grips with my new job at Jones Bros. I received a bombshell in the form of a letter requesting my attendance at Swansea's Guildhall again, this time on jury service!! Oh no! That was all I wanted! Anita, poor girl, must have privately (and quite understandably) wondered whether she had become engaged to me or to my somewhat unpredictable life and most importantly, what kind of future lay in store for her! So there I was stuck in the court again, listening to cases in which frankly, I wasn't the slightest bit interested. My thoughts quite naturally, were focussed on the Neath set-up and I was extremely frustrated at this pointless waste of time, even if I did get fairly generous travel and subsistence expenses.

However, one case was intriguing, to say the least: readers may be quite surprised to discover that there were drug barons making a very lucrative living in Swansea in the 1950s! One character arrested for supplying a drug of some kind around the town was very confident that he would get off Scot-free. He was a particularly oily specimen of mankind, very sure of himself, dripping with (and almost weighed down by) a huge gold watch, massive gold bracelet, glittering diamond rings on his talon-like fingers and a trio of heavy gold chains around his neck. How the NKVD would have loved to have got hold of this guy and put him to work in Kolyma. Remember? 'The land of gold and death'? He was eventually found guilty and the verdict wiped the smirk off his face: he was fined £2,000, which was payable immediately or he faced a prison sentence. His fine must have been the present day equivalent of £20,000. The sudden realisation that his ill-gotten wealth would soon vanish hit him like a train and after a frantic discussion with his lawyer, he requested paying the fine off at just £10 a month! This insulting offer was of course rejected out of hand by the judge, so the dealer's hitherto lucrative career was abruptly terminated!

I thankfully escaped from the frustrating, cloying atmosphere of Swansea Court and returned once more to my responsibilities at Jones Bros. I was glad to be back in action with them and also to help the Fornari's, who were to be my future in-laws. Anita's current priority was her parents, who were trying to get the fish shop and restaurant in Windsor road up and running. One day I walked from Neath to Briton Ferry and was shocked to count at least ten cafes, ice cream parlours and restaurants. I later got to know the individual proprietors and discovered that some businesses had been handed down for generations. For instance, the Plaza café overlooking lovely Victoria Gardens, which had been established by Giovanni Minetti in 1927 and is now run by his niece Angela Marzella, is celebrating its eightieth year serving the Neath community.

The harsh realisation of what he had taken on immediately hit home to Antonio: being strangers who had arrived from 'down west', viable trading would undoubtedly be a battle, but Antonio relished a fight. His previous experience in the Mumbles train terminus café was to prove invaluable and Adele was an excellent worker. Anyway, what was the alternative? Going to work for somebody as unscrupulous as Ernie Hughes again? Never! The first weeks were very quiet and they realised that it would take several months to build up trade. Time, but not money was on their side, so the couple would have to go carefully for a while and watch every penny. Antonio decided that the restaurant would not open on Sundays and would close at lunchtime on Good Friday, as in those days there was a big demand for fish on that sacred day. In the first months of the 'Model' they couldn't afford to hire additional staff, but Anita was proving to be extremely capable, working alongside her father. In fairness, they couldn't expect help from Maria and Rina who were very busy in their respective jobs with the N and C Bus Company and a furniture shop. Although Neath was a world apart from the slow-paced life of Llandeilo, they were both very close-knit communities in their own special ways and as they settled down, the Fornari's discovered that the Neath people were very warm hearted and friendly. Slowly the family got to know other Italian families, either working in, or running their own catering businesses.

One such young lady was Angela Malvecini, who had come to Wales in 1948. Angela hailed from the Bettola Commune in the Piacenza region of North Italy and worked in the Transport café, just off the Neath-Briton Ferry roundabout. The business opened each day at 6.00 a.m. until 2.00 p.m. and Angela soon found out what work in a busy transport café entailed. An astonishing 300 to 400 breakfasts and dinners were served up every day to long distance lorry drivers and workers at local factories, which in those dreary post-war days didn't have staff canteens. Angela later married Peter Dimaio who was ambidextrous and thus a key 'roller-man' at the Eaglesbush tin works, but who suffered several severe strokes in 1997, which affected his left side. Unfortunately, his left leg had to be amputated, sadly incapacitating him to a wheelchair. Angela was really outstanding and selfless in her nursing and care for her husband. I visited Peter every week, until his death in January 2006.

March 5th 1957: a very, very, special day. Anita and I were married in St. Joseph's church! The reception was in our house at the Ropewalk, followed by a two week honeymoon in London. As well as exploring the sights of the big city, we attended the Grace Kelly, Bob Hope and Frank Sinatra smash hit 'High Society' at the Odeon cinema, Leicester Square. The Odeon was about a hundred times larger than the picture house in Llandeilo and the Empire and Windsor cinemas in Neath. Being well into the second week of our holiday, our funds were now becoming seriously depleted, so it had to be the cheapest seats. Big mistake! A snooty usherette escorted us to the very front row. We looked up in horror at the screen which appeared to be a mile high and as wide as four football pitches! Within half an hour we had aching necks, were blinded by the new 'Cinemascope' technology and our ears were buzzing from the deafening music. After the film ended we staggered out into the badly lit street and the Leicester Square darkness; dazed and bewildered. My neck was sore for days and I don't recall that I had such a bad neck and back even when I was looking up at those tall firs in the Volga Basin! Luckily we soon forgot our discomfort at the Odeon, as being newly weds, there were far more interesting diversions to enjoy! Here's a thought: why didn't Vera Lynn make any films? *

We returned to Neath and were soon busy with the move to our first married home at Penrhiwtyn, near Neath Hospital. Trade was really improving at the 'Model'; as the business was near the Empire and Windsor cinemas and the Post Office, customers from all three establishments regularly frequented us. Antonio started extending the opening hours to facilitate the new upstairs restaurant which we had renovated. Eventually, the restaurant could seat 40 guests, with another table for 10 on the ground floor and definitively established the 'Model' as an excellent venue for diners. As both the fish and chip trade and the restaurant took off, I became more involved in the business. My day with Jones Bros. commenced at 7.30 a.m., but before dashing off to the site, I started preparatory work in the café kitchen at 5.30 a.m. cleaning kilos and kilos of potatoes, preparing the fish and anything else that was necessary before Antonio and Anita arrived at 11.00 a.m. The restaurant served meals until 11.00 p.m. and on Saturday nights I cleaned the machines, range and premises, sometimes not finishing until 3.00 a.m.! On reflection, I should have opened a large hotel somewhere in Wales and that would really have kept us in clover! Anita had more than her fair share of long hours, whilst trying to enjoy some form of social life. If, for example, she signed up for the all too brief luxury of a pre-Christmas shopping trip to London, Cheltenham or Bath on a Saturday, there was a hard price to pay at home for this enjoyment. On arrival back at Neath around midnight, she always stayed up for the remainder of the night preparing the family's Sunday lunch!

It was in 1957 that Anita became pregnant with the first of our three children and naturally I did all I could to ensure she had a safe, happy, confinement. However, one evening she was alarmed to learn that her parents had experienced the shock of discovering that two well-fed diners had attempted to depart without settling their bill. These lads had ravenously worked their greedy way through the menu and after their dessert, Antonio spotted them abruptly leaving their table and hurrying to the toilets. He rushed outside and some cinemagoers queuing for the evening's films at the Empire pointed out the pair, who had climbed out of the upstairs window of the restaurant and were running down Windsor road. Antonio was incandescent with fury at this breach of trust and telephoned the police. The two freeloading opportunists were soon picked up and thankfully this type of theft didn't occur again. There were however other unpleasant instances of customers in the fish shop attempting to defraud the couple by inventing implausible stories to obtain refunds. One such person barged into the premises demanding compensation from Antonio for damage to vinyl long-playing records: she remonstrated that they were in her shopping bag, but she had stupidly put her fish and chips in the same bag! Naturally when she arrived home, the records had melted and were ruined. The outraged customer demanded money from Antonio to replace the records, as in her opinion the fish and chips were too hot!

Another fraudster regularly used to return to the shop two days after being served, to complain that she had been short-changed by several pounds. She was always passing the premises, but waited for two days to elapse before returning to demand her 'missing' change. Antonio soon put her in her place after several attempts at this type of blatant fraud, by counting out her change aloud and having another person to verify the transaction. On another occasion, a customer attempted to extort money from the couple by the lying assertion that he had found a large piece of glass in his fried fish. Antonio was furious and told him to leave immediately before he called the police. Perhaps this nice customer expected the Fornari's to believe that a fish had bitten off the top of a bottle that a castaway on a desert island had thrown into the sea! In this sorry reminiscence of disreputable customers, the pick of a bad bunch must surely be the one who after purchasing her lunch, spent the next three quarters of an hour gossiping outside the 'Model'. The next day she stormed into the shop, screaming and demanding a refund, complaining that by the time she arrived home her lunch was cold!

By 1958, the Fornari's had been running the 'Model' for four years. Anita was imminently expecting our first child and her parents were struggling to keep on top of what had now become a very busy, popular fish shop and restaurant. On May 27th 1958, Adele gave her husband his breakfast then went off to open the shop. On completion of his meal, Antonio went into the next room to finish off his repaste with an apple. Suddenly, there was a sickening crash. Anita tore downstairs and seeing the lifeless form of her Dad slumped centimetres from the blazing coal fire, rushed next door to call her neighbour Clementina Underwood. They managed to drag Antonio away from the flames, but he failed to respond to their desperate attempts to wake him. Anita frantically telephoned the family doctor who on arrival immediately pronounced her father dead from a massive heart attack. It often happens in families that when one of the older members dies, a new baby arrives shortly afterwards. So it was with Anita and I, as our first child, Linda Patricia, came into the world soon after the death of my beloved, hard-working father-in-law, Antonio Fornari. The Bester family increased again in 1960, when our son Anthony Francis was born, followed in 1965 by a second daughter, Helen Adele.

On April 15th 1966, Adele and Anita went shopping in Swansea to buy a dress for Helen's first birthday. On arriving home, Adele said that she felt very tired. After tea, she dozed in the armchair for the rest of the evening, but at 11.00 p.m. she failed to respond to attempts by Anita to wake her. Like her husband eight years earlier, she too had suffered a massive, fatal heart attack. A somewhat strange occurrence took place during the days after Adele's funeral: the children were staying with friends at the time and one after another, Helen, Linda and Anthony all contracted measles!

I spent a lot of time at the restaurant and during research for this book, several people have mentioned that I always seemed to be at the 'Model.' Quite simply, I wanted to make certain that Anita, who was in charge now had all the additional help and support she needed. Everything has its time and by now Anita was fully occupied with looking after our three children as well having as the onerous business to manage. I found it harder and harder to continue burning the candle at both ends as well as in the middle, so we wisely decided to finish at the 'Model' in 1967. The shop was taken over by Denis and Clementina Underwood, who had three children: Carla, Adrian and Paul. Clementina and Adrian were the mainstays of the business and long hours and hard unrelenting work were part and parcel of restaurant life in those days. The business flourished successfully for twenty one years until 1988. As contemporaries, we were very pleased when they asked Anita to work for them, when the children's schooling and activities permitted. Prior to the end of our time at the 'Model' we had been looking for a larger home. We eventually found the ideal house at London Road in Neath and have happily lived there for the past thirty-three years.

* Author's notes: I have been informed by Dame Vera's son-in-law, Tom Jones, that she did in fact make three films. The first was a war fundraiser, followed by a comedy, then finally a musical. She had no desire to make more films and continued with her illustrious singing career, until her retirement in 1995.

Julian at the Model Fish Shop and Restaurant 1954

CHAPTER 33
'Julian's Gang'

Robert Cole of Cimla, Neath, was Julian's protégé and worked with him for thirty years in the construction industry in South Wales: they have remained good friends ever since. I asked Robert, or Rob as he's known, if he would consider writing a few thoughts about his early days with Julian and their subsequent time together. He readily agreed and this is his story.

"One miserable Monday morning in November 1970, I met the man who was to have an enormous impact on my entire life for the next thirty years. I was the youngest of seven children, having two older brothers and four sisters. I had finished my education in Neath and having hardly been the most dedicated of pupils, was unable to read or write at the end of the course. Like many pupils (even in these so-called enlightened times), I had far greater interest in friends and activities outside the school walls, so only attended if I felt like it. Predictably, the end result was illiteracy, but my selfless, hardworking mother had other ideas for her errant son. She worked at the local hospital and having heard that Chestnut Construction, a local firm, needed a lad, she contacted the company. I'd been instructed to meet the work's transport vehicle at a pre-arranged meeting point near Neath bus station. My heart sank when an old battered pickup truck arrived and the driver, a burly tough looking guy with a guttural foreign voice enquired, 'Robert?' I nodded nervously. 'Get in the back boy!' I climbed up onto the truck and endured an hour's cold, wet and uncomfortable journey, as we travelled to the house building site at Trimsaran, West Wales.

On arrival at the cluttered, miserable looking site, my driver introduced himself: 'I'm Julian the foreman, come with me Robert.' I was handed a shovel and Julian showed me how to mix concrete. Initially I found the work arduous and demanding, but I was determined to succeed for Mum's sake. Indeed, I soon realised that my foreign mentor Julian, who everyone called 'Jule', was a master of his craft and was unrivalled in his knowledge, skill and experience in every conceivable area of house construction. He knew absolutely everything and everybody in the trade and above all was highly respected by his workers. This tough man led by example and as I later discovered, his Polish village upbringing and wartime experiences had moulded him into a man of iron-like temperament, who always overcame the many problems that arose on site.

We were all supremely confident that if Julian had upped sticks and gone to North America, Canada, Australia or even Europe with his beloved wife Anita and their three children, he could well have owned his own very successful construction business and have become very wealthy. Incidentally, if employees tried to con Jule by lying about their skills and previous experience in order to get work, our Polish leader immediately sussed them out. He set prospective workers a short trade test to assess their skills or, as he often discovered, their lack of them! Julian's face betrayed what he thought about their efforts, but he always gave them a second chance to redeem themselves. Instead of screaming at them and sacking them instantly for their lies and incompetence, he showed them how a job should be correctly approached and completed. It always worked. In my case, he encouraged me to read and write, advising me that these basic skills were absolutely imperative and of course Jule was absolutely correct!

Jule was light years ahead of his time in all areas of man-management and as well as securing meaningful employment for initially recalcitrant workers, he stored up a currency in his bank account that could never be measured in monetary terms: respect! This quality rarely, if ever, pervaded the harsh world of the construction industry. It can be defined in terms of esteem, honesty, integrity and even admiration. Respect is what Julian reaped in abundance from all his hundreds of workers; respect that is undimmed, despite the intervening years and as Julian meets former workers today, their admiration and gratitude is plain to see. I shall always be especially grateful to Julian for helping me to read and write and there must have been many innumerable instances of his kindness and encouragement to youngsters like me, learning the ropes.

As the seemingly endless demand for houses accelerated across South Wales, Chestnut Construction expanded its operations, becoming a huge company almost overnight. Imagine working with a handful of men one week, jogging along with a straightforward house-building job, then suddenly being plunged into part of a gigantic operation involving literally hundreds of men of all ages and capabilities, from all parts of West Glamorgan. The people who now live at Talycoppa, on the outskirts of Swansea, may be surprised to learn that nearly thirty years ago the surrounding area was agricultural land with just one small cottage and a farm: the arrival of a vast team of builders soon changed all that. There were major obstacles to be overcome before any properties could be built at Llansamlet, but this site would eventually become the largest private housing estate in Swansea. To their shock, Julian and the surveyors discovered that the land was not soil, but the hardest rock base since the Stone Age! In those days, there was no advanced machinery available and the foundations had to be dug with jackhammers, picks and shovels, like miners. Believe me; today's labourers have it easy, but for Julian and the rest of us, on many days it seemed akin to working in a forced labour camp. It really was hell working on this site and only our grit and sheer determination overcame these totally unexpected conditions.

We all looked up to Julian for his expertise and advice in surmounting the initial problems at Talycoppa and the workforce became known as 'Julian's gang', with a reputation for unrelenting graft and achievement. No matter what difficulties we encountered, we gradually melded into a solid, reliable unit used to working in any adverse conditions and weather. The site preparation was just a taste of what lay in store at Talycoppa, where literally miles of foundations, roads and paths had to be dug by hand for the hundreds of houses. Being a young, very fit man in those days, the unrelenting hard work became just another day at the office. Later, when I began to get to know Julian, who was a very private person, I realised that our labours at Talycoppa were insignificant in comparison to the conditions and starvation he and his family had endured in Russia and his later war service. As my respect and admiration for Julian increased during our working relationship, I became more and more curious about his background, his early life in Poland and the difficulties he encountered and over which he prevailed. During our years together, from my first day on site with Julian at the tender age of sixteen, I slowly pieced together fragments of his astonishing life. During our chats I was very careful not to become irritating and overtly inquisitive. As his story unfolded, week by week, I became absolutely amazed at what he and his family had gone through in Russia and the many battles he had fought in Italy and had thankfully survived. His strong voice and distinctive Polish accent reverberated around all our sites. His method of summoning me for instance was rather unusual; he would shout, 'Robert, like a lion!' Did I really resemble the King of the Jungle? Anyway, that was Julian's 'call' every day, so I just used to laugh, or should that be 'roar' in reply!

Of course life on site with Julian wasn't all hard work and there were plenty of laughs, as he had an infectious sense of humour. During the course of my long, happy working relationship with Julian we often came up against massive logistical and technical problems on site. Probably the most dangerous episode of my experience involved the laying of huge concrete pipes through a stream at Ynystawe. The pipeline extended for about 200 metres downstream and we intended to build houses above it. However, we predicted that due to the site conditions, we would eventually experience operational difficulties and these soon began to manifest themselves. The pipes were lowered onto the bed of the stream and then the real nightmare began. The only way to link the concrete pipes together was by using a hand winch, and to successfully achieve this, a worker had to drop down into the freezing waters of the stream and climb inside the pipes. A steel cable then had to be very carefully winched through the pipes to link them together. The cable tension would increase minute by minute, until it was as taught as a military snare-drum skin, and gently flicking the cable at its maximum tension produced a disturbing' pinging' sound. If the cable had snapped, we were in no doubt that the workman would have been cut in half, but thankfully that nightmare scenario never materialised

Health and Safety officers would never countenance such dangerous operations today and quite rightly so. Twenty five years ago there was no such watchdog in the construction industry, as the emphasis was on speed and completion of contracts in record times, with mistakes and injuries often occurring. On another occasion, as an illustration of the problems

205

we encountered almost weekly, (and at a serious risk of boring readers!) I shall relate another hairy experience that befell 'Julian's Gang'. A few weeks later, that same pain of a stream had become swollen by floodwater from the Upper Swansea Valley. About 300 metres downstream, flood debris had created a major bottleneck below a small bridge. Urgent action was called for in order to prevent potentially serious flooding, which could have caused major problems on the site. There was no way of removing the accumulation of forty-five gallon drums, branches, pieces of timber and general building refuse that blocked the stream other than by somebody going into the water and physically handing up the junk to men on the banks. As the stream's level had nearly doubled, it would have been extremely foolish to have waded in and attempted to clear the blockage unsecured. Of course you won't be surprised to learn that this hazardous task was delegated to the youngest 'gang' member: me! For two hours I stood up to my chest in the freezing stream, with a rope tied around my legs, held by a colleague on the bank. I could see by the self-satisfied grins on the faces of my mates that they were extremely glad that Jule hadn't delegated this one to them! I eventually completed the horrible job; frozen, exhausted and thoroughly fed up and carefully made my way to the bank. Jule took me straight home to thaw out after this ordeal. Listening to my catalogue of moans and groans during the journey, he casually mentioned that the slaves who tied the rafts together on the Volga river spent a nine hour shift in water, which was deeper and much colder, but with no ropes securing them. Oh dear! After that revelation, one very subdued pupil spent the remainder of the journey in regretful silence!

The above tales are just a few examples of our work together. Let's be absolutely clear about one thing: the remuneration Julian received for this tireless planning and organisation on so many construction sites across South Wales, was in my opinion, totally inadequate. He made several site owners very rich men indeed.

In conclusion, I salute Julian Bester a man I have been privileged to know and work alongside. He is a generous, cheerful, loyal and dedicated family man, a true friend to those in need and a credit to his native country.

Robert Cole

Swansea City A.F.C. was founded in 1912 and based at the Vetch Field. Its first professional match was against Cardiff City on September 7th 1912, with the result a creditable 1-1 draw. Over the next seventy years the club's fortunes had ebbed and flowed and there was the usual mix of highs and lows for the faithful supporters. I have no real interest in sport, but on May 2nd 1981 nobody who lived in South Wales could be unaware that victory in an away game against Preston North End would propel the club up to the dizzy heights of the First Division of the Football League. The 'Swans' pulled off an amazing 3-1 win and their destiny was assured, with the prospect of large gates in the new season and financial stability. As things turned out it didn't quite work out like that, but in the meantime I was brought into the Vetch picture for a very good reason.

I was working for the local building firm of Sharpe and Ayres at the time and one day received a message to go to the Vetch to meet the council clerk of works. I walked with him across the hallowed turf of the strangely asymmetrical ground, towards the North Bank double-decker stand. It had certainly seen better days and was in urgent need of demolishing and re-building. However, there was a huge caveat: the inspector told me that our firm's part of the work, which involved replacing the concrete steps, had to be completed in the short close season; a time scale of just ten short weeks. The inspector would monitor our progress on a daily basis and when we completed the steps, the contractors would move in to assemble the new stand. As the 'North Bank' was the stamping ground for legions of loyal supporters, it would be unthinkable and potentially very embarrassing for the club and directors for them not to be cheering their team on when the new season began. Unlike today's new Liberty Stadium, there was no seating on this area, so club expectations of very large crowds necessitated the installation of new safety barriers. A lot of work then, plus a very tight deadline with no leeway for any hitches or delays in materials. Looking back, I'm pretty sure that for me the challenge was pretty irresistible and gave my team the necessary impetus: plus of course the lure of a nice early completion bonus!

I contacted Rob Cole and Norman Price and told them about our massive challenge. They naturally wondered whether the job could be completed in such a tight timeframe, but we decided to go for it. The top section of the stand had to be removed by contractors with cranes and the site was carefully prepared before we started. This was going to be a frantic race against two unremitting opponents: time and weather. All the materials were brought to the Vetch daily, so there would be no delays. We started off like an express train and thankfully, being a lovely summer, the work could go on until 10.00 p.m. if necessary. Norman Price mixed the phenomenal amount of concrete needed, Rob Cole barrowed the mix to me and together we laid the steps. Lady Luck was on our side: believe it or not, the seemingly impossible job was fully completed in the amazing time of eight weeks!! When the eagerly awaited first game of the season arrived, I was given tickets in the best seats for Anita, Helen and myself. Of course readers won't be surprised to learn that I spent most of the game keeping a beady eye on the jam-packed new stand, half expecting it to suddenly collapse!

After official recognition from the club of our huge effort to finish the North Bank on schedule, we were always kept busy at the Vetch with general building maintenance. Sometimes things didn't quite go according to plan. The concrete floor of the player's tunnel at the Vetch had become broken up and needed renewing. I asked one of our lads, the driver of a small digger, to rake up the crumbling concrete prior to replacement. He dug a small section up, but luckily I noticed three thick black cables and I immediately told him to halt any further excavation until I investigated. The workmen who had installed the new Vetch flood-lights before the new season hadn't sunk the electricity cables deep enough: if the digger had struck the cables, it would have resulted in the entire city being blacked out!

Throughout the exciting first season in the First Division, I was often given 'comps' to watch the games. On one occasion, I noticed that Swansea fans throughout the game were repeatedly kicking a fence, which enclosed the North Bank area and also segregated the opposing team's supporters. Consequently some sections had become badly torn, so after the final whistle I walked across to examine the fence. In its present weakened state it would never survive another 'attack' in the next home game and I decided that it would be pointless just to replace the damaged sections. The remedy? The thickest, most tensile steel mesh I could locate, which later proved to be impossible for the excited fans to destroy and is still in situ today at the abandoned ground.

One day, I received a telephone call from a site agent named Harry

Thomas, who was primarily responsible for the smooth running of a huge building project of three hundred houses. The problems he was having in getting this large contract finished were many indeed. His site foreman, a Canadian named Bob, had a very free and easy manner and as there were so many workers involved he just couldn't keep tabs on them. As Bob had gone back to Canada for a holiday, Harry Thomas asked me to come and see what was going wrong: I soon found out! For months, the workers had been taking it in turns to sleep in the lofts of partially finished houses, and they slyly took full advantage of their Canadian boss's 'laissez-faire' approach!

I was slowly getting a name in the trade as a trouble-shooter for building problems that invariably came to light a few months after the initial building phase. For example, we were always back and forth to the giant Talycoppa estate over the next three years, attending to resident's complaints and problems with their properties. But the crisis I came across on one visit would take all my experience to put right: a young and enthusiastic engineer, who was responsible for the installation of the main sewers on the site, hadn't made allowance in his initial calculations for the hilly, rocky ground. The pipes had therefore been laid with insufficient 'fall' and were about five feet higher than their required position. This gaffe on his part led to a number of blocked drains on the site, but as there were 500 houses at Talycoppa, the engineer's mistake had to be rectified as quickly as possible, to prevent catastrophic flooding of the properties. The only way of sorting out this big headache was for my men to dig tunnels in the rock under the pipes, for about 200 metres across the estate, then crawl along the very narrow tunnel and carefully uncouple and reset them. We completed this very difficult, dangerous operation in just one week!

Oxwich Bay is a jewel in the world-renowned Gower Coast and every summer the family enjoyed many trips to either Oxwich or Porteynon. In those days there weren't many beaches in Britain that were so easily accessible, with wonderful scenery and safe bathing. Helen, my youngest daughter, loved camping with her friends in the field adjoining the large caravan-park, which was situated above Oxwich Bay. As the weather that summer was remarkable, with endless sunny days and cloudless skies, the girls decided to stay on a further week, so Anita and I went down to see them and enjoy a quiet drink at the site club. I had exchanged a few words, (in my customary subdued manner) with Eric the site owner on previous visits to the club. When he learned that for a living, I endured the strife and vagaries of the building trade, he told me about an ongoing problem at the caravan-park. Pre-season building work at the site had been carried out by builders who made the same mistake as our young engineer at Talycoppa. Again, allowance hadn't been made for adequate 'fall' in the pipe laying and flooding had frequently occurred, much to Eric's undisguised fury.

When the caravan and tent site closed down in October, after the pressures of the non-stop summer season, Eric and his wife always relaxed in Spain for a month. He asked me could I sort out the drains while they were away. I agreed and said I would carry out the work at weekends. My 'gang of three' soon sorted out Eric's problem, as the sandy soil was easy to dig and the nightmare of Talycoppa didn't reoccur. Eric was delighted with our work, so the next summer, on our visits to Oxwich as a family, we really had the red carpet treatment, with free meals and drinks in the club and the use of a caravan at any time. Very nice!

The Mond works at Clydach in the Swansea Valley have been established in the small town for over a century. The bust of the founder, Gustav Mond, is positione 1 at the corner of the road passing the plant and his stern features gaze onto the town. The factory produces silica sand for glass manufacture and I was brought in to put down a new cement floor in the main hall before new processing machines were installed. Yet again, this one was another very difficult job, which had to be completed quickly before the new equipment arrived. (Why was I always given the really hard jobs?). To pull this one off, my 'gang of three' really went for it and completed the daunting task in just four days!

I often smile to myself when I walk past building sites these days. The Health and Safety people have really gone to town now with notices such as:
'No hard hat- no job!' and several other dire warnings adorning the site entrances, challenging all and sundry to obey, or else! I'm the first to admit that years ago, the building trade had more than its fair share of dangers lurking to trap and often seriously injure,the unwary , careless, or even experienced workers. On one terrifying occasion, a dreadful accident almost cost the life of Norman Price,

one of my most able and reliable 'gang'members.   We were working at a site at Cwmavon , near Port Talbot, for a local firm called Concrete Products.   On this unforgettable day, Rob and I were working on the top floor of a group of houses.   We were about 12 metres above the ground and finishing the morning's work when suddenly a spine-chilling scream rent the air.   Rob and I dashed to the edge of the house to see Norman Price lying motionless on the ground.   Another man rushed to help and I yelled to him not to touch Norman, otherwise we'd have two fatalities on our hands.   I realised that the J.C.B. driver had cut through the electricity cable connecting Norman's cement mixer and as there was no insulation on the mixer handles, the poor man had been instantly electrocuted, I then shouted to the site manager to knock off the power and call an ambulance.   Rob and I descended abseil-style down the front of the house, grabbing anything to slow down our headlong plunge.   I dashed over to the lifeless man and by now his face was blue and he had stopped breathing.   I started an attempt to resuscitate Norman, frantically massaging his heart and giving him the 'kiss of life',but to no avail.   Rob then took over when I was exhausted and very soon, Norman started moaning,moving his head from side to side and miraculously breathing again. Two ambulances arrived very quickly and the medics took over, placing him on a stretcher and quickly administered oxygen, then one of the ambulances took him at high speed to Neath Hospital.   Thankfully Norman eventually made a complete recovery and a few months later rejoined the 'gang'!

(After yet another episode in my memoirs of a person I worked with, or myself cheating death, readers would naturally be quite entitled to ask themselves why wasn't this chap's life story called: '200 Lucky Escapes?')

In all works of life there are some nice people and some not so nice. In the murky waters that swirl around the building trade, there are quite a number of unscrupulous sharks out there, who rip apart anybody they get their razor-sharp teeth into. I personally encountered several such creatures who took every possible advantage of their fellow men, to garner their ill-gotten gains. I got caught once for £150 by such a creature in Neath. This householder's request for a building grant from the council had been agreed and he contacted my mates Eric Carpenter, Bryn Meyer and myself to carry out the work. A few weeks into the job, this odious scab, having received a large cheque from the council for the work, immediately pocketed the money, left his poor, long suffering wife and ran off with a woman with whom he'd been having an affair for years!

Another well-planned scam took place in Neath in the late eighties. This time a 'gentleman', from England informed everybody of his intentions to renovate a run-down mansion at Longford Woods and turn it into a club. On arrival, he made it clear to all and sundry that his establishment was going to be the finest in South Wales, would provide jobs for locals and of course would make him his fortune! He needed reliable carpenters to begin with and soon hired three local lads to start work. As the first weekend approached, he asked them to forego their wages until the end of the month. The excuse he used was that as he was just starting his wonderful project, he was short of funds. In lieu of the money, he offered them free meals every day. Unfortunately, because they needed the work the carpenters accepted his proposal. One of the lads was very unhappy and came to see me to discuss this very unusual arrangement. I immediately smelt a very large rodent indeed! I warned the carpenter, 'Watch it! This is a very strange business. You fellas don't know anything about this bloke's background. Take my advice. Leave the job!' Of course they didn't and were strung along with more lies and vague promises from their employer of 'huge' bonus payments on completion. As I expected, he soon approached me and lads from the 'gang', asking us to carry out building work on his new venture. I made it absolutely clear at our meeting that I expected weekly payment and of course, never heard from him again.

Incredibly, just one month after the club opened, with all the enticing brewery advertising and razzmatazz it closed and the owner disappeared! Months later, I learned that this crafty Englishman had embezzled the brewery out of thousands of pounds. They had stocked the club cellar to capacity and equipped the building and bars with, of course, luxurious fittings and plush seating. When all the drink had been sold after the first successful month, he ignored the statements from the brewery and local suppliers landing on his slippery doormat and he vanished. A sad lesson for the young carpenters, and an equally big shock for the brewery and local wholesalers. He probably made his furtive way across the Severn Bridge after dark, then a few months later started a similar profitable scam with a false name and identity, to fleece another unsuspecting brewery.

A few months later one of the 'gang' members was caught for £15,000! In this murky saga, he had paid in advance for the materials needed for a large job in a local house, so he was heavily out of pocket before he even took off his coat. When he completed the work (which had been superbly executed), the owner of the property refused to pay him, saying that he didn't have any money! This was another example of people taking advantage of a worker who trusted the householder, believing from day one that he would be promptly paid on completion. My colleague, who needed the money, made a big mistake: he was so anxious to start the job that he didn't get the householder to sign a contract. Thus when the man refused to pay him, my pal had nothing in writing to support his assertion that the work had been professionally carried out. It is really difficult for those of us who are honest to comprehend such an obscene attempt to gain a pecuniary advantage by one person over another. At least the existence of a mutually signed binding contract would have enabled the builder to take the rat to court and may have secured some, if not all of the money owing to him, plus costs. The lesson to everyone in the 'gang' was very clear: don't believe anyone or trust anybody who asks you to do work and above all get a contract, no matter how small the job!

The same year, another loathsome reptile slithered out of the undergrowth and approached me for help with his house. Now this character was a real star! Having left the Services flush with a hefty pay-off, he decided he would become a builder, despite having had no previous training or experience. (In retrospect, he should have taken a course, funded with his service money, but he was confident he would make a good living without such trivialities). From time to time, the word got around on the circuit that this 'builder' had failed to complete any job satisfactorily and was definitely in the wrong trade. He was borrowing money left, right and centre to carry on his shabby, ill-conceived venture and building suppliers were watching him very closely, insisting upon cash payment before releasing any goods. With his dodgy financial background there was no question of him obtaining any credit from these companies, so he lived from hand to mouth and from job to job.

One day he told me the sorry story of his latest fiasco, which this time involved his own house: he had mistakenly believed that he was sufficiently experienced as a builder to carry out a very straightforward renovation. I soon surmised that he was in really big trouble. He asked me to come and see the mess he was in, and having heard about his building 'skills', I decided to take a look at his latest masterpiece. He had knocked down the retaining wall between the ground floor front room and the living room, but his plans and the execution of them were unbelievable. It was certainly one of the worst DIY disasters I'd ever seen: a real amateur, penny-pinching shambles. After knocking down the wall, the clown had positioned a wooden beam unsupported by jacks and there was no doubt the entire house would eventually collapse! Of course this snake had obtained a nice grant from the council hadn't he? When the council inspector turned up a week later to examine the progress on the house, he was horrified at the prospect of imminent disaster. He immediately slapped an enforcement order on the property, stopping all further work and insisting that the damage had to be rectified to the inspector's satisfaction, by another builder.

A few weeks later, the householder's wife turned up on my doorstep. She was distraught, beside herself with worry and crying hysterically that her husband had left her and her two children. In floods of tears, she pleaded with me to sort out the state the house was in. Being the decent chap that I am, I just couldn't drive the desperate woman away. Against my better judgement, I fell for her sob story and decided to remedy the botched job. The big uncertainty was of course who was going to pay me, but in the meantime I decided to start on the house and fit it in with our existing daytime contracts. The next weekend, Norman and I arrived to start the big salvation job. When Norm saw the state of the room he nearly fainted. Staring in disbelief at the dire condition it was in he gasped, 'My God Jule, is this guy supposed to be a builder? He doesn't know the difference between a jackhammer and a jackdaw!' The floor of the house had originally been covered in large ugly slabs and as well as the mess he'd made of the ceiling, the idiot had ripped them up, prior to concreting the area, so that would have to be sorted out as well.

Oh yes, I'd really stumbled into a nightmare with this one and it was going to take hours of hard work to put right. The woman and her children were living in the upper floor, so there was no need for them to move out, as we usually worked in the evenings and at weekends. The final nail in my coffin of goodwill came when I asked the wife what had happened to the grant money. She of course, had no idea and hadn't seen a penny of it since it came into the greedy paws of her husband and she thought that he'd used some of it to settle his outstanding debts. (I doubted very much if that was the case: it was far more likely he'd dissolutely squandered the lot before he did a runner from her and his children). She insisted that he hadn't been in contact and had no idea where he was living.

Norm and I completed the job, but every time I came to discuss my outstanding bill, she resolutely ignored my frantic banging on the scarred, peeling, front door. I was certain she was lurking somewhere in that hole of a house, waiting for me to go away. I hated the sight of her fat, lazy, cat, which was always lying across the weed-choked path as if waiting for me, or nearly hidden in the overgrown, rubbish-strewn garden. It had eyes like a lynx, which coldly and dispassionately watched me arrive and leave, as usual, empty-handed. There were times when I'm sure the creature appeared to be grinning at my frustration, after yet another fruitless visit.

Then the biggest atom bomb since Hiroshima landed on my unsuspecting head. A well-meaning neighbour, who had previous dealings with the couple's skulduggery, which always ended in vicious, unrelenting acrimony, warned me that the husband had returned!! I was knocked sideways by this totally unexpected news. Now it began to slowly dawn on me that I was the victim of a pair of callous rogues who had fabricated the whole tale of desertion and thus tricked me into carrying out the vital remedial work gratis! I chased the slimy parasite for a year, but unsurprisingly didn't get a cent: in my case it wasn't the absence of a contract, but an evil, well planned con trick!

Swansea Marina was more than a dream in the plans of the local authority; it was going to become reality and guess who was going to be a huge cog in its creation? This project was undoubtedly the authority's flagship development for the decade and would radically change the old dock area into a first class yachting centre for sailing in the panoramic Swansea Bay, which has been favourably compared to the Bay of Naples. The large boating marina, which extended from the river Tawe to the docks, was accessed for water traffic by a swing bridge and the maritime backup for the marina consisted of several yacht chandlers and repair shops. Hundreds of workers had been recruited for this one and the prestigious development would consist of flats, waterfront homes, shops and restaurants. Eventually, a waterside community would be established, thus revitalising an area of the city, where previously old sheds and derelict, decaying buildings had stood for decades.

Come the 'gang of three', to add their undoubted skills to the creation of the city dream. Our responsibility was the laying of foundations, footings, kerbs and drains for the new properties and for covering the entire Marina site with slabs and blocks. Reinforced concrete was used for the foundations, followed by the drain and pipe laying and believe me, this was just the beginning. Now I have had a lot of experience in laying paving slabs and blocks in my building career, but the logistics of the marina project were definitely a completely different ball game. For three men to even attempt to carry out what we were lined up to do would be declared 'impossible!' But time and again, we three have proved any doubters wrong and this time was no different. As with the Vetch job, which of course was very finely balanced, we were determined to succeed.

Teamwork par excellence is the key to carrying out successfully what at first sight seems a very doubtful undertaking. We all had to work hard in unison and were very careful and systematic from start to finish every shift. First, hundreds of metres of drains had to be dug and pipes laid, then tons of hardcore was brought to the site and disgorged by a fleet of lorries and spread over the area designated for the blocking and slab laying. When the hardcore had been spread, the area resembled a field of volcanic lava deposits and then it was our turn to complete the creation of the much-heralded Swansea Marina. Creation is a somewhat fanciful term for what took place. Each day I would lay around 2000 blocks and 40 to 60 slabs. In the next nine months that it took us three men to complete the Marina site, I could well have laid upwards of a 250,000 blocks! No wonder I never failed to reach my 'norm' quota in the Volga forests! The next time any reader strolls around Swansea Marina, do me a favour and take a look at the ground. Then try and work out how three men laid the foundations, drains, kerbs, blocks and slabs in nine months!

Another thing, if you come across any broken or missing slabs or blocks please don't contact me! On and on, the building contracts marched. There just seemed to be no end to the remorseless house-building frenzy of that era. (On the other hand, the Marina these days is a another hive of building activity and perhaps the city waterfront will eventually rival Monte Carlo, Cannes, or even Cardiff!).

Over the next years there were so many other construction projects in which I was involved, from small site work to building roads and factory units on the new Swansea Enterprise Zone. I'm often asked how many housing projects I've been involved in around South Wales: without a doubt the figures were in hundreds, leading to the building of thousands of houses during my career. One achievement I'm very proud of was that I trained hundreds of youngsters in the building game. I proved to so many that if they were good timekeepers, sensible and diligent, they would eventually learn a very useful trade. On reflection, I think I did my bit to keep them away from false illusions and distractions that may have led to a spell in one of Her Majesty's hotels and a very uncertain future.

Readers are perfectly entitled to wonder if I was ever in a position with my work at the 'Model' and the construction industry to take Anita and the children for days out. I assure you that I did promise them on many occasions to do this, but invariably my sincere endeavours foundered, when an unexpected crisis surfaced on a building project. Anita always reminds me of one well-intentioned episode, which if repeated, could well have resulted in divorce court proceedings. One bright sunny day, I promised to take Anita and the family to our favourite Gower beach, Porteynon, but of course on that particular day I was embroiled in a major crisis at the site where I was working at the time. In desperation and well aware of the consequences at home, I pleaded with the manager to let me get away. He reluctantly acquiesced and I roared home like a Formula One driver, desperate not to disappoint the family, as had happened on countless occasions before. I arrived home an hour late and dashed into the house. I couldn't hear a sound. Surely they hadn't left without me? Unthinkable, but possible. I slowly opened the front room door to be confronted by a deathly silence, three impeccably dressed children and a wife who looked as if she was about to explode. The children looked at me sadly and reproachfully. I sensibly realised that now was definitely not the time for my usual apologetic litany of tired, well-worn excuses. I slowly retreated from the room, replaced my trusty black beret on my head, jumped into the truck and headed back to the safety of the building site!

I could go on and on with stories about my unforgettable days in the construction industry. Without doubt, my fierce, fanatical determination to survive slavery in Stalin's Russia and my army career embedded in me the ruthlessness necessary to overcome any problems on the sites. Perhaps most importantly, I derived lasting pleasure and a great sense of personal achievement from each successive project, which I knew had been carried out to the best of both my ability and that of the 'gang' workers. I started work on the farm in Rogozno when I was just five, helping Mum and Dad to feed the animals and gathering eggs from the henhouse. Sixty long, satisfying years later in retirement, I could at last look forward to spending holidays and quality time with Anita.

CHAPTER 34
Retirement

In May 1990, I reached the landmark of my sixty-fifth birthday and decided to retire from the civil engineering and construction industry. The event was marked by a meal with all the 'gang' and there were congratulory messages from building firms for whom I had worked. The 'gang' members, in a very nice gesture, presented me with a suitably inscribed tankard.

Having journeyed with me through sixty years of farm work, imprisonment, war service and civil engineering, readers may be surprised that I finally decided to retire. Retire? What does that word conjure up? Stopping work? Yes, I suppose so. Shutting oneself away? Definitely not! Withdrawing? Perhaps a little. Retreating or pulling back? What, with my military training? Never! Disengaging? Maybe, but keeping my options open of course! Going to bed? Yes, but I don't really need much sleep. Calling it a day? Well, that's a bit nearer, isn't it friends?

Now that we've all agreed a picture of me wearing carpet slippers and dozing in front of daytime TV is very unlikely, lets find out how long my 'retirement' lasted for. A hesitant knock on the door of my London Road house on a wet, miserable day, just one week into my 'retirement', dispelled any hazy illusion that Anita and I may have had regarding the twilight of our lives together. The caller was a local builder who was having difficulty with a job he was involved in and he needed my advice. I went with him to the house he was working on and soon sorted out the relatively minor problem. The word soon got about that 'Julian was available for advice on any building problem, just call at his house and ask him!' Anita soon made it clear that 'Julian was definitely NOT available at present, nor would he be at any time in the future for advice on building problems of any description, so DON'T call at OUR house!'

Unfortunately, as wives who have been in a similar situation will ruefully recall, this impasse soon crumbled, as the financial stakes for this prized 'advice' steadily increased. The sight of their 'retired' husbands slowly replacing the telephone receiver, with a glazed expression on their faces, as the reality of their stoic refusal of such an enticing 'offer' immediately hit home. Yes, you've guessed it! The procession of builders urgently needing my 'advice' has therefore continued unabated up to the present day!

During my 'retirement', as you can imagine, I was in constant demand for general house repairs in his area. In addition I was now able to keep an eye on elderly neighbours, especially if they were disabled or housebound.or as in one particular case, sadly neglected and forgotten.

On May 15ᵗʰ 2007, Anita and I celebrated our Golden Wedding! We attended a Thanksgiving Sunday Mass at St. Joseph's Catholic Church at Westernmoor Avenue, Neath, followed by an enjoyable celebratory family lunch.

The church, presbytery and grounds are surrounded by hedges, lawns and lush gardens and do you know who has been their watchful horticulturalist for the past twenty years? During my 'retirement' of course! My co-workers in the church gardens are appropriately named Luke and John. No, I know what some of you are thinking ! Now I am a bit of a Praying Mantis, but my intercessionary endeavours have, up to now,not resulted in weekly assistance in the church gardens by the original Apostles!!

Anita and I have been blessed with three wonderful children. Linda is single, lives with them and looks after Tiggy, her cat and the famous Tony the tortoise, who is over fifty years old! Anthony, also unmarried, lives in Spain and is a flat letting agent. Helen, a former clerk with South Wales Police, is married to Flight Lieutenant Gary James, who was born in Glyneath. They have three children: Holly, Jenson and Katy.

I conclude my life story with sincere thanks to Almighty God, for protecting me on countless occasions throughout my life, for enriching it with so many graces, a wonderful marriage, children, grandchildren and so many happy memories.

THE END

EPILOGUE

It is June 2007, sixty years after the wartime events described in this book. Another beautiful summer's day dawns on the Volga River, a gentle mist lingering along its banks and slowly rising into the deep forest, presaging another hot day. The birds have ended their chorus and retreated into the shade of the trees. A sleek cruise ship lies quietly at its sheltered berth at a new jetty; a few crew members are cleaning the decks and polishing the brass rails, preparing for another long day of sightseeing and entertainment. A delivery truck, its engines disturbing the peaceful air, pulls alongside the ship and two men start unloading provisions. The low chug of the engine of a coal barge is heard, as it valiantly battles against the rivers turgid flow, bound for a distant depot. Inland, the forest stretches interminably: it has virtually covered two old huts, which collapsed and decayed a lifetime ago. All that remains is rusting corrugated-iron sheets and pieces of scrap metal. Further on through the trees, ruins of smaller huts are barely visible. Again, just iron sheets remain and rusting battered stoves poke through the undergrowth, as if trying to escape from their forest tomb.

A muddy, torn up road, almost suffocated in undergrowth, leads to the ruins of a barely visible village. The houses have gaping holes in the roofs and walls and the overgrown gardens are a wilderness of dereliction and despair. What happened to the villagers? How many times did the monsters of steel and fire smash through this village, locked in a titanic battle for supremacy, all those ages ago? Did any of the combatants notice the small, earth-covered grave, at the roadside and read the inscription on the cross?

Anniela Bester - 1888-1940. R.I.P.

Only the tall forest sentinels know and they have kept their secret. The river, slowly meandering, twisting and turning on its long journey to the welcoming sea, also has its secrets of those times, buried in its black, cold, watery embrace forever.

APPENDIX
Two heroes: a tribute
General Wladyslaw Anders: 1892- 1970

Wladyslaw Anders is a revered hero of the Polish nation and his military and political achievements will always remembered. He was born on August 11 1892, in the village of Krosniewiche-Blonie, near Kutno, not far from Lodz. He served in the army of Tsar Nicholas the 2nd, as a young officer in the 1st Krechowiecki Lancers Regiment during the First World War. After the cessation of hostilities, he joined the newly formed Polish Army and led the 15th Poznanski Lancers in the 1919-1920 war against the Soviets, when Poland decided to reclaim her rightful territories. Twenty short years later, in 1939, exactly the opposite happened when the Russians took advantage of Poland's desperate fight against Hitler's invading armies and seized huge tracts of Polish land.

Wladyslaw's rise to prominence in the army was very swift and he was made a General of the Krechowiecki Lancers and later commander of the Novogradek Cavalry Regiment. At the battle of Lidzbark Warminski, near Elbag, after initial successes his unit was forced into a tactical withdrawal in the face of overwhelming German air and armoured attacks. He tried to escape with his troops through Hungary but Russian forces surrounded them at Rajgrodek. In the ensuing battle he was wounded and separated from his men. During his time in hospital, the Russians started to put into operation Stalin's carefully prepared plans for dealing with the fighters of the Polish army who were now his prisoners.

Over the next weeks, as many as one and a half million soldiers were put on cattle trucks and deported to slave-camps in Siberia. Later, their families also suffered the same fate, many never returning. However, the most evil part of Stalin's plan was the murder of thousands of Polish army officers, who were shot by the NKVD and buried in mass graves in Katyn Forest, near Smolensk. This massacre was uncovered in 1941 by the invading Germans, but the Soviets denied any complicity, blaming the Nazi SS Einsatzgruppen death squads. The actual number of officers who were shot is uncertain but a figure of ten thousand is conceivable. When the Polish Ambassador to Moscow, Stanislaw Kok, became aware of the unexplained disappearance of so many Polish fighters, he requested a meeting with Stalin to discuss this serious situation. The meeting didn't last long: after carefully listening to the Ambassador's concerns, Stalin blithely dismissed his anxiety by remarking, 'O well, perhaps they all must have gone to Mongolia!' These denials continued for fifty years until 1984, when as part of his new programme of 'glasnost' or 'openness', Russia's Prime Minister Mikhail Gorbachov grudgingly admitted that the NKVD were the perpetrators of this heinous crime. (Stalin had a bizarre attitude to any deaths. He considered a single person's death as a 'tragedy', but a hundred thousand deaths as a 'mere statistic').

Along with other Poles, Wladyslaw was imprisoned in Lvov prison then taken to the dreaded Lubianka jail in Moscow. He was regularly interrogated, beaten, starved and eventually kept in solitary confinement, but Stalin needed him for the next part of his plans for the Poles.

After twenty months in captivity, Wladyslaw was released on the orders of Lavrenti Beria (head of internal security and Stalin's closest henchman). He enjoyed his newly found freedom as a guest of the Soviets, almost as if they were trying to make it up to him for his disgraceful incarceration and treatment. The real reason was that after the German invasion of Russia in June 1941, Stalin had decided that he was a very experienced reliable officer, who could set up a new Polish army to fight for the Allies. From then on, Wladyslaw became totally immersed in the complicated arrangements needed to bring together all the Poles from Siberia and other labour camps across Russia. He flew to Teheran to start the planning, but later flew back to Moscow with General Wladyslaw Sikorski for a meeting with Stalin to discuss in detail arrangements for the proposed new Polish Army. Also present at the meeting was the Soviet Foreign Minister Molotov, joint signatory of the iniquitous 'non-aggression' pact with Germany's Ribbentrop in 1939, which effectively sealed the fate of millions of Poles. Stalin and Molotov promised to release the thousands of Polish soldiers and their families from labour camps and they were to be sent to the new Polish garrison at Yangi-Yul in Iran.

In March 1942, the exodus of Polish soldiers and their families from Russia began, but Stalin wanted the Poles out of Russia in just a few weeks, making it clear that the borders would be closed and any stragglers would remain. He authorised his top General, Georgy Zhukov, to speed up the departures. Sikorski and Anders vehemently protested to Stalin that the people should travel immediately to the warm climate of the Middle East. However, as Zhukov's brief was to get the Poles out of Russia as quickly as possible, no arrangements were made for the people to have food rations, adequate clothing and shelter in the sub-zero conditions. Tragically, many died of cold and hunger, huddled in tents on the windswept freezing plains of Kazakhstan, hundreds of kilometres from warmth and safety.

The General's Second Polish Corps joined up with the British Eighth Army and were outstanding combatants in the battles of Monte Cassino, Ancona and finally Bologna. However, at a conference held in Teheran a year earlier in November 1943 between Churchill, Roosevelt and Stalin, it was decided that at the end of the war, the Eastern half of Poland would be annexed to the Russians! Two additional Allied conferences, at Yalta on the Black Sea coast and Potsdam, further strengthened Stalin's control over Poland. He promised so much to the Allies, but lied repeatedly; eventually coming away with everything he wanted and in return gave Churchill, Roosevelt and later Truman (after Roosevelt's death) nothing but empty promises. After the Yalta agreement, Anders announced bitterly, 'It is impossible to imagine that humanity has suddenly become blind and has really lost the consciousness of mortal danger!' Stalin had given Britain and the U.S.A. his personal guarantee that Polish soldiers returning to their cities, towns and villages after the war would be warmly welcomed as they had indeed been worthy allies in the fight against the Hitlerite tyranny. His sly deception instead meant that there was a very real danger that returning Polish soldiers, far from being hailed as heroes, would be handed over to the NKVD and shipped back to Siberia!!

Wladyslaw was very much aware of these potential problems, but failed to get any reassurances from the Russians. Surprisingly, at the end of the war, Stalin gave Wladyslaw a present of a white horse! Being an ex-cavalryman Anders soon took to his new charge. Not so Stalin: at the rehearsal in Moscow for the Soviet Victory Parade in Red Square in 1945, Stalin ignominiously fell off his horse! He was so humiliated that he delegated Zhukov to lead the parade on horseback, while he watched from his Kremlin podium in a jealous rage! As they took more and more control in Poland, the Soviet authorities were so alarmed by Ander's influence that they forced the Communist government in Poland to withdraw his Polish citizenship. Now, sadly, every region of the entire country was held in the vice-like grip of the Soviet bear and the very breath of the nation was being choked and stifled by its oppressors steel claws. For years, the General fought tirelessly for his soldiers, being a prominent member of the Polish Government in exile. He must have been heartbroken when certain British officials decided that his army would not be permitted to take part in the 1945 Victory Parade in London for fear of upsetting Stalin! His outstanding record as a general and indefatigable opposition to Communism has led to many schools, public buildings and roads being named in his honour throughout Poland. Recognition of his distinguished military and political achievements resulted in him being awarded forty medals and honours from governments and royalty world-wide. These included the Legion of Merit and the order of Lafayette from the U.S.A., the Companion of the Order of the Bath and Defence medal from Great Britain and the Italian Star. From France he received the Legion of Honour, Croix de Guerre and the Medaille Interalle.

General Anders died in London on May 12th 1970 and was buried, in accordance with his wishes, among his men, at the Polish Military Cemetery at Monte Cassino.

Joseph Bester: 1917 - 1978

My brother Joseph, you may recall, was involved in the Polish Army's desperate attempts to halt the Nazi invasion in September 1939. After his unit was virtually wiped out, he was captured along with thousands of Polish soldiers and marched through the Rogozno district, to be taken by train to a prison camp in Germany. As the long column trudged through the countryside, he seized his chance at a bend on a lane at Wacud and jumped into a hedge. He hid in the hedge for hours and, when darkness

Julian and Joseph at the Military Convalescent Home Wrexham, 1946. Julian's army chauffeurs '100,000 miles Silver Wheels' award medal is below his left epaulette

fell, walked to a farm for shelter. Despite the great risk, the family kept him hidden in a loft and sent word to Mum and Dad that he was safe. He stayed with them for a month, and then bought a small boat, intending to cross the Sludwia River to Zduny. Unfortunately for Joseph, the area he chose for his escape was already in the hands of the Soviets. One evening after midnight, he paddled across the calm river, confident that he would be successful. As he reached the far bank, two Russian guard dogs viciously attacked him. The commotion alerted the soldiers guarding the river and they quickly seized Joseph, who luckily hadn't been badly injured by the dogs, but was very frightened.

He was kept in a room at the guardhouse for a day and then thrown into prison in Zduny, where he stayed for a week. In late November, he was taken b train along with hundreds of other Polish men, women and children on the long journey to Russia. He arrived at the logging camp three months before us and was working in another tree-cutting brigade. He was shocked when we arrived, as he had hoped we would be left in peace by the Soviets to get on with our lives at Kamionka.

Joseph was in the other large hut, but as there was room because of recent deaths, he managed to get his friends Martin, Tadek and Edek accommodated there. In the aftermath of the Christmas Day strike and the announcement of the proposed formation of the new Polish army, he came to see me to discuss his future plans. He wanted to leave the camp immediately for Tashkent, so he persuaded Edek, Tadek and Martin to join him. The four lads caught the troop train at Swieregorske and went down to Tashkent, but a few days after they arrived, Martin and Edek began to have second thoughts about joining the army. Martin especially was missing his wife Honorka so he wanted to return to Oserki and the other two also decided to go back to Russia. Joseph was undeterred and reluctantly said goodbye to them and signed up. His unit trained for four months in Tashkent, before arriving at the army base in Kinokin in June 1942. I have related our eventual reunion at Kinokin in Chapter 12 and from then on we often met on exercises in the Middle East.

Tragically, he was badly injured in the first assault of the Fourth Battle at Monte Cassino, sustaining severe injuries and losing his left arm below the shoulder. His entire body was embedded with shrapnel and he had lost a lot of blood. His comrades brought him down the mountain and he was taken to the Military Hospital at Brindisi, a town on the Strait of Otranto, near Taranto. After the battle ended, I went down to Brindisi to see Joseph on May 14th 1944. He was bandaged from head to foot and heavily sedated but thankfully he did recognise me, although he was deeply traumatised by the loss of his arm. When he eventually came around, he spoke very quietly and hesitatingly and appeared very relieved that I had survived the terrible meat-grinder that was Monte Cassino without injury. (He knew only too well the hazards that lay in wait for sappers in combat zones). Joseph drifted off to sleep, so I went to see the medical staff. The doctors told me that Joseph would remain in Brindisi for at least two months, but nothing had yet been finalised regarding his future hospitalisation. They had been kind, attentive and thoroughly professional in their care and I gratefully thanked the medical staff before returning to Campo.

Joseph stayed in Brindisi until July 1944, and then was flown to a military hospital in Glasgow, where he stayed for four months. His injury meant that he would eventually be fitted with a prosthetic arm and this would be changed periodically. He was then moved to the Military Convalescent Hospital at Wrexham, North Wales staying there for a year. Eventually he settled in Shipley in Yorkshire, where he later met and married a Polish girl, named Honorka, who was working in a textile factory in Bradford. They had a baby girl, Danuta and spent the rest of their lives in Shipley. Amazingly, despite his severe disability, Joseph trained as a welder in a factory and was able to carry out his duties successfully. Unfortunately, the increasing number of operations he had to undergo to remove the shrapnel in his body, eventually told on him and he had to finish work, receiving a 90% war disability pension. Luckily, as he and Honorka owned a large house in Shipley, they were able to take in Polish couples, which improved their finances after Joseph retired.

I visited Joseph, Honorka and Danuta fairly regularly and always had a great welcome but I could see he was slowly deteriorating: in 1978, he suffered a massive heart attack and died.

So there it is. Two undoubted Polish heroes: one a fearless, inspirational General, the other, one of his dedicated soldiers. I conclude this tribute, with the inscription carved for posterity on the marble monument at the Polish cemetery in Monte Cassino:

We Polish soldiers
For our freedom and yours
Have given our souls to God,
Our bodies to the soil of Italy
And our hearts to Poland.

The Polish Military Cemetary at Monte Cassino

Interior of the Arandora Star Memorial Chapel in Bardi

Dorino Moruzzi of Neath with his father's wallet, gold watch and passport returned to him by the Catholic priest at Bodden, Donegal, Eire

The marble memorial depicting the names, photographs and Italian communities of the 487 men who died on July 2nd 1940.

THE AFTERMATH

Maria and Rina Fornari:
Maria married Raymond Jenkins and had two children, Andrea and Christopher. Rina never married.

Wlatka, Salka and Stefa:
Stayed in Rhodesia until the end of the war and then decided they wished to live in Britain. Julian wrote to the War Office on their behalf and permission was granted. They were employed at the Airport Hotel in Cambridge for a year and then Wlatka and Salka moved to Bradford, whilst Stefa settled in Leeds. They all married Polish boys. Wlatka gave birth to two girls, Alina and Elizabeth. Salka also a girl, Danuta. Stefa didn't have any children. Salka died in 1986 and both Wlatka and Stefa died in 1991.

Helena:
It is believed she returned to Poland after the war, but no contact was made and Julian has failed to ascertain her whereabouts.

Edek:
After leaving Joseph in Tashkent, he went back to Russia with Martin and later married a Russian girl and had three daughters. After the war they moved to Tozym, on the Polish-German border, where they had a small-holding, and remained there until his death in 2002.

Martin:
Remained in Russia with Honorka, and had a daughter, Danuta. Moved to Saratov, further up the Volga River. Edek tried to contact them, with

a sum of money for Danuta from Joseph. Tragically, famine swept the region in the post-war years and first Danuta died, then Honorka and Martin in 1946.

Tadek:
After returning from Tashkent with Martin and Edek, he remained in the Saravan region until the war ended. He later moved to the Polish border near Frankfurt-an-der-Oder, where he had a smallholding. He reached the grand old age of ninety last year.

Zybyshek and Mietek:
Nothing was heard from them again.

General Wladyslaw Sikorski:
Died in a plane crash off the coast of Gibraltar in July 1943. Suspicion has always remained that his death was not an accident, but nothing has ever been proved.

General Bor Komorovski:
After the failure of the 1944 Warsaw Uprising, he was imprisoned in the famous Colditz Castle in Saxony and kept with a group of other prisoners, who the Germans called the 'Prominente' In the event of Germany losing the war, the 'Prominente' would be held hostage and used as bargaining chips in negotiations between the Allies and the SS and Gestapo. Luckily, Colditz was suddenly liberated by the Americans before any such plans were put into operation. The General made his way to Austria with the help of a German officer who was a pre-war show-jumping competitor. Eventually he was handed over to the Americans at Innsbruck. He settled in England after the war, and died in Buckinghamshire in 1966.

Lavrenti Beria:
Minister of the Interior and Stalin's accomplice in mass murder. Suspected of complicity in Stalin's death,he was arrested by the MVD,(successors to the NKVD in 1946), and shot in a bunker in a suburb of Moscow on December 22nd 1953.

Marshall Georgy Zhukov:
Commander of the defence of Moscow, Leningrad and Stalingrad. His popular acclaim after the Allies victory was too much for Stalin, who

had him exiled to Odessa on the Black Sea. Reinstated as Commander-in-Chief of Soviet and Warsaw Pact forces after Stalin's death. Later became Soviet Defence Minister and was responsible for the brutal suppression of the East German Workers' Strike in July 1953 and the Hungarian Uprising in October 1956. Died in Moscow in 1974.

Field Marshall Albert Kesselring:
After the Allied victories in Italy, he was sent to Germany in 1945, in a last attempt by Hitler to stem the Russian advance. Arrested in 1947 by the British, he was tried and sentenced to death for allegedly organising the killing of three hundred and thirty five Italian civilians in the Ardeantine caves near Rome in 1944. Although many Italians were convinced that Kesselring had authorised similar reprisals, he was reprieved in 1952, when it was proved that the SS were responsible for the crime. Died in 1960 at Bad Nauheim, near Frankfurt-am-Rhein, aged seventy nine.

Lieutenant-General Sir Oliver Leese:
After the Battle of Monte Cassino, he was sent to Burma and became Commander-in-Chief of Allied land forces, South East Asia. He was not successful in his new command and was replaced in 1945 by Field Marshall William Slim. Retired from the army in 1946 and later became a noted horticulturalist. Died in 1978.

Field Marshall Brian Alexander:
Accepted German surrender in Italy on April 29th 1945. Became Governor of Canada, serving from 1946-1952. In addition to his many military decorations, he was awarded honorary degrees at Harvard and Princeton Universities in Boston. Died on June 16th 1969 and being a Member of the Order of the Garter, his funeral was held at Windsor Castle.

SS-Gruppenfuhrer Heinz Reitefarth:
Commander of SS Divisions in the Warsaw Uprising, 1944. Inexplicably never arraigned for war crimes, despite his appalling record. His lawyers successfully blocked repeated demands from Poland for his extradition. In 1951, he incredibly became mayor of Westerand ,on the Frisian Islands off the coast of Denmark and on his retirement, was granted a full General's pension by the West German government! Died in 1979 in his manor on the holiday island of Syllt.

SS-Brigadefuhrer Jurgen Stroop:
Commander of the SS and police units during the Warsaw ghetto uprising in 1943. Hanged in Warsaw in 1951.

SS-Sturmbannfuhrer Walter Reder:
Organiser of the massacres in the Marzabotto area, in 1944. Extradited from Austria to Italy in 1948 and found guilty at a court in Bologna of war crimes. Sentenced to life imprisonment in 1951, but released in 1984 after serving thirty-three years in a fortress prison in Naples. Sent a letter expressing his deep repentance and remorse to the descendants of the villagers killed by his men and begging their forgiveness. Died in Vienna in 1991.

U-87 Commander Gunter Prien:
Died on August 7th 1941, when his submarine was hunted down and destroyed with depth charges from the corvette escort for the OB 293 North Atlantic convoy.

Michai! Onufrejczk:
Killed by a lorry while crossing a road in Manchester in 1964.

Megan Williams:
Now 92, she lives in her own home at Penygroes, near Ammanford. Well cared for by her daughter and son-in-law. Anita and Julian have always kept in touch and visited Megan, who did so much for the Fornari family when they lived in Llandeilo.

Dame Vera Lynn O.B.E. D.B.E.
Achieved her ninetieth birthday on March 20th 2007. She thoroughly enjoyed the celebrations on this auspicious occasion, which included a birthday tea with local children and events at the Imperial War Museum. She lives in her own home in the East Sussex village of Ingfield, next to her daughter Virginia and son-in-law Tom. She is regarded with great affection by the villagers and takes an active interest in local events.

Vice- Admiral Harry de Wolf R.C.N.:
Canada's highest decorated naval officer and Commander of the destroyer St. Laurent which rescued 880 survivors after the S.S.Arandora Star sank on July 2nd 1940. De Wolf was decorated for

this mission and his exemplary wartime service by Britain, America, France and Norway. He died in the Canadian capital, Ottawa, on December 18th 2001, aged 97.

The Mumbles Train - 1804-1960

Just twenty years after the Fornari family fled from Swansea in September 1940 the historic train left its terminusat Rutland Street around 11.00pm on January 5th 1960 for its final journey. Large crowds lined the route to Mumbles Pier on a bleak, wet, night and there were poignant farewells at every stop. Many bystanders were in tears and just couldn't believe they were witnessing the end of the working life of what was acknowledged to be the World's First Passenger Railway. There was precious sentiment shown by its new owners, the South Wales Transport Company once the line had closed and in a very short time the carriages and ancilliary equipment was reduced to scrap iron. Even now, 47 years later, its demise is continually lamented by Mumbles and Swansea people, that a unique, world-famous tourist attraction has been lost to future generations forever.

Finally, my former employer: Josef Vissaroniovitch Stalin:

Died in his Kremlin apartment on March 5th 1953, at the age of 74, suffering a stroke after an all night party at Beria's house on March 1st. The circumstances of his death are shrouded in mystery. No medical help was summoned by the Politburo for twelve hours and it is strongly believed that he was murdered. Beria, in fact, later gleefully boasted to Molotov that rat poison had been mixed with Stalin's food at the party! Over a thousand Muscovites died in a stampede at Red Square on the day of his funeral: I'm pretty sure he enjoyed that send off! The latest conservative estimate of the number of people who died during Stalin's dictatorship from 1929-1953 is forty million.

BIBLIOGRAPHY

Title	Author	Publisher	Year
A new history of Wales	Jeremy Blade	Sutton Publishing Ltd	2000
Army in Exile	Wladyslaw Anders	Macmillan & Co	1946
A Walk in the Park	Vernon Hopkins	Private	2004
Beachhead Assault	David Lee	Greenhill Books	2005
Berlin	Anthony Beever	Penguin	2002
Defeat in the West	Milton Schulman	Cassell	1947
From war to Westminster	Stefan Terlezki	Military Pen & Sword	2005
Harvest of Sorrow	Robert Conquest	Hutchinson	1986
Hitler and Stalin	Alan Bullock	Omnia Books	1991
Hitler's Mediterranean Gamble	Douglas Porch	Weidenfeld & Nicholson	2005
In the ruins if the Reich	Douglas Botting	Methuen	1985
Koba the Dread	Martin Amis	Jonathon Cape (London)	2002
Men at Arnhem	Geoffrey Powell	Military Pen & Sword	2003

Monte Cassino	Mathew Parker	Headline Publishing	2003
Stalin	Robert Service	Macmillan	2004
Stalin	Simon Sebag Montefiore Weidenfeld & Nicholson		2003
The Battle of Monte Cassino	George Forth	Ian Allan LH	2004
The Forgotten Few	Adam Zamoyski	Military Pen and Sword	2004
The Desert War	George Forty	Simon Publishing	2002
The Great Terror (a re-assessment)	Robert Conquest	Hutchinson	1968
The Gulag Archipelago	Alexander Solzhenitsin	Fontana	1982
The Holocaust	Martin Gilbert	Collins, Glasgow	1986
The Last Battle	Cornelius Ryan	Coronet U.K.	1959
The Longest Day	Cornelius Ryan	Coronet U.K.	1959
The Pianist	Wladyslaw Szpilman	Clays, St.Ives	1998
Unpunished Crimes	Latvian Relief Society	Memento	2004
Uprising '44	Norman Davies	Pan Books	2004
Wales	Jan Morris	Viking	1998
World War Two	Ivor Matanie	Colour Library Books	1985
Philips Concise Atlas	Reference Edition	George Philips	2005
The Times World Atlas	Reference Edition	Times Books	2006
Penguin Encyclopaedia	Reference Edition	Penguin Books	2006
Wikipedia	the Internet Encyclopaedia		2007

The names and Welsh Towns of the 49 Italian men who died on July 2nd 1940, from the following Italian Communities; Albareto, Bardi, Bedonia, Bettola, Crederola, Fanna Varsi. Grezza di Bardi, Morfasso, Picinisco, San Gallo.

Albertelli C.(Pontypridd) Antoniazzi B.(Newtown) Basini B (Treherbert) Belli I.(Maesteg) Bombelli.M.(Cardiff) Carini F. (Pontypridd) Carini G.(Ebbw Vale) Carpagnini Giovanni (Briton Ferry) Carpagnini Giuseppe (Cwmcarn) Castelli A. (Aberdare) Cavalli G.(Neath) Chiappa E. (Bridgend) Conti Guido (Newport) Conti Giuseppe (Treharris) D'Ambrosio F.(Swansea) Di Marco M.(Swansea) Ferrari L. (Aberdare) Franci G. (New Tredegar) Fulgoni Giacomo (Hirwaun) Fulgoni Giuseppe (Pontygwarth) Gazzi A. (Gorseinon) Gazzi F.(Pontnewydd) Gazzi L.(Ferndale) Lusardi F.(Llanharan) Marenghi G.(Pontypridd) Minetti G. (Neath) Moruzzi E. (Neath) Moruzzi P. (Neath) Pinchiavolli L.(Pontypridd) Pompa F.(Swansea) Rabaiotti A.(Newport) Rabaiotti B.(Pontypridd) Rabaiotti D. (Ogmore Vale) Rabaiotti F.(Swansea) Rabaioti L.(Swansea) Ricci L. (Treharris) Rossi E. (Mountain Ash) Rossi G.(Cardiff) Rossi L.(Swansea) Sidoli G.(Glyncorrwg) Solari L.(Neath) Spagna A.(Maesteg) Stelloni G.(Newport0 Sterlini M.(Tenby) Strinati M.(Cwmamman) Taffurelli G. (Dowlais) Tambini G.(Newport) Zanelli E.(Tonypandy) Zanetti A.(Swansea).

May they Rest in Peace

Through Hell to Freedom